"Kevin Cawley has produced a thoughtful and extremely readable introduction to the history of religions and philosophical systems in Korea. This work, as well as illuminating Korea's fascinating and diverse religious landscape also thoroughly situates the traditions discussed within the broader East Asian context making this an invaluable companion for the student of East Asian thought."

James Kapaló, *University College Cork, Ireland*

"Kevin Cawley's *Religious and Philosophical Traditions of Korea* is an excellent phenomenological and chronological overview suitable for undergraduates or for post-graduates wanting to understand the distinctive character of these traditions in Korea. Written in a highly readable style, Cawley's book illustrates how these traditions continue to influence contemporary culture. Highly recommended."

James H. Grayson, Emeritus Professor, *The University of Sheffield, UK*

"Until Cawley's textbook, there has been no text in the Anglophone literature that explains the religious and philosophical traditions of Korea in a historically comprehensive manner. It fills this significant gap in a way that will be appealing to a range of students and scholars, and will be tremendously useful pedagogically."

David H. Kim, *University of San Francisco, USA*

"Korean history is often interpreted from a political perspective, but Kevin Cawley has innovatively applied a religio-philosophical insight of transnational East Asia in which the nation is depicted as a transformative peninsula. The highlight of the book is the encountering dialogues of Catholics, NRMs, chuch'e and cyber-*mudang* within the context of modernity for readers in Asian studies, history, philosophy, sociology and religious studies."

David W. Kim, *Australian National University, Australia*

Religious and Philosophical Traditions of Korea

Religious and Philosophical Traditions of Korea addresses a wide range of traditions, serving as a guide to those interested in Buddhism, Confucianism, Shamanism, Christianity and many others. It brings readers along a journey from the past to the present, moving beyond the confines of the Korean peninsula. In this book Kevin N. Cawley examines the different ideas which have shaped a vibrant and exciting intellectual history and engages with some of the key texts and figures from Korea's intellectual traditions. This comprehensive and riveting text emphasises how some of these ideas have real relevance in the world today and how they have practical value for our lives in the twenty-first century.

Students, researchers and academics in the growing area of Korean Studies will find this book indispensable. It will also be of interest to undergraduates and graduate students interested in the comparative study of Asian religions, philosophies and cultures.

Kevin N. Cawley is Head of the Department of Asian Studies at University College Cork (UCC), Ireland. He established Korean Studies as a new discipline in Ireland when he was appointed as the first ever lecturer in Korean Studies there. He has researched and published extensively on Korea's intellectual history.

Religious and Philosophical Traditions of Korea

Kevin N. Cawley

LONDON AND NEW YORK

First published 2019
by Routledge
2 Park Square, Milton Park, Abingdon, Oxon OX14 4RN

and by Routledge
52 Vanderbilt Avenue, New York, NY 10017

Routledge is an imprint of the Taylor & Francis Group, an informa business

British Library Cataloguing-in-Publication Data
A catalogue record for this book is available from the British Library

Library of Congress Cataloging-in-Publication Data
A catalog record for this book has been requested

ISBN: 978-1-138-19339-0 (hbk)
ISBN: 978-1-138-19340-6 (pbk)
ISBN: 978-1-315-63936-9 (ebk)

Typeset in Sabon
by Apex CoVantage, LLC

All photos are the author's unless indicated otherwise

In memory of my wonderful mother,
Mary Cawley (née Mc Quillan),
for her love, lessons and laughter!

Contents

Figures

Language note

Chinese names and terms have been romanised using the Pinyin system unless quoted from another system, or unless the authors use a different system for their own names. There are two major exceptions, Confucius and Mencius, whose names are generally written this way.

Japanese names and terms have been romanised using the Hepburn system.

Korean names and terms have been romanised using the McCune-Reischauer system unless quoted from another system. However, some names and terms, such as Kim Il-sung and Juche, will appear as they more commonly appear in print, as will the names of some of the newer religions, which corresponds to how the practitioners of those religions write them, and how it appears on their websites. In such instances, I will also include the McCune-Reischauer transliteration the first time the term is used.

I have also respected the romanisation of authors who do not write their names according to the McCune-Reischauer system.

Acknowledgements

This book would never have been possible without the encouragement and support of Emeritus Professor James H. Grayson, whose classes first inspired my interest in Korean religion and philosophy. His guidance has been on many levels for which I will always be thankful.

I am grateful to Dr James Lewis of Wolfson College, University of Oxford, for inviting me there during my sabbatical, which permitted me the time to finish this book.

Many thanks to all of the people at Routledge who have been involved with this book at every step of the way.

I am indebted to the comments and suggestions of the several reviewers for helping me to refine the final manuscript.

I would like to thank the Korea Foundation and the Academy of Korean Studies for their generous funding over the years.

'Sage' Roseleen Falconer and 'enlightened' Ingrid Hanson, thank you both for your insightful comments on all sorts of drafts of my work throughout the years.

Till Weingärtner, thank you for your collegiality and friendship, and for the calmness and enthusiasm you bring to work each day. Chiara Giuliani, Sarah Baccianti and Michael Nott, for helping me over the final hurdles writing this book with friendship and laughter.

I would like to express my deepest gratitude to my lifelong friends, especially Bríd and the Falconers (in Fermanagh), and Gene and the Rooneys (in Limerick): your kindness, love and support has guided me along my own pathway. Shira Brady, Goretti Connaughton, Anne Corcoran, Maeve Henry, Ita Kennelly, Claire McAvinia and Carol O'Sullivan – thank you all for many years of friendship!

My wonderful friends Dusty Stevens and Alvin Burch – thank you for so many Korean adventures and for accompanying me on road trips, even to Kangjin. Tasan would be proud of you! Kane Mason and Sung Jeonghyang, for fun times every summer in Busan and Seoul.

Thanks to my very dear Korean friends, especially Lee Sunhak, Joo Susan (and her family), Lee Daseul, Kim Hyeoncheol, Kang Wongu, Kwak Fely, Master Kim (my Taekwondo master, who introduced me to Korean culture) and the Jang family from Jinju. When I first went to Korea in 2001 I had the pleasure of teaching some amazing children who are now adults – you made me fall in love with your country – thank you for also teaching me!

Emilie Petersen, Hori Emo, Omura Wakako, Monty Sullivan (his husband and sons) and Andrea Petruzella, for many fond memories – and many more to come. Mary and Denise Kenneally, my Cavan friends, thank you. Mary Tilson and Bernadette Hughes, my mother's wonderful best friends, with love and deep appreciation always.

To my sister and brothers – none of us saw this coming when we were growing up in Northern Ireland during 'the troubles'.

Deep gratitude to my Aunt Rose (sadly departed) and Uncle Felix, for encouraging me to study as a child, and for so much more. Aunt Betty and Uncle Mike, in appreciation of so many magical parcels from America as a child.

I would especially like to thank two very important people who are always there for me: my aunt Margaret "Nana" and my uncle Seán. Without your support I could never have gone to university in the first place, and so I am utterly indebted to you for any success I have! There are not enough words to thank you both.

Figure 0.1 A glimpse inside a Korean temple
Courtesy of Dustin Stevens

Prologue

On April 15, 2014, the MV Sewol ferry boarded 496 passengers in Incheon, a port not far from the capital of the Republic of Korea (ROK), Seoul. The majority of passengers (325) were excited students from Danwon High-school, which is in Ansan, a city Southwest of Seoul. The students, accompanied by a dozen teachers, were going on a fieldtrip to the beautiful island of Cheju, the largest island off the Southern coast of ROK, a well-known spot for honeymooners. While their initial boarding had been delayed by a few hours due to fog, everything else appeared normal. However, tragedy struck early the next morning between 8:49 and 8:50 when a sharp turn in treacherous waters was further exacerbated by falling cargo which had not only been overloaded, but also insecurely fastened, causing the ferry to tilt towards the water. What followed was gross negligence. By 8:52 a.m. announcements were repeatedly being made over the ferry's intercom system, with the following advice: "Do not move. Just stay where you are. It's dangerous if you move, so just stay where you are" (Park 2014). At the same time, a very bright student on board, Choi Duk-ha, who was only 17 years old, decided to call the national emergency number and eventually was put through to the Mokpo Coast Guard who dispatched a patrol vessel – before members of the staff on board did three minutes later – while water continued to pour in. Duk-ha's call saved lives. Other students called their parents, sending images of what was happening on board via their smartphones, where the announcements to remain in place could be heard very clearly (Stevens 2014). Until this point, the children and other passengers were never ordered to wear life jackets; this order came after the Jindo Coastal VTS (Vessel Traffic Services) urged the crew members to inform them do so. The captain of the Sewol finally made the call for evacuation at 9:30 a.m., and he, along with several senior crew members were the first people to be rescued. Meanwhile, 304 passengers and crew members lost their lives, among them Duk-ha, whose call had saved the lives of many others who were rescued.

But what has this to do with the religious and philosophical traditions of Korea, the reader may be wondering? Authority in Korea in rooted in hierarchical relations, which for almost two millennia, have been shaped by Confucian ideals, where authority is also inextricably linked with moral responsibility for those under one's charge. Confucianism will be dealt with in much more detail later, but for now, if we relate this idea of 'moral authority' to the captain in charge of Sewol and all those on board, mainly teenagers, we soon see how it was abused. This may be described as 'Corrupt Confucianism', in which people did not fulfil their roles and duties in a moral manner, from the owner of the ferry company, to those who overloaded its cargo at the expense of the lives of children. The captain should have seen to the safety of the passengers, before he had disgracefully fled from his sinking ship. At the other end of the hierarchical relationship were the many Korean teenagers who were taught to respect and heed the word of their elders, a basic Confucian teaching, which they would have all learned in school and at home. But again, their reaction also displays their unwillingness (for the most part) to question authority – even as water poured in on top of them. They were dutiful, fulfilling their roles at the other end of the hierarchal spectrum, remaining where they had been told to remain. This highlights another basic teaching of Confucianism that is engrained in every young Korean, though they themselves may not realise it, and that is the link between learning, and putting into practice what one has learned: in this case, obeying one's seniors and people in positions of authority. So the students remained, simply through good manners or etiquette, but also because they would have considered that the captain and senior crew members had their well-being and safety as their prime goal, which was sadly untrue. Ironically, it was Duk-ha, whose family was Catholic, who assumed moral responsibility by contacting the emergency services, and in so doing, saved some of his classmates and other passengers – including the captain who had failed in his own duties and responsibilities.

In the many images which brought the ROK to the forefront of global consciousness due to this preventable disaster, one thing became clear – that the Koreans were uniting in their grief through recourse to a wide variety of religious and cultural practices, such as Buddhism, Catholicism, Shamanism and Protestantism. The many reports on the tragedy, though they did not in themselves focus in on it, broadcast many images of different ceremonies along the coast where the tragedy had taken place. They indirectly illustrated the pivotal importance of Korea's religious and philosophical traditions, which are absolutely necessary to understand in order to assess the influence of the various traditions on the present, shaped by the past, which also shape the future. Understanding these traditions will enable us to understand how Koreans think, live and practice religions, which in the Korean context are inseparable from a long philosophical tradition.

Korea has a long, proud intellectual history, often unknown to foreigners who often assume that most Asians are Buddhists. Korea is an enigma in this regards. This book hopes to bring readers along a journey from the past to the present, through different traditions, moving beyond the confines of the Korean peninsula, highlighting the intellectual interactions with

Figure 0.2 Buddhist lanterns at a temple

neighbouring countries and also those far away, where ideas from the past reverberate in the present. It provides an overview of the history which influenced ideas, while examining some of the key texts, now available in English, of some of the most important figures from Korea's intellectual traditions. It is an introduction to this subject, and not a comprehensive compendium, as that would require many volumes, but it should provide readers with enough background information to then be able to delve deeper. The religious and philosophical traditions of Korea may at first seem very foreign, but they are relatable to all of us, as they provide different *ways* to guide people to lead a better life, for themselves, their families, their countries and the world.

Chapter guides

Chapter 1 – Religions and philosophies in East Asia: 'pathways' for self-transformation

Chapter 1 discusses what is meant by 'religion' and 'philosophy' and examines the relation between the two as modes of "self-cultivation" in a Korean/ East Asian context. It will outline how both have always been historically and intellectually intertwined in Korea, and to varying degrees inseparable, beginning with a look at some key terms, such as 'religion' and 'philosophy'. This gives a better understanding of how they were understood by people who belonged to a multi-faceted cultural system where there was not a singular homogenous religious hegemony, nor any prerequisite for 'belief' in dogma or doctrines associated with religions such as Catholicism. At the same time, this chapter considers the etymology of the Western/Latin word 'religion' which was initially used to describe traditions in East Asia by Europeans who were generally Christian (missionaries), and shows that what they encountered in East Asia did not really fit the western nomenclature, and in fact, led to misunderstandings. It also highlights that some of the terms Europeans used to describe Asian traditions, such as Confucianism, were misnomers that could also lead to confusion.

From this point, it is already clear that to understand the religious and philosophical traditions of Korea one must engage with ideas and traditions that did not necessarily originate on the Korean peninsula. Indeed, to understand the earlier development of important traditions such as Confucianism, Buddhism and Daoism, the reader will be provided with a brief introduction to some of the key figures, and the most important tenets of these different schools of thought, which may be described as 'path*ways*' for transforming oneself, drawing on many traditions at the same time, creating a heterogeneous collage which navigated through religion and philosophy. It will also discuss Shamanism, which reflects the indigenous traditions of the peninsular people, before the Chinese traditions became absorbed into society and the political system, but which also interacted with them, and which still has an important place in Korea today in the twenty-first century.

Chapter 2 – Adaptations and interactions: Chinese traditions and Korean ways

Chapter 2 examines the initial reception by Koreans of the important Sinitic traditions outlined in Chapter 1. It shows the importance of the socio-political context in order for ideas, both religious and philosophical, to gain acceptance on the Korean peninsula during the Three Kingdom period, when Korea was made up of Koguryŏ, Paekche and Silla, while also discussing Korea's 'origin' myth, which reflects the earlier culture. Each kingdom reacted differently, but in general would be accepting of traditions that had made their way onto the peninsula from the prestigious 'Middle Kingdom' as China was known. This chapter will highlight several key developments by Korean thinkers as well their application to a very different context from whence the ideas had come, adapted to new contexts, blending with folk traditions and shamanism, which pre-dated the arrival of Buddhism and Confucianism, and which already embodied many ideas associated with Daoism. These new traditions were used by different governments to cement their authority, spiritually through Buddhism and politically through

Buddhism and Confucianism. It draws attention to the immense religious, philosophical and cultural importance of Korean missionaries to Japan during the seventh century, shaping Japan's own religious and philosophical traditions, bringing Chinese characters to the Japanese, long used by the elite in Korea, linking them to the highly developed cultural realm of the Sinosphere. This chapter will detail the development of Korean Buddhism, its relationship with royal leadership (kingship and queenship), as well as its interaction with Daoist ideas.

One of the focal points in this chapter will be Monk Wŏn'gwang (541–640?), whose secular teachings, blending Buddhism with Confucianism, were used by a band of elite warriors, the *Hwarang* or Flower youths, as their guiding principles. After an examination of some of the new intellectual trends of Buddhism in China, that would influence Korean Buddhists who studied there, the reader will be provided with a more in-depth look at one of Korea's greatest thinkers, Wŏnhyo (617–686), whose intellectual ingenuity still guarantees his place as a key figure of Buddhist thought in Korea and East Asia, and whose ideas on resolving disputes and achieving harmony have as much to contribute to intellectual thought today as they did during his own lifetime – maybe even more. Lastly, Ŭisang, a friend of Wŏnhyo, will be discussed, especially for his contribution to spreading the Hwaŏm branch of Buddhism in Korea. These Buddhist intellectual developments are necessary to understand as they pave the way for a later metaphysical recalibration of Confucianism.

Chapter 3 – From Buddhism to Neo-Confucianism: hegemony and metaphysics

In Korea, the meditational Buddhist tradition emerged towards the end of the Unified Silla period, which absorbed the Three Kingdoms. This new tradition was founded on the peninsula by Korean monks who had studied with the great masters in China, linked with some of the original lineages there. Their ideas and the monasteries they founded would emerge as important intellectual centres, which had gained prestige by the inauguration of Koryŏ (918–1392), protected by King T'aejo (877–943), the first ruler of the new dynasty in his 'Ten Injunctions' which are examined. While Buddhism was considered to provide spiritual protection to the state, it also bolstered the prestige of Korea's place as an intellectual hub in East Asia where writing and printing were advanced and promoted. This period saw the rise of Buddhism crystallised though such timeless works as the carving of the complete Buddhist scriptures onto over 80,000 woodblocks, known as the *Tripitaka Koreana*, and the first ever use of movable metal print. However, this same period also saw the decline of Buddhism, compounded by the issue of conflict between the doctrinal sects, and the meditational schools who were responsible for cementing the Sŏn tradition in Korea (known as Zen in Japan, but which had originated in China as Ch'an Buddhism). This chapter will deal with Ŭichon (1055–1101), who attempted to resolve some of the emerging issues, but in particular, it will focus on the role Monk Chinul (1158–1210) who attempted to rejuvenate the Buddhist orders, and whose contribution to the consolidation of the Sŏn tradition in Korea cannot be emphasised enough. Some of his key ideas will be examined, as well as the practice of *Kanhwa Sŏn*, one of the salient features of Korean Buddhism.

A new philosophy would again come from China, Neo-Confucianism, this time brought by Koreans themselves, based on the ideas of Chinese philosophers from the Song dynasty, especially those of the Cheng brothers, but most importantly Zhu Xi (1130–1200). Zhu's influence on Korean Neo-Confucianism was immense, outlined in the second part of this chapter. This philosophy, which was a more metaphysical rejuvenation of earlier Confucianism, nevertheless still reinforced original Confucian values, and emphasised the role of the king, much needed in Korea at a time when the kingship had been devoid of real leadership or moral authority. The time had come for a new dynasty, which would be called Chosŏn (1392–1910), established according to the new Neo-Confucian principles that the Confucian elite would use to construct a patriarchal society where they wielded utmost power and sway over the King, eradicating the sway previously held by the Buddhists, who along with Shamans were rejected and repressed for several hundred years. For the first time, Korea had a hegemonic ruling philosophy, which used metaphysics and rites to organise people into different classes, diminishing the rights of women who had enjoyed similar privileges to men in their families until then. The final part of this chapter outlines the great Buddhist-Confucian confrontation of the early Chosŏn period through an examination of the writings of Confucian Chŏng Tojŏn (1342–1398) and Buddhist Kihwa (1376–1433). Chŏng lambasts the basic tenets of Buddhist belief, considering Confucianism more socially relevant, but the rebuttal by Kihwa, on the other hand, displays a sophisticated understanding of not only Buddhism, but also Confucianism and Daoism, drawing all these different strands of 'being' together into a holistic fabric.

Chapter 4 – Sagehood meets 'Western' learning: from 'Principle' to 'The Lord of Heaven'

Chapter 4 continues to explore the importance of Neo-Confucian ideas to Korean scholars, especially the concept of Sagehood, which will be examined in relation to two of the most important scholars in Korea's intellectual history, T'oegye (1501–1570) and Yulgok (1536–1584). In particular, T'oegye's *Ten Diagrams on Sage Learning* is given due consideration, as one of the most important texts of the entire Chosŏn dynasty, also shaping Yulgok's text on Sage Learning. The metaphysical 'Four-Seven' debate spurred on by the ideas of both philosophers is also dealt with, followed by a review of Yulgok's 'community compacts', an attempt at improving the social reality of those in more rural communities. By the sixteenth century, Koreans had already become aware of European 'Western Learning', including the sciences and Catholicism. Chosŏn scholars would engage with these ideas from beyond China, including the religious ideas of the Italian Jesuit Matteo Ricci (1552–1610), whose text, *The True Meaning of the Lord of Heaven*, first published in 1603, sought to blend together religious strands from the earlier Confucian tradition with Christian teachings, ideas that would exert more influence in Korea than in China.

While Korean Confucians continued to write commentaries on the canonical Confucian texts, many of them initially criticised Catholic ideas. The next key focus point of this chapter is a group of scholars who converted to the new Western religion, soon drawing the ire of the Confucian state, which saw Catholicism as a 'dangerous' teaching, which was encouraging dissent among lower classes and growing rapidly in adherents who were women. This section will look at key figures among the early Catholic Church who contributed to the earliest Catholic literature in Korean history, written by elite Confucians, soon using *Han'gul*, the language associated with women and the poor masses, described then as the 'vulgar script'. It will pay particular attention to the first Korean Catholic Catechism written in *Han'gul* by Chŏng Yakchong (1760–1801), which spread the ideas of the early Church among women and men, many from poorer backgrounds, who soon united in their 'belief' of a monotheistic God, moving away from the metaphysics of Neo-Confucianism, which emphasised the idea of a universal guiding *Principle*. Women became a force to be reckoned with, and for the first time in Korean history, a religious movement had begun where texts were read and disseminated by women, granting them *equality* with men, something even Shamans could not boast of. This chapter ends with a discussion of Tasan, Chŏng Yagyong (1762–1836), the younger brother of Chŏng Yakchong, highlighting his contribution to Korea's history of ideas, but also exploring his vulnerable position as a Confucian who had become a Catholic, only to renounce his affiliation after a series of executions and widespread persecutions had taken the lives of many of his close friends and family members, forcing him and many others into lonely exile. His writings embody the times they were written in, full of conflict between different Confucian factions, where poverty and hunger were not uncommon, facts bluntly recounted in his poetry. Tasan challenged the system of endemic abuse and injustice at the hands of magistrates who were supposed to enforce the law and morality. This is the subject of one of his main texts, examined closely. The Chosŏn dynasty was in demise, Confucianism no longer provided for the people, and no longer solidified the state, gradually weakening until it would collapse and fall into the hands of its colonising neighbour, Japan. This sets the scene for other uniquely Korean spiritual responses, which emerged from the end of the nineteenth century, and which also encountered Protestant Christianity.

Chapter 5 – 'Eastern' learning and Protestant Christianity: new religions and a 'Korean' God

Though Catholicism was outlawed and Catholics were persecuted, their ideas sowed the seeds of other movements, even if some of those movements would reject all forms of 'Western' religion, such as the Tonghak (Eastern Learning) movement. This religious movement, developed by Ch'oe Ch'e-u (1824–1864), known as Su-un, sought to provide Koreans with a new path-*way* to deal with their difficult social conditions, and it blended different facets of the religious traditions that had been practiced on the peninsula for hundreds of years, adopting and amalgamating ideas from Buddhism, Daoism, Shamanism and Confucianism. However, even Catholicism had influenced Tonghak, including one of the terms they used for God. These intersecting ideas are examined in the writings of Su-un, which outline his encounter with the 'Sovereign on High', who, for the first time, speaks and gives instructions. These ideas would be developed by subsequent leaders, and the name of the religion would be changed to Ch'ŏndogyo – the 'Religion of the Way of Heaven'. The ideas of Su-un would also inspire other new religions, such as Chŭngsando, whose leader would declare himself to be the Korean incarnation of *Shangdi*, known as *Sangje* in Korean, developing its own unique scriptures and doctrines.

As Protestant Christianity started to grow quite quickly from the late 1880s, and the Japanese had made their intentions of conquering Korea clear, already forcing Korea to sign its first unequal treaty by 1876, a strong sense of nationalism surged. Nationalistic scholars emerged, hoping to protect Korea's cultural legacy from degradation, but also to rejuvenate it, to meet the needs of the Korean people, finding their past undervalued and their future unsure, in a new desperate socio-political situation. The Tan'gun myth would get a modern reboot, giving rise to a religion in its honour, *Taejonggyo* – the Religion of the Great Ancestor – presenting the three male figures in the myth as a trinity, clearly as a rival to the Christian trinity, which thousands of Koreans by that time believed in. The Christians, starting with Revd. John Ross, would translate the Bible into *Han'gŭl*, settling on a Korean term for God, *Hananim*, 'the Great One', and as with Catholicism earlier, Korean women would become active evangelisers, known as 'Bible Women', operating from the Anbang, or inner female quarters, a space also shared with the Korean Shaman, or *mudang*, explored in the final section. As Protestantism spread, shaping Korea's educational system and introducing new modern medical facilities, it would also become linked with Korea's independence movement.

Chapter 6 – Korea(s) complex modernity: Buddhist renewals, post-Christianities, Juche and Shamanism

The transition to modernity was a traumatic experience for the Koreans, linked with colonisation, followed by the devastating Korean War, which saw the peninsula divided. The Buddhists, who had been oppressed for several hundred years, saw the collapse of Chosŏn as a time to reassert themselves. Korean monks such as Han Yongun (1879–1944) championed this movement, confronted by Japanese assimilation colonial policies, which sought to turn Koreans into Japanese citizens, a project that failed. Han's revitalisation strategy, outlined in this chapter, sought to awaken the Buddhists to their own important role in Korea's intellectual history, but, as well, to make them more socially engaged, clearly motivated to some degree by the growth of Christianity and its social relevance. This would also inspire a new form of Buddhism, known as Wŏn Buddhism, developed by Sot'aesan (1891–1843), who would take the religion along a new trajectory, making it more inclusive and making social activism one of its core tenets, examined along with its other innovations and successful expansion abroad.

Offshoots of 'Christianity' such as the Olive Tree Church and the Unification Church, both founded by former Presbyterians, and both originally from the Northern part of the now divided peninsula, would consider themselves as the central figures of their religions, as promised prophets, or God incarnate, envisaging a special role for Korea in the new millennium. The Unification Church, led by the infamous Revd. Mun, would be extremely successful in exporting itself globally; spreading to Japan, the United States, South America and Europe; growing in power and wealth; as well as weathering negative backlashes from former followers who labelled it a cult. It continues today to spread its teachings, which are outlined in some detail, drawing attention to some of its more problematic practices.

To the North, religion was suppressed after the division of the peninsula, but it was also replaced by a new ideology with a cult figure constructed around Kim Il-sung. This reformulation of Marxism-Leninism would gradually overpower the ideologies that had influenced and shaped it, making it the *de facto* religion of the people, in terms of what linked them to their 'Dear Leader' and each other, known as Juche (also written Chuch'e), which is discussed in relation to the speeches of Kim Il-sung and Kim Jong-il, which outline its development. To the South, the mainstream religious denominations, Buddhism, Protestantism and Catholicism, saw growth but Shamanism, examined in the final section of this chapter, rose to meet the challenges of the modern world with *mudang* becoming 'early-adapters' to new technologies, but who also provide their services to their clientele in the cities, catering for newer, modern, urban needs and providing alternative ways to deal with the stress of the world we live in today.

References

Park, Madison. 2014. "Ferry Accident". *CNN*, 18 April. Available at: http://edition.cnn.com/2014/04/18/world/asia/south-korea-ship-survivor/ [accessed on 18 January 2016].

Stevens, Andrew. 2014. "South Koreans Mourn Teen Hero Who Made the First Emergency Call from Ferry". *CNN*, 27 April. Available at: http://edition.cnn.com/2014/04/27/world/asia/ferry-south-korea-teen-remembered/ [accessed on 18 January 2016].

1 Religions and philosophies in East Asia

'Pathways' for self-transformation

Introduction

The peoples who have inhabited the Korean peninsula have from time immemorial remembered their dead. This is evident in the many dolmens which can be found scattered around the peninsula dating from the first millennium BCE. In fact, while dolmens can also be found in many other countries such as Ireland and India, Korea accounts for more than anywhere else – up to 40 percent of all the dolmens in the world are located on the Korean peninsula. The Koch'ang, Hwasun and Kangwha (also written Gochang, Hwasun and Ganghwa) dolmen sites are listed on the UNESCO World Heritage list since 2000 (UNESCO 2018a). The construction of Dolmens can be said to represent an ancient method of remembering the dead using stone structures, but they clearly brought people together to erect them, and to commemorate the dead person(s), and so, had an important social function within communities. In contrast, Koguryŏ (37 BCE–668 CE), a kingdom that extended into northeast China as well as the northern part of the Korean peninsula (which will be discussed in Chapter 2) left a complex of tombs (currently in North Korea and China), which is also listed on the UNESCO World Heritage list (2018b). These tombs, considered to be for the elite of that society, including royalty and the aristocracy, have wall paintings that give us some insight into the lives of the people from that time, with many colourful images of processions, dancing, and portraits of the owner of the tomb, as well as depictions of what are often interpreted as immortals or various gods and aspects of nature, but also what appears to be monks. What this illustrates is that the link between the living and the dead was something that was taken seriously by these different communities, linking them through specific traditions. It also highlights that they considered the afterlife, prepared for it carefully, and had religious rituals that were, even by this point, quite elaborate and very beautiful (if the paintings are anything to go by). More importantly, it shows a syncretic attitude that blended beliefs of immortality, probably from traditional folk beliefs, with teachings from Buddhism, which was clearly respected. Hence, these tombs and dolmens represent the material manifestations of ideas, beliefs and rituals that linked people in their society together. From this time, it is evident that people in East Asia, and in this specific case, the Korean peninsula, were brought together through their beliefs and ritual practices which inextricably bound the individual into a group where hierarchy was important, but also very evident, discernible from clothing, and shaping their cultural world.

These early people then accepted teachings from various schools of thought which shaped their culture and worldviews, where philosophy, or guides to communal living and morality, intermingled with the religious aspects of how they considered death and an afterlife, as well as the gods they held in common and revered.

Religion and philosophy: modes of self-cultivation

Ideas from China clearly exerted growing influence on ideas on the Korean peninsula from the first millennium BCE. The 'Three Teachings' in the form of Buddhism, Confucianism and Daoism (sometimes written 'Taoism'), which made their way into Korea, demonstrate how religion and philosophy converge in East Asia, rather than diverge, as may often be the case in the West, where they still occupy very different spaces, especially in universities. For East Asians, the three teachings represent different paths that assist and enable the individual to become the best person they can become. These paths are usually referred to as a *way* in East Asia, from the word Dao (道, K. *To*), hence, I have chosen the term path*way*, which reflects the idea that these teachings represent different routes to becoming a better person. These teachings act as guides to help the individual become a beneficial member in their family, their society, and in short, in their own way, contribute to making the world a better place. The individual as such was always considered as part of a greater whole: a family, a state, a country, the world, even the universe.

There have been many books written in the West on religion; it is after all a Western concept (European to be precise). Especially from the nineteenth century, different scholars emerged who had different takes on religion, but most were conceptualised in relation to the monotheistic traditions of Christianity (in particular), Islam and Judaism as the standards against which other 'religious' value systems were to be measured. This meant that they clearly revolved around the concept of a singular, creator God, a transcendental entity with human characteristics, also known as anthropomorphism. Many peoples' traditions have not been so fixated on the idea of creation, and many were not interested in proving or even acknowledging a world of spirits or gods, or a transcendental existence beyond the world they lived in. In his essay "Religion, Religions, Religious", Jonathan Z. Smith (1998: 281) investigates different attempts to define religion, concluding that "it can be defined, with greater or lesser success, in more than fifty ways". This illustrates that the term is fluid and not rigid, and often depends on the context of the individuals and their communities, shaped by different traditions. Jacques Derrida (1998: 29–30), in his discussion of religion in an edited volume of essays simply called *Religion*, notes that any discussion of 'Religion' is already "speaking Latin". He is referring to the Latin origin of the term which may have two etymologies: *'relegere'*, which is to gather, or *'religare'*, which is to bind together, which entails a sense of obligation – such as to god(s). He also emphasises that *religion* reflects what he calls 'globalatinization', the influence of the Latin world shaped by the Latin language which still persists today, especially revolving around discussions of religion, and more centrally around Christianity. This draws our attention to the anachronistic application of a Euro-Latinised concept of *religion* onto traditions, which have both religious and philosophical underpinnings, formed in very different contexts, and sometimes not concerned with gods or spirits: Confucianism, Buddhism and Daoism. Indeed, philosophy in Chinese is known as *Zhexue* (哲學, K. *Ch'ŏrhak*), literally the 'study of wisdom', or simply, 'how to become wise', which would better reflect its more dynamic and proactive implications in the East Asian context.

These Asian traditions were first brought to the attention of Europeans in a serious manner by Jesuit missionaries to Asia during the late sixteenth, early seventeenth century. In particular, Matteo Ricci (1552–1610), an Italian Jesuit missionary, was greatly responsible for this transcultural exchange through his "translational apostolate" (Cawley 2013). Ricci had mastered the Chinese language and translated Western works on science, mathematics and religion into Chinese. Additionally, his journals and letters provided information on China, its language and customs, as well as descriptions of Confucianism, Buddhism and Daoism, which made their way back to Europe. As Gallagher (1953: xix) writes, "[Ricci's journal] probably had more effect on the literary and scientific, the philosophical and the religious, phases of life in Europe than any other historical volume in the 17th century". Indeed, Ricci, who as a missionary, was clearly on a mission to convert the Chinese to Catholicism; and he engaged with Confucianism in a positive way, while rejecting Buddhism and Daoism, considering them as rival 'religions'. He considered Confucianism to be a social philosophy with moral teachings that were complementary to Christian ones, which he would expand upon. Ricci's biases would make their way into the writings of European philosophers, such as Voltaire, who evoke them through their praise of Confucius, while other Europeans would also engage with these 'new' ideas emerging from the East, which were actually older than any of their European antecedents (see: Dawson 1971; Fuchs 2006).

Confucianism has been considered as a philosophy and/or (not) a religion, and in this sense it is not easily defined by the western terms of 'religion' or 'philosophy'. Though it started out by being understood as a socio-political philosophy, it nevertheless does refer to the spirit world and boasts of intricate and elaborate rites for the ancestors, for example. Buddhism, which is generally considered to be one of the great world religions, also has a deeply philosophical, even psychological side to it. Daoism, which began as a philosophy for living a good life in tune with nature, saw certain practitioners adapt it as a religious 'way' seeking health and longevity, even immortality, blending it with indigenous beliefs about spirits and gods. These different schools emerged during the Warring States period (fifth to third centuries BCE), when Chinese society was in chaos and divided, providing the contextual impetus to promote teachings to help stabilise the state and shape its ruler's ethos, as well as bolster emotional and spiritual support for the general populous. The next section provides a basic overview of these important traditions as they provide both the foundation and catalyst for intellectual developments in Korea for almost two millennia, examined throughout the rest of this book. It also includes a discussion on Shamanism, which has been practiced on the Korean peninsula before Chinese traditions gained importance there, and which continues to have an important place in the twenty-first century.

Confucianism: *an overview and some key concepts*

The use of 'Confucianism' as a proper noun is significant as it already hints at the misunderstanding of key terms, their mis-translation into European languages, and their misuse in Europe – something which continues until today – as a result of the globalatinisation mentioned above, where religious and philosophical ideas are subsumed into a Eurocentric (now Western) understanding of them. As Paul Rule (1986: 195) emphasises, 'Confucianism' only became known in Europe after Nicolaus Trigault published Matteo Ricci's journals in 1615, noting that Ricci was responsible for having "transmutated the tradition of the Ju [Ru] or Chinese 'scholars' into an '-ism', Confucianism". Ricci had been made aware that the great Chinese scholar *Kong Fuzi* (from the Chinese characters 孔夫子) was greatly revered, and it is from the Latinised version of the scholar's name 'Confucius' that 'Confucianism' as a school of thought comes, as understood in the West. However, this term does not reflect how it was referred to in Asia. The Chinese (and later Koreans) referred to a corpus of literature that pre-dated Confucius, which had been compiled by various writers who referred to both mythical and real figures from the past as exemplars of moral behaviour, for example, legendary 'sage' kings such as Yao (堯) and Shun (舜), whose dates are usually suggested as the third millennium BCE. Confucius systematised these texts and their main socio-political ideas, teaching them to his students, who only after his death compiled the 'sayings' of their master, much the same as the Gospels in the *Bible* were compiled after the death of Jesus. The text which recounts the collected sayings of Confucius is known as *Lunyu* in Chinese (論語, K. *Nonŏ*), translated as *The Analects*. We do not have much information on the life of Confucius, but we know that he was a peripatetic teacher who travelled to spread his teachings, not unlike Jesus and the Buddha, although he sought to have his ideas adapted by rulers, and therefore was more closely aligned with the elite. His ideas were not adapted during his lifetime in any meaningful way. The tradition which Confucius belonged to, drew upon and developed is known as *Ru-xue* (儒學, K. *Yuhak*) [study of the scholars] or *Ru-jiao* (儒敎, K. *Yugyo*) [teachings of the scholars].

Figure 1.1 A painting of Confucius enshrined in Jeonju (Chŏnju), South Korea

There seems to have been a development in the roles and function of the 'Ru', who during the Shang dynasty (商朝; c.1600–c.1046 BCE) may have been ritual specialists who through dance and music supplicated the spirits, gods or ancestors for good harvests and rain, which would have been important for agricultural communities, as well as the study of astronomy and astrology to predict the weather. In this regard, they performed the functions that shamans or folk priests would later. By the Zhou dynasty (周朝; c.1046–c.256 BCE), as 'Ru' positions became more official and professional, their posts would have been linked with developing statecraft, while focusing on education which was linked with morality, culminating in the teachings of the great master Confucius himself. The goal of such teachings is to become a sage, one who developed himself to the utmost of his innate potential as a human being (Yao 2000: 17–21). There was no need in this context to ask for help from or to pray to gods or deities: we as humans are expected to solve our own problems.

The main texts associated with the 'Ru scholars', which were later edited and probably re-organised by Confucius himself, are generally grouped together and known as the *Five Classics* (五經, C. *Wujing*, K. *Ogyŏng*):

The Five Classics

Yijing (易經) [Classic of Changes]
Shujing (書經) [Classic of History]
Shijing (詩經) [Classic of Poetry]
Liji (禮記) [Records of Rites]
Chunqiu (春秋) [Spring and Autumn Annals]

These texts of different genres would have been compiled by different authors over a long period of time, much like the Old Testament in the Bible, probably corresponding to the late Zhou Dynasty (1050–256 BCE), up to and after Confucius. They all recount the importance of the remote deity *Shangdi* (上帝, K. *Sangje*), or the Sovereign on High, who was clearly revered during the Shang Dynasty, though whose importance had diminished by the time of Confucius – in the *Analects* there is not even a single reference to this rather distant and evasive entity, who had been replaced with a focus on a more enigmatic conceptualisation of 'Heaven', known as '*Tian*' (天, K. *Ch'ŏn*). The *Analects* itself would much later be grouped into a new set of texts collectively known as *The Four Books* (四書, C. *Sishu*, K. *Sasŏ*), which will be outlined in more detail in Chapter 3:

The Four Books

Lunyu (論語) [The Analects]
Daxue (大學) [The Great Learning]*
Zhongyong (中庸) [The Doctrine of the Mean]*
Mengzi (孟子) [The Mencius]

* originally separate chapters in the *Liji* (Record of Rites)

Confucianism places a special emphasis on the notion of *Dao* (different from that of Daoism, discussed later). For Confucians it is a practical 'way' that can be studied and then put into practice, which reflects the practical nature of Confucianism in general, introduced in the opening line of *The Analects* 1.1: "The Master said: Having studied, to then repeatedly apply what you have learned – is this not a source of pleasure" (Ames and Rosemont (Tr.) 1998: 71). This is also the basis of 'self-cultivation' (修己, C. *xiuji*, K. *sugi*) (see: *The Analects* 14:42): an ongoing path*way* of learning and an implementation strategy for Confucian scholars, which will be examined in more detail later in relation to Korean Confucians. The Dao of Confucianism is quite rigidly organised and is conceived of in a social context through clearly defined hierarchical relationships between individuals and linked with the most important Confucian virtue: usually written as *ren* (仁, K. *in*) in English (though sometimes written '*jen*'), which Confucius himself expounded on greatly. It is a combination of the character for a human being and the number '2', in other words – what connects two people. This character therefore highlights the link between people, or emphasises that the most basic thing that makes us 'humans' is our interaction with other people: we (animals) exist as 'social beings' because there are at least two such beings.

This bring us to the 'Five Cardinal Relationships' (五倫, C. *wulun*, K. *oryun*) of Confucianism, providing the basic guidelines for a moral community where kinship and age are important for maintaining vertical hierarchies. These relationships were taught to children, both male and female, from an early age and considered the most basic, but necessary guidelines, for a well-functioning 'harmonious' society, whereby harmony was achieved through fulfilling one's specific role (see: *Mencius* 3A:4; *Doctrine of the Mean* Ch. 20; *The Great Learning* Ch. 3):

The Five Cardinal Relationships

Between father and son
Between ruler and minister

> Between husband and wife
> Between old and young
> Between friends

The other relationship, emphasised much more in Korea than even in China where it is still important, is the idea of filial piety (孝, C. *xiao*, K. *hyo*). *Hyo* is often referred to as the defining feature of Korean Confucian familial virtues, a term that all foreigners in Korea soon learn about, especially when invited into a Korean home by friends, where the eldest male is the most respected person in the family. Filial obligations are referred to very early on in *The Analects* (1:2), where it is in turn followed by and linked with the terms discussed above, *Dao* (道) and *ren* (仁):

> Master You said: "It is a rare thing for someone who has a sense of filial and fraternal responsibility (xiaodi) to have a taste for defying authority. [. . .] Exemplary persons (junzi) concentrate their efforts on the root, for the root having taken hold, the way (*dao*) will grow there from. As for filial and fraternal responsibility, it is, I suspect, the root of authoritative conduct (ren)?"
>
> (Ames & Rosemont 1998: 71)

This passage encapsulates the main concerns of a Confucian 'exemplary person', sometimes translated as 'the superior person' or 'gentleman', though the term is linguistically gender neutral in Chinese, referring to one who is morally and socially responsible – the end goal of self-cultivation. Indeed, all Confucian teachings are to guide one on the path*way* to become an exemplary person: one who exemplifies and embodies *ren*. This then develops into a philosophy on developing social relationships in a beneficial manner and the term is often translated as humane, humaneness, benevolent and so on. In their 'philosophical translation' of *The Analects*, Ames and Rosemont (1998) translate *ren* as "authoritative conduct", which exemplifies the hierarchy and sense of obligation that is embodied by all relationships in a Confucian society, which is made up of the moral and social, which inevitably shapes Confucian political discourse too. Even the leader *should* be a morally and socially responsible individual who has obligations to the population (s)he governs.

Confucius advocates a leader who embodies 'virtue' (德, C. *De*, K. *Dŏk*); one who practices self-cultivation to the highest degree, but who also organises people through observing ritual propriety (禮, C. *li*, K. *Ye*), rather than by force. This is another recurrent theme in Confucianism, whereby ritual carries with it moral obligations as well as personifying the refined behaviour associated with a (self-)cultivated person. Rites and rituals, especially towards ancestors, can be a serious (and expensive) business. But, as Naoaki Hiraishi (2003: 187) stresses, "Rites had the advantage of inculcating people with social norms rather than teaching with words or social ordering with criminal law and other physical punishment". Confucian morality and their reinforcement through ritual propriety as such, reflects another goal of a Confucian education (but for more details on ritual in Confucianism, see: Yao 2000: ch. 4).

The benefits of, and the need for education, then, is another important idea that is closely linked with Confucian self-cultivation. It is also a theme that was taken on board by two later Confucians, Mencius (sometimes written as Mengzi) (c.372–289 BCE) and Xunzi (also written Hsun Tzu) (c.313–238), though with diametrically opposing views. Mencius wrote that 'human nature' (性, C. *xing*, K. *song*) was good, and hence education was to refine one's inherent good and promote one's virtuous nature; Xunzi wrote that human nature was evil, and that education, as well as strict laws were necessary to deter people from acting out according to it (See: Chan 1973: chs. 3, 6). Xunzi would actually influence a school of thought in China known as Legalism (法家, C. *Fa-jia*), which validated the strict rule of law under the First Emperor, Qin Shi Huang (260–210 BCE), who unified the warring states under the Qin Dynasty (秦朝; 221–206 BCE). Under his very violent and brutal reign, he enforced the infamous 'burning of the books', which included many Confucian texts, as well as the live burial of Confucian scholars (see: Chan 1972: 101–108). Mencius would become extremely important much later, and his ideas on human nature would stimulate a renewed interest in Confucianism towards the end of the Tang dynasty (唐朝; 618–907CE) in China, becoming one of the salient features of the later development of Neo-Confucianism. In the Korean context, it would not be an exaggeration to say that Mencius' ideas became more important, in terms of intellectual stimulation and provocation, than those of Confucius himself, given due consideration in Chapter 4. But, Neo-Confucianism was also influenced by another school which focused on the idea of Dao, though in a different manner, which became known as Daoism. Daoism was also important for the development of Korea's religious and philosophical traditions, though more indirectly than Confucianism, demonstrated later in this book.

Daoism: *an overview and some key concepts*

The origins of what is known as philosophical Daoism (sometimes written as Taoism) (道家, C. *Daojia*, K. *Dogyo*) or Classical Daoism begins with the teachings in one of the most translated texts in history – the *Dao De Ching* (道德經) – attributed to Laozi. Usually grouped with this text is the *Zhuangzi* (莊子), named after its supposed author. Little is known about either of the authors of these important texts, and some even doubt the existence of Laozi, which simply means the old master(s), and as Julia Ching (1993: 87) notes, "We are not even certain [. . .] whether his name was Lao (Lao Tan) or Li (Li Erh, Li Tan)". While it is generally accepted that Zhuangzi was a contemporary of Mencius, only the first seven chapters of his text are actually attributed to him, known as the 'inner chapters', while the other chapters are generally considered to be the compilation of Daoist ideas by other scholars over a substantial period of time (Palmer *et al.* 2006: xviii–xix). What is clear is that these texts were critical of Confucianism and sought to undermine rigid applications of its ideals and over-attachment to any man-made '*way*', which is problematised through issues regarding language itself, in an attempt to dissolve artificially constructed and delimiting boundaries, a project which in modern times (in the West) is not dissimilar to Jacque Derrida's 'De-Construction' (originally discussed in *Of Grammatology*, 1976).

Dao De Ching (verse 1) begins with the famous phrase:

> Way-making (*dao*道) that can be put into words is not really way-making, And naming (*ming*名) that can assign fixed reference to things is not really naming.
>
> (Ames & Hall 2003: 77)

The first issue highlighted is then one of 'fixing' names to things, and then becoming attached to the rigid meanings implied by these names, which impose boundaries on ideas and path*ways* for self-cultivation, and therefore on our existence under the aegis of how we think. This is most definitely a pun at the expense of Confucians who considered naming to be extremely important, reflected in their teachings on the 'rectification of names' (正名, C. *zhengming*), explained in *The Analects* of Confucius himself:

> When names are not used properly, language will not be used effectively; when language is not used effectively, matters will not be taken care of; when matters are not taken care of, the observance of ritual propriety (*li*禮)[. . .] will not flourish.
>
> (Ames & Rosement 1998: 162)

The Dao, according to the early Daoists (as they would be known only much later), should not be limited to certain rigid interpretations and then refracted even further by strict application though rites and propriety, which are then deemed to have some intrinsic meaning in and of themselves by Confucians. Laozi overturns such constructed notions of humanity, wisdom, and sageliness, and even questions the important Confucian relations, suggesting they are antithetical to 'way-making' or the *Dao* (see verses 18 and 19). Laozi challenges the force of tradition, which was championed by Confucius himself, but later forced on people by an authoritarian hegemony which enforces its own boundaries on society through restrictive societal norms and artificial relationships which further reinforced hierarchy, discriminating against women in particular: a recurrent theme in this book.

Conversely, Laozi is someone who eulogises the female/femininity and his text has several respectful and affirmative references to the "mother" and to "femininity". If the West was created (and structured) by "God the Father", then the East spontaneously emerged (unstructured) from "Dao the Mother". Un-learning/Un-knowing conventions opens a possibility for a reversion to a stage of limitless (im)possibilities like infancy, a pure state like an uncarved block of wood, *pu* (樸) (verse 28). Initially, a child is open to an ocean of un-fixed ideas, before a "structuring" education imposes itself upon the mind, and so the mind which was receptive to everything, and fluid like water, becomes rigid with Confucian dogma (which was learned by rote by aspiring students!). Virtue, or *De*, was something Confucians were busy teaching how to recognise by the "invention" of conventions (both linguistic and ritual). By contrast, Laozi (and later Zhuangzi) challenged such interference in the natural way-making of *dao*, promoting instead, "*wu-wei*" (無爲), non-action, a most important Daoist principle (see: verse 63). This may be explained as letting things follow their natural course, allowing things to originate without unnatural constraints and limitations from their onset. If we apply this to a real-life situation today, take the example of a boss at work who lets the workers carry out their work without undue interference: the individuals have been hired because they have their own skillset, so as long as they carry out their work to the best of their capacities then things should turn out well. Over interference may lead to stress, which may lead to less productive work, even mental illness on the part of the employee who is then prevented from carrying out her/his work to the best of her/his abilities – again – the mind is the engine which generates all actions.

There is also a notion of meditation developing in the *Dao De Ching*:

> In carrying about your more spiritual and more physical aspects and embracing their oneness, are you able to keep them from separating? In concentrating your *qi* [氣] and making it pliant, are you able to become the newborn babe? In scrubbing and cleansing your profound mirror, are you able to rid it of imperfections?
>
> (Ames & Hall 2003: verse 10)

The mirror imagery, usually related to the mind, emphasises the importance of removing imperfections, or having pure thoughts, ridding the mind of delusions or simply put, negative thoughts. Breathing exercises focusing on *qi/chi* (*ki* in Korean) would also be developed by religious Daoism, and incorporated into martial practices such as *Qigong* and *Taiji-chuan*, later developed by Buddhists into meditational Buddhism, which will be discussed in subsequent chapters.

Zhuangzi (399–295 BCE) developed Laozi's theme of non-attachment to fixed ways, also focusing on the "unnatural" limitations one is exposed to, reinforced through language, as well as rules and regulations imposed by institutions. Watson (1968: 3) in the "introduction" to his translation of the Zhuangzi emphasises that "the central theme [. . .] may be summed up in a single word: freedom". Zhuangzi acknowledges the inter-relatedness of all things which are constantly changing, where perceptions depend on the perceiver – depending on their contexts – which always alters and transforms things, which are in a (non)state of flux. Zhuangzi (in Hinton 1998: 23) explains:

> This is that, and that is this. That makes yes this and no that the same, and this makes yes this and no that the same. So is there a that and a this? Or is there not a that and a this? Where that and this cease to be opposites, you'll find the hinge of Dao. [. . .] Then yes this is whole and inexhaustible, and no that is whole and inexhaustible.

Confucian scholars, as noted above, were very different, trying to attach exact meanings to words, a process called "the rectification of names". For Zhuangzi language and words had one purpose – to express meaning; then the words themselves became redundant:

> The fish trap exists because of the fish; once you've gotten the fish, you can forget the trap. The rabbit snare exists because of the rabbit; once you've gotten the rabbit, you can forget the snare. Words exist because of meaning; once you've gotten the meaning, you can forget the words.
> (Watson1968: 302)

Zhuangzi (Watson 1968: 305) emphasises that meanings change depending on our own perceptions and these perceptions are shaped by our own context. In other words, someone in another place and time may (quite correctly) view things differently. This was also poking fun at the Confucians who sought to "fix" language within boundaries, suggesting that, "What at the beginning he used to call right he has ended up calling wrong", playing again with the idea of reversals between "this" and "that" which have a plurality of meanings depending on context(s), thereby destabilising fixed ideas of "yes this" and "no that", opening language and existence itself to "Other" possibilities, that follow the natural pattern of Dao inherent in all things. In other words, there are many ways to achieve similar goals, and the goals themselves may evolve and change.

The *Yi Ching* (Classic of Changes), mentioned above as one of the Confucian Classics, was also of great importance to Daoism and its later developments, especially through its ideas on Yin (陰) and Yang (陽), highlighted in the *Dao De Ching* itself which discusses them. These ideas were also used and developed by the Yin-Yang school that then linked them with the Five Elements (五行, C. *Wujing*, K. *Ohaeng*): fire, water, earth, wood and metal. Yin and yang literally mean the shaded side and the sunny side of a mountain respectively, in other words, reflecting upon the different aspects/attributes of the same thing, or the inherent changes that take place within things and their transformation depending on the situation or context. So from a Daoist point of view, cold becomes hot, hot becomes cold; dark becomes light, light becomes dark, and as such, a complementarity is acknowledged between the different phases/cycles of nature, rather than considering them as diametrically opposing forces. This text was also used for predicting the future, through the different arrangements of the hexagrams, and reading these became associated with Daoist priests, linked with the more religious form of Daoism, *Daojiao*, which blended with folk religion, deifying figures such as Laozi, along with many other deities.

This religious strain of Daoism which initially developed at the start of the Han Dynasty as the Huang-Lao school (where Huang referred to the legendary Yellow Emperor, Huangdi), had a set of texts compiled and known as the Huainanzi, but Confucianism was already gaining power at this point in China, and would soon be transmitted to Korea. Around 142 CE, religious Daoism took on a greater development when Laozi apparently appeared in visions to Zhang Daoling (34–156 CE) with instructions on "morality, meditation, the cure of diseases through rituals of petition to various deities [. . .] and social organisation", leading to a religious order that would further be developed by his descendants and followers (Adler 2002: 67). Eventually reaching its zenith during the Tang dynasty, *Dao-jiao*, by this point, emphasised ideas about physical well-being and longevity, developing teachings about the importance of certain exercises coupled with preserving and nourishing *Qi/Chi* energy (K. *ki*), in turn linked with a new goal: immortality (67–73). Daoist priests were also important figures who selected propitious days for weddings and feasts, as well as the best sites for graves to guarantee peace for the spirits of the dead, developing the art of *Feng Shui* (風水, K. *Pungsu*). Many of these ideas would be adapted in Korea, but the functions associated with Daoist clergy in China, would be carried out by Buddhist monks in Korea, leaving no place for a long-lasting separate Daoist school there. This may be quite possibly due to the fact that Korea was much smaller than China and hence, there was less population in need of ritual or spiritual alternatives, as Confucianism and Buddhism were flourishing, adopted by the elite, and shaping the spiritual lives of those on the entire Korean peninsula, along with Shamanism.

Buddhism: *an overview and some key concepts*

Buddhism is a missionary religion based on the teachings of the original Shakyamuni (also known as Guatama/Siddhārta) Buddha who probably lived during the sixth century BC in Lumbinī, now in southern Nepal (for an overview of his life, see Choi 2011: 33–49). His teachings entered China at some point during the early first century CE, though the earliest records of Buddhist texts arriving in China date from the first century BCE (Chan 1973: 336). Clearly shaped by the cultural and religious context in which it originated and developed, Buddhism was influenced by Hinduism, especially ideas such as karma and reincarnation, but also meditation and the importance of the mind (for more on Hinduism, see Narayanan 2005). Its encounter with China and the Chinese context would also mean that its form would be shaped by the beliefs and traditions it encountered there, especially Daoism. An initial stage in the spread of one religion into a new cultural and linguistic sphere is translation. The early Buddhists who made their way into China had loosely (and sometimes inaccurately) borrowed concepts from Daoism. This led many to think that Buddhism was simply a different version of the traditional and indigenous Chinese tradition – so much so that there were even claims that the Buddha was none other than a reincarnation of Laozi (Ching 1993: 126). It would also, like Daoism, be criticised by Confucians, who felt that its teachings and celibate priesthood did not provide a path*way* for dealing with the real world and real issues, something the Confucians exalted in their own teachings. In particular, Confucians critiqued the apparent lack of social responsibility, especially in relation to their parents, that monks eschewed, and suggested that Buddhists rejected the basic fabric of a well-organised society by not having their own children or families (Adler 2002: 17). In sum, they alleged that Buddhism had nothing 'real' to teach humans because it was too far removed from our social existence and too interested in speculative metaphysics, which is simply not true.

Contrarily, Buddhism reflects teachings that reify the unhappiness and injustices that humans experience in their lives and provides a detailed path*way* to help them. This is obvious from the first sermon of the historical Buddha (see: Lin 1942: 359–362), in which we encounter the basis of his teachings, called 'Dharma'. Usually translated in East Asia using the character 法 (C. *Fa*; K. *Pŏp*), meaning law, it may be more appropriate to translate it as 'guidelines', which is a less rigid term, open to change and interpretation. The Dharma is embodied by the Buddha's teachings on suffering or non-satisfactoriness, from *dukkha* in Pāli, and the basis of the Four Noble Truths (Hardy 1990: 61–64):

The Four Noble Truths

1   Life is *dukkha* (starting from birth itself).
2   The cause of *dukkha* is desire and craving (both sensual and material).
3   To remedy *dukkha* one must eliminate desire and craving.
4   To eliminate desire and craving one must follow the Eightfold Path.

The Eightfold Path (Adler 2002: 76–77) delineates the Buddhist practical guide for adherents, which is devoid of faith, a necessary component of the Abrahamic traditions, but rather, emphasises: wisdom and discernment (1–2); ethical behaviour (3–5); and discipline of the mind (6–8):

The Eightfold Path

1   Right views
2   Right intention
3   Right speech
4   Right action
5   Right livelihood
6   Right effort
7   Right mindfulness
8   Right concentration

One thing that is important to signpost here, is that the solution to *dukkha* was to 'awaken' the actual need for 'liberation' from desire and craving. Indeed, the title of 'the Buddha', means 'the awakened one', or one who is awakened to the precariousness of our attachments. Or conversely, it could mean an awakening to the need to strive for non-attachment to things/fixed ideas/reality/the world, which the Buddha taught were illusory, or 'empty' coming from the Sanskrit term Śūnyatā, meaning 'nothing-ness', an issue that will be dealt with in more detail later. The ultimate goal of the Eightfold Path is to extinguish attachments, which can lead to Nirvana (which means 'to blow out') or the cessation of samsara, a cycle of rebirths, which remember, inevitably begin with *dukkha* and an ongoing cycle of suffering and trying to alleviate that suffering in subsequent lives.

Those who followed the Buddha and his teachings were collectively known as the Sangha, comprising of laypeople as well as monks and nuns, who took a series of vows of abstinence. For laypeople, they had to abstain from (1) taking life; (2) stealing; (3) sexual misconduct; (4) false speech; (5) intoxicating agents (drink and drugs). These teachings reinforce the Buddha's espousal of the 'middle path*way*', which avoids the extremes of being overly ascetic, unlike the adherents of a rival religion during this early period, Jainism, with which it has some similarities (for more on Jainism, see Caillat 2002: 97–110). Members of the Buddhist clergy had to follow five additional precepts of abstention: (6) eating after noon; (7) forms of entertainment (singing and dancing); (8) adorning the body with cloths, perfumes and garlands; (9) sleeping in high or luxurious places; (10) receiving gold or money (Adler 2002: 76). In a nutshell, the Buddha discourages us from being overly self-indulgent, and encourages us to be considerate of others at all times – in other words – to *be* compassionate.

An important factor that influenced the style of Buddhism that developed in East Asia was the particular branch that became deep-rooted there, known as Mahayana, or the 'Greater Vehicle'. This contrasted with the branch known as Theravada (school of the elders), which considered itself to be more closely aligned with the earliest teachings of the Buddha, and also considered itself more 'purist', now generally practiced in South-East Asia. The Mahayana branch emphasises that everyone had the potential to achieve Nirvana in a single lifetime, which is an attractive aspect of its teachings. The Mahayana's appeal in China may well have been due to the intellectual climate where both Daoism and Confucianism taught about the innate perfectibility of everyone (while at the same time discriminating against women). Indeed, Mahayana Buddhism is the form of Buddhism that became pervasive not only in China, but also Korea and Japan.

But, as mentioned above, the translations of Buddhist texts had not been refined in the early stages of its development, anachronistically "matching concepts" from Daoism. One example using this technique known as "*Geyi*" 格義 (sometimes written *ko-i*), was to equate the 'emptiness' known as *Śūnyatā* in Buddhism with the 'nothingness' or *wu* (無) of Daoism, despite

Figure 1.2 A Korean Shaman performing a ritual
Courtesy of David J. Kim

their very different meanings and implications (see: Mair 2012). It was not until the fourth century that monks such as Kumārajīva (344–413 CE) really started to consider the importance of translational issues, while retranslating Buddhist texts from Sanskrit to Chinese. Kumārajīva and his followers focused particularly on the teachings of the great Indian Buddhist philosopher Nāgārjuna (c.150–c.250 CE), who himself had shaped the development of Mahāyāna Buddhism. It is important to underscore that by this time Buddhism had already made its way to the Korean peninsula, clearly influenced by the Sinitic Mahāyāna tradition that was developing and being promoted in China. Before long, Buddhism, as well as Confucianism, and more indirectly, Daoism, would be adapted, but also transformed and refined by a number of great Korean intellectuals that readers will meet as they journey through this book, which assesses their contexts and ideas, as well as their important contributions to the history of ideas.

Shamanism: *an overview and some key concepts*

It is almost impossible to look at Korea's religious history without also mentioning Shamanism from the outset. Though the intellectual (and written) traditions of Confucianism, Buddhism and Daoism, undoubtedly shaped Korea's intellectual heritage immensely, Shamanism always loomed, sometimes closer to the forefront of things, sometimes in the background, especially during the Chosŏn dynasty (朝鮮; 1392–1910) when it was virtually outlawed, but never eradicated. Nevertheless, it was an integral part of Korea's socio-religious historical context, and often analysed as a part of 'folk religion', or *musokkyo* (무속교) in Korean. As early records and writings on these religious elements fall between scarce and virtually nonexistent, it is sometimes difficult to form a clear picture of these traditions, opening the door to much conjecture by some (especially modern nationalists) who turn myths into reality, outlined in later chapters. Shamanism is the embodiment of a myriad of interwoven religious elements such as animism and totemism, incorporating various aspects of the traditional culture of the Korean peninsula and its people before recorded time into its current polytheistic pantheon. Shamanism should be understood in this regards, reflecting the long oral historical transmission of Korean culture, drawing from other religious traditions, such as Buddhism, as well as legends and folktales, representing the collective consciousness of the people, reflecting what cultural anthropologist Claude Lévi-Strauss (1908–2009) described as "bricolage". At the same time, it should *not* be seen as something old-fashioned, out-dated or 'primitive', but something that is transformative and dynamic in the globalised and internet-driven Korea of the twenty-first century, discussed in more detail in Chapter 6.

The history of Shamanism in Korea is a long one, dating from the early first millenium BCE, hence, Shamanism predates all the textual traditions discussed earlier in this chapter. The word 'shaman' seems to be derived from a Tungusic word, *saman*, but the Korean word for shaman, known as '*mudang*' (무당) is based on the Chinese character '巫' (pronounced *mu* in Korea), which represents a link Heaven and Earth and the entities from both worlds through an axis mundi (Hogarth Kim 1999: 2). Shaman are mostly female in Korea, referred to as *mudang*, but also known as *mansin* (만신, literally meaning 'ten thousand gods), whereas male shamans are known as *paksu* (박수). Kim Tae-gon (1998: 16) notes that many of the classic definitions of Shamanism "emphasise the idea of trance, ecstasy, and possession", such as that by Eliade (1964: 5, 190), but this reflects only part of the functions of the *mudang* in the Korean context. The *mudang* are professional spiritual ritualists who often have close relationships with their clients who pay for their services, which may include various rites, known as *kut* (굿in Korean), which involves spirit-possession, accompanied by music and dance and other 'performance arts', but they were historically often adepts in shamanic medicine, and consulted for revelation and prognostication, which many still are today.

In Korea, there are two types of *mudang*: (1) *Kangsin-mu* (강신무/降神巫) – a *mudang* who is initially possessed by a spirit, accompanied by a 'spiritual illness' or *sinbyŏng* (신병), and who is eventually guided by a more experienced *mudang* who will initiate the novice into the spirit world by performing a *naerim kut* (내림굿), or descent ritual; (2) *Sesŭp-mu* (세습무/世襲巫) – a *mudang* who inherits her spiritual abilities through the female line, hence matrilineal, in direct contrast to Confucian patriarchy and its focus on agnatic kinship or patrilineality. The men in such families would often play the instruments to accompany the rituals – supporting the women – again, the opposite of Confucian norms (Yim *et al.* 2002: 334–336). The *mudang* interact with a vast variety of deities, reflecting their connection with nature and the spaces and lives of the people they intercede for: Mountain God, Earth God, Dragon King God, Smallpox God (as the disease was common in the past), Seven-Star God (the Big Dipper), God of Luck, God of the House, Kitchen God, Birth God, and so on (336–337). The *mudang* will be mentioned throughout this book hovering around other traditions, while sometimes subtly shaping them, and explored in more detail in the final chapter.

Conclusion

This chapter has outlined how religion and philosophy are not mutually exclusive terms in East Asia, though they remain quite separate disciplines and concepts in the West. Considering 'religions' in a more pluralistic way, as sets of practices and rituals, and sometimes tenets of belief, which unify a group within a community, is a more helpful way of looking at traditions in East Asia. Philosophy in an East Asian context is considered as a set of teachings by morally cultivated scholars, that when studied, should ultimately be applied to one's daily life, with the ultimate goal of becoming a better person, who will then contribute to society. Wisdom then is something that is considered to be a realistic and achievable goal, which emphasises that learning should transform how one thinks, and this will in turn transform how one lives: thought and action are inextricably intertwined, it is teaching for understanding how *'to practice' a better life*. It is also something that can be attained by following path*ways* of self-cultivation: Confucianism, Daoism and Buddhism, as well as others, discussed later in this book, some considered Western, others which originated in Korea itself. Indeed, people in East Asia would have seen these approaches as non-exclusivistic, with followers of Buddhism also adhering to Confucian social ideals and rituals, who may also have been scholars of Daoism, and later prayed to Daoist deities, which could also include the Buddha, while all could consult a shaman depending on their individual (or family) needs.

Confucianism, a misnomer of European Jesuit origin, is a large body of scholarship consisting of a tradition which pre-dates Confucius, represented by the *Five Classics*, as well as a collection of other texts, the *Four Books*, which include the *Analects* of Confucius, but also the important text which expounds the teachings of Mencius. Confucianism shaped one's social being by reinforcing a code of ethics based on the Five Cardinal Relationships, which were hierarchical and unfortunately manipulated to discriminate against women in particular. This social philosophy also reinforced itself through moral principles such as *'ren'* or 'humanity', which again places great importance on our interaction with other people as a defining feature of a morally superior individual. This was further bolstered within the family through the concept of filial piety, of great importance in Korea. Daoism too had a textual basis, drawing from the rich ideas represented by Laozi and Zhuangzi, who both diverge from the quite rigid interpretations and rituals conceptualised by Confucians. They emphasised the 'naturalness' of non-interference by recommending *'wu-wei'*, only necessary action when needed, to balance our relationships with each other and with nature as part of an interconnected universe. Their sense of Dao or 'way-making' is something that cannot be concretely defined as 'this' or 'that': such polarities lead to rivalry and conflict, all too obvious in the world we live in today. Buddhism, based on the sermons or teachings of the Buddha, also attempts to remove conflict. The Buddhists draw our attention to their 'Four Noble Truths', starting with the source of suffering, which emanates from the mind due our perceptions of things and then our subsequent attachment to those things. Monks and laypeople are provided with a set of guidelines to assist them along the 'Eightfold Path', which is a continual and gradual process, which aims to alleviate their suffering and lead them to nirvana. Finally, shamanism, briefly discussed in this chapter, pre-dates all the other textual traditions in Korea, but historically would have interacted with them, and the image of spirits descending into the Korean *mudang* has been embroidered into other Korean religions throughout history, especially those which developed in the late nineteenth century, right down until the present, in which shamanism remains relevant.

These ideas are intended to help all of us on our own path*ways*, and so we do not need to be Korean or Asian to benefit from their wisdom. Nor should we be afraid to question and sometimes criticise some of their implications and biases that are unsuitable and untenable for our lives in the early twenty-first century, where freedom and equality are important rights that we should not take for granted.

References and further reading

Adler, Joseph A. 2002. *Chinese Religions*. Routledge: London.

Ames, Roger T. and David L. Hall. 2003. *Daodejing 'Making This Life Significant': A Philosophical Translation*. Ballantine Books: New York.

Ames, Roger T. and Henry Rosemont, Jr. (trans.). 1998. *The Analects of Confucius: A Philosophical Translation*. Ballantine Books: New York.

Caillat, Colette. 2002. "Jainism". *The Religious Traditions of Asia*, ed. Joseph M. Kitagawa. Routledge Curzon: London and New York. 97–110.

Cawley, Kevin. 2013. "In the Name(s) of God: Matteo Ricci's Translational Apostolate". *Translation Studies*, 6(3): 293–308.

Chan, Lois Mai. 1972. "The Burning of the Books in China, 213 B.C.". *The Journal of Library History*, 7(2): 101–108.

Chan, Wing-Tsit. 1973. *A Sourcebook in Chinese Philosophy*, Princeton University Press: Princeton, NJ. Chapters 3, 6, 12.

Ching, Julia. 1993. *Chinese Religions*. Macmillan Press: London.

Choi, Joon-sik. 2011. *Buddhism: Religion in Korea*. Ewha Women's University Press: Seoul. Part One.

Dawson, Raymond. 1971. "Western Conceptions of Chinese Civilization". *The Legacy of China*. The Clarendon Press: Oxford. 1–27.

Derrida, Jacques. 1976. *Of Grammatology*. Translated by Gayatari Chakravorty Spivak. The John Hopkins University Press: Baltimore and London.

———. 1998. "Faith and Knowledge: The Two Sources of 'Religion' and the Limits of reason Alone". *Religion*, eds. Jacques Derrida and Gianni Vattimo. Stanford University Press: Stanford. 1–78.

Eliade, Mircea. 1964. *Shamanism: Archaic Techniques of Ecstasy*. Translated by William R. Trask. Routledge and Kegan Paul: London.

Fuchs, Thomas. 2006. "The European China-Reception from Leibniz to Kant". Translated by Martin Schönfeld. *Journal of Chinese Philosophy*, 33(1): 35–49.

Gallagher, Louis J. (trans.). 1953. *China in the Sixteenth Century: The Journals of Matteo Ricci*. Random House: New York.

Graham, A.C. 2003. *Disputers of Tao: Philosophical Argument in Ancient China*. Open Court Publishing: Chicago.

Hardy, Friedheim. 1990. "The Classical Religions of India". *The World's Religions: The Religions of Asia*, ed. Friedheim Hardy. Routledge: London. 37–127.

Hinton, David. (trans.). 1998. *Chuang Tzu: The Inner Chapters*. Counterpoint: Washington, DC.

Hogarth Kim, Hyun-key. 1999. *Korean Shamanism and Cultural Nationalism*. Jimoondang Publishing Company: Seoul.

Kim Tae-gon. 1998. "What Is Shamanism?" *Korean Shamanism*, ed. Keith Howard. The Royal Asiatic Society, Korea Branch: Seoul. 15–31.

Lin Yutang. (ed.). 1942. *The Wisdom of China and India*. The Modern Library: New York.

Mair, Victor H. 2012. "What Is Geyi, After All?" *China Report*, 48(1–2): 29–59.

Naoaki, Hiraishi. 2003. "The Essence of Li (Rites) and Its Modern Significance". *Sungkyun Journal of East Asian Studies*, 13(2): 179–189.

Narayanan, Vasudha. 2005. "Hinduism". *Eastern Religions*, ed. Michael D. Coogan. Duncan Baird Publishers: London. Part One.

Palmer, Martin *et al.* (trans.) 2006. *The Book of Chuang Tzu*. Penguin Books: London.

Rule, Paul A. 1986. *K'ung-Tzu or Confucius – The Jesuit Interpretation of Confucianism*. Allen and Unwen: London.

Smith, Jonathan Z. 1998. "Religion, Religions, Religious". *Critical Terms for Religious Studies*, ed. Mark C. Taylor. University of Chicago Press: Chicago. 269–284.

UNESCO World Heritage. 2018a. Gochang, Hwasun and Ganghwa Dolmen Sites. Available at: http://whc.unesco.org/pg.cfm?cid=31&id_site=977 [accessed on 13 June 2018].

UNESCO World Heritage. 2018b. Complex of Koguryo Tombs. Available at: http://whc.unesco.org/en/list/1091 [accessed on 13 June 2018].

Watson, Burton. (trans.). 1968. *Chuang Tzu: Basic Writings*. Columbia University Press: New York.

Yao, Xinzhong. 2000. *An Introduction to Confucianism*. Cambridge University Press: Cambridge.

Yim, Suk-jay, Roger L. Janelli and Dawnhee Yim Janelli. 2002. "Korean Religion". *The Religious Traditions of Asia: Religion, History and Culture*, ed. Joseph M. Kitagawa. Routledge Curzon: London. 333–347.

2 Adaptations and interactions
Chinese traditions and Korean ways

Introduction

Due to its close geographical proximity to Korea, Chinese ideas were easily adapted and then developed in Korea, particularly during the Three Kingdoms period (*ca.* 57 CE–668), where Koguryŏ (高句麗) (which extended well into Manchuria), Paekche (百濟) and Silla (新羅) would vie for control of the peninsula, as well as cultural supremacy to validate their political control (see Figure 2.1). Whether they are Buddhist, Confucian or Daoist, these ideas attempt to provide society with a *modus vivendi*. They seek to provide path*ways* to help humans to reconcile themselves with life, and also death. In order to reconcile themselves with life, the scholars of ancient China adopted the ideas of Confucianism and sought to create an ethical and societal discourse. Buddhism, whilst it also deals with the complexities of living a life of goodness, focused on the machinations of the mind in an attempt to purify and reconcile it before death and the consequences of an afterlife. Daoism also sought to help people live balanced lives with each other without the hierarchy of Confucianism, while respecting nature and the world around us and acknowledging the role of moral leadership. When transmitted to Korea these teachings clearly were encountered by people who had already pre-existing traditions and beliefs of their own into which new ideas were assimilated, as still happens today with knowledge and technology around the world.

Mythical origins

As Homer B. Hulbert (1906: 69) and James Scarth Gale (1972: 121), Western missionaries active in Korea from the end of the nineteenth century surmised, the history ancient Korea is hard to grasp due to the paucity of documents, so that *myths* and facts have been mixed up – often difficult to extricate one from the other. Nevertheless, these myths are important repositories of knowledge about Korea's proto-history, reflecting on the 'origins' of a distinctive culture in an attempt to construct an idea of uniqueness which connects a certain group, or even different groups of people.

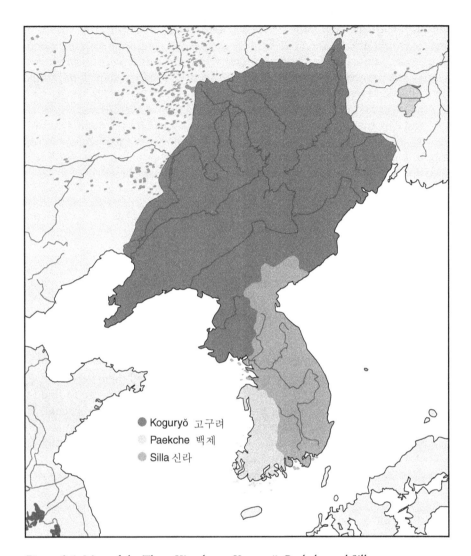

Figure 2.1 Map of the Three Kingdoms: Koguryŏ, Paekche and Silla

Myths also relate what earlier groups considered sacred or divine. The most important myth for understanding Korea in this regards is undoubtedly that of Tan'gun (also written Dangun). The earliest extant account of the myth dates only from the thirteenth century, where it appeared in the *Legends and History of the Three Kingdoms* (sometimes referred to as *Memorabilia of the Three Kingdoms* in English) (三國遺事, K. *Samguk Yusa*), composed by the Buddhist monk Iryŏn (1206–1289) – allegedly based on earlier (lost) sources. Though the text dates from a much later period, it sketches how Koreans during this later period considered their distinctive culture at a time when the Mongols were busy expanding their empire, which would also include the Korean peninsula. The myth would become even more important for Korean identity in the twentieth century, when it would assume a very different role for Korean nationalists during the tragic period of Japanese imperialism, discussed in Chapter 5.

This myth and others in the *Legends and History of the Three Kingdoms*, also indicate that the inhabitants of the peninsula had a pre-existing culture that was enriched with ideas from China, but also that these ideas entered into a distinctive Weltanschauung, shaped by another cultural and political identity, which the Tan'gun myth describes summarised here:

The Myth of Tan'gun*

According to the myth, Hwanung, a secondary son of Hwanin, the ruler of heaven, had descended with followers to a sacred place on a mountain in Korea, bringing culture and civilisation, but motivated to help human beings, assisted by the earl of wind, rain and the clouds. A bear and a tiger wishing to become human prayed to Hwanung, who gave them a task of eating specific herbs while remaining for a specific period of time in darkness in a cave. The tiger did not fulfil these obligations and ran away while the bear fulfilled them becoming a woman who prayed at an altar tree to have a child, unable to find a husband. Later Hwanung mated with this woman, and the child of this union was Tan'gun, who established a city at P'yŏngyang and called his nation Chosŏn (now known as Old Chosŏn, or Kojosŏn), before finally becoming a mountain god at the age of 1908. Kija then governed the state, who had been a refugee from the Shang dynasty in China.

* For a full translation of the myth see: Grayson 2002: 240

But what does the myth tell us about primeval Korea's religious and philosophical traditions? Firstly, it relates the idea of a ruler of heaven, showing a belief in the existence of deities, spirits, or beings beyond the mundane world who exert some influence over it. The king of heaven, while having some sort of control over the world below, is not its creator, hence there is no explanation of 'how' the world and its peoples have come into being. This idea of creation and 'origin' was clearly not a concern in earlier times when the myth was first constructed, just as it was not a concern for Confucians, while it seems to be an obsession of Western traditions (both religious and scientific). Secondly, the myth intertwines hierarchy with authority, where only certain people are leaders and set the rules, which others should follow – again, not entirely different from Confucianism, but in this case the king seems to possess some of the traits associated with Shamanism, possessing a deep connection with the spirit world and a deep connection with special 'sacred places', be it a mountain (where he descended) or an altar tree (where he has heard the prayers of the transformed bear). Thirdly, this also underscores that rituals are performed in sacred places which have special connections with spirits or gods. Korea is a very mountainous country, so it is hardly surprising that a mountain has been chosen as a place for the son of heaven to descend to – or that Tan'gun finally becomes a 'mountain god' – and this must be one of the earliest cults to have gained an extensive following throughout the peninsula. Fourthly, the myth explains the tribal interactions of a previous period, reflecting a belief in animism or totemism. From an anthropological point of view, the bear and tiger could represent totems of different tribes, just as heaven represents the object of worship of the most important tribe – the tribe that assumes its power or mandate from heaven through Hwanung. The 'heaven' worshipping tribe clearly is the strongest, and marriage into this tribe has benefits, hence the bear and tiger tribes are willing to undergo trials to join, and when the tiger failed, the tribe may have been expelled or overthrown from some position of power that they vied for against the bear tribe. It may have been that only unions from these two tribes could ascend the throne, something similar to what would happen in Silla.

The much later Confucian dynasty, Chosŏn (朝鮮; 1392–1910), would draw its name from the kingdom founded by Tan'gun in this myth. There are many other myths relating to the founding of other states, and the later Koryŏ dynasty (高慮; 918–1392) would affiliate itself with another such myth, the *Foundation Myth of Koguryŏ*, whose founding hero is Chumong: a great warrior and skilful archer whose birth occurs when he cracked out of a mysterious egg (see Grayson 2002: 243–244). This myth is also recounted in the *Legends and History of the Three Kingdoms*, and, unlike the Tan'gun myth, is also included in the earlier *History of the Three Kingdoms* (三國史記, K. *Samguk sagi*), compiled by Kim Pusik in 1145. But, a much earlier text of the myth is to be found carved in stone on the famous stele dedicated to King Kwanggaet'o the Great (374–413), dating from 414, which is to be found today in Ji'an, Manchuria, the former capital of Koguryŏ. The myth relays the foundation of a state, but does not include such detailed cultural and religious information as the Tan'gun myth. However, King Kwanggaet'o, known for having expanded Korean territory into Manchuria, is also remembered for having adopted Buddhism as the state religion. It is worth noting that the Tan'gun myth also indicates that another name for Hwanung was Chesŏk, originally a Hindu deity, but also a noted guardian deity in Buddhism (Grayson 2001: 34). While this may have been a later interpolation on the part of Iryŏn, the Buddhist raconteur of the myth, these early myths clearly reflect transcultural elements of the religious and philosophical traditions in Asia, which shaped and interpenetrated each other, showing us that ideas travelled from India to China and from China to Korea quite freely in this proto-cosmopolitan age.

The arrival of Buddhism: its early growth and dissemination

Spread by travelling monks who must have been aware of the influence of China in the region, Buddhism had started to make an impact on the Korean peninsula by the fourth century. As Eckert *et al.* (1990: 10) point out, it is clear that Kojosŏn, having been taken over by a Chinese refugee, Kija, would inevitably "[bear] some of the hallmarks of the Chinese political, economic and cultural influences". These influences would include Chinese characters, used by the elite in Korea up until the end of the nineteenth century, as well as Confucianism and Buddhism, the latter of which would produce some of the greatest intellectual scholars in East Asian history already by the end of the Silla kingdom. The *Samguk Yusa*, source of the Tan'gun myth, also recounts the entry of Buddhism into Korea, much of which was based on another Koryŏ text *Lives of Eminent Korean Monks* (海東高僧傳, K. *Haedong kosŭng chŏn*), compiled by another Buddhist, Kakhun, at the bequest of the king in 1215. These texts recount the arrival of Buddhist missionaries to Koguryŏ in 372, to Paekche in 384, and to Silla during the reign of King Nulji (r. 417–458) (Iryŏn 2004: 177–179). *The Lives of Eminent Monks* (Lee 1969) provides hagiographical details about the first missionaries: Sundo to Koguryŏ, having travelled throughout China (pp. 30–32); Mālānanda from Serindia to Paekche (pp. 45–49); Ado, possibly from Wu China or India (pp. 50–56). By this time, in the mid-sixth century, Buddhism had been adopted by Silla, and it is clear that it had become the main religion of the Three Kingdoms, and would reach its zenith during the Koryŏ dynasty, before entering a period of decline during the Chosŏn dynasty with the rise of Neo-Confucianism.

Early on, through state sponsorship, temples were erected throughout the peninsula, spreading Buddhist architecture and art. Soon, Koreans were sending missionaries to Japan, and while Silla and Koguryŏ monks definitely made their way to their island neighbours, it was the relations between the Paekche royal family and the Yamamoto imperial household which have most documented evidence, particularly in Japanese sources such as the *Records of Ancient Matters* (古事記, J. *Kojiki*) and the *Chronicles of Japan* (日本書紀, J. *Nihon Shoki*), both dating from the early eighth century. These texts recount how Paekche scholars such as Wang In, known as Wani in Japanese, tutored elite members of the Japanese Imperial household, and were responsible for teaching Chinese characters, as well as transmitting the sophisticated religious and philosophical teachings of the Sinosphere: Buddhism and Confucianism, but also Daoism. Grayson (2002: 33) emphasises the immense influence that Paekche monks had on the development of Buddhism in Japan, noting that:

> It was Paekche which initiated Buddhist missions in Japan. It was Paekche which over several generations transmitted the sophisticated art and architecture of the Chinese world, notably the Northern Wei Style. It was Paekche which was largely responsible for the early training of Japanese monks and nuns. Paekche, in this century of cultural ferment, was the principal transmitter and active agent in the early development of Japanese Buddhist Civilization.

Additionally, already during the reign of King Widŏk (r.554–598), masters of Sŏn Buddhism would make their way to Japan, helping to sow the seeds for Japanese Zen Buddhism, well-known to most Westerners, who are often unaware of its Chinese roots and Korean transmission.

If in the proto-historical period the king's reign was validated through his connection with various spirits, from the middle of the Three Kingdoms period, this mandate would be validated through an affiliation and devotion to Buddhism, reaching maturity in Silla. Buddhism was adopted later in Silla than in the other kingdoms, which may have been a result of the pre-existing and rigidly stratified, but nevertheless sophisticated 'bone-rank' (骨品, K. *kolp'um*) system, where one's place in society and one's roles in that society were largely determined by one's genealogy – and one's family background still influences social position in modern Korea. At the top of the bone-rank system was the hallowed [sage]-bone lineage (聖骨, K. *sŏnggol*), followed by those of the true bone status (眞骨, K. *chin'gol*) who had claims to the throne, and who could marry into the royal family, and then there were several other bone ranks descending in order until there were the lowly and distained slaves and outcasts (Kim 1971: 43–69). The sŏng (聖) character is an interesting choice as this is the character which would have been used to describe a sage, such as Confucius, but also one of the characteristics emphasised by Mencius as the measure of a King, who should be wise and sagacious, and indeed the character is also made up in part of the character for a king, 王, pronounced *wang* in Korean. These titles indicate just how important the role of King was considered, something that is gradually heightened over time, reaching its climax in the later Chosŏn dynasty which would have a particular focus on 'sagehood', discussed in more detail in the following chapters. For Silla, the kingship would have to incorporate a Buddhist motif for the *hwabaek* (elected council of nobles) to accept it and for the state to then begin to promote it, and this is exactly what happened.

King Pŏphŭng (r.514–540 CE), who championed the adoption of Buddhism, bore a name which literally means, Promoter [*hŭng*] of Dharma [*pŏp*], described in both the *Legends and History of the Three Kingdoms* and *Lives of Eminent Korean Monks*. Both accounts testify to the resistance of Silla to accept Buddhism; however, due to the miracles that accompanied martyrdom of the Grand Secretary Pak Yŏmch'ŏk, also known as Ich'adon, the Buddhist teachings were finally adopted as the court became convinced of their power: accounts relate how milk poured from Ich'adon's decapitated body and descended as flowers. From this point, it appears that Buddhism based on the teachings of the original Buddha, the man Siddhārtha Gautama, had been blended with the more miraculous aspects of folk religions and possibly Daoist tales where such feats were not unheard of, and eventually incorporated into accounts of the various Buddhas themselves. Such beliefs would have further bolstered the idea that Buddhism would protect the state as it was mandated by the Heavens (of which there were many) and the gods, evoked through Ich'adon's prayer before his execution, suggesting the adoption of Buddhism would generate peace.

King Pŏphŭng took the Chinese title of 'Wang' (王) as king, not the Korean title of Marikpan, reflecting a greater integration of Korea into the realm of Chinese cultural influence, which would only continue to grow. Inspired by King Pŏphŭng, future kings would also acquire Buddhist inspired titles, gaining prestige by doing so, which also bolstered their political power during this warring period with Paekche and Koguryŏ. These Buddhist titles, also adopted by King Chinhŭng (r.540–576), whose name literally meaning the 'Promoter of [Buddhist] Truth' were drawing on the Sanskrit term of *Cakravartin-raja* or benevolent ruler, not entirely unlike the sage-king championed by the Confucians, but suggesting a compassionate Buddhist king whose lineage was linked with that of the original Buddha. This had also been the case in China, specifically King Wen Di (r.581–605) of the Sui dynasty (隋朝; 581–605), who had presented himself as the *cakravartin*, but also the *mahādānapati*, a great patron of the religious faith, influencing King Mu (r.600–641) of Paekche (Best 2007: 36–38). However, this too would also have suited the Korean regal vista as it had a long tradition of the 'Shaman-King', echoing back to the Tan'gun myth, whereby the king was also considered a spiritual force which validated their rule. Indeed, Queen Sŏndŏk (r.632–647) 'the visionary', drew on this Shamanic symbolism which today has mostly female practitioners in Korea, and was noted to have predicted events that saved the state from enemy attacks, invoking the 'state-protection' consciousness associated with worthy rulers, who were also spiritual adepts. Accounts of these deeds appear in the *Legends and History of the Three Kingdoms* (in ch. 31 of that text), explicitly highlighting the importance of Buddhism, as well as its link with the throne and the military elite, as in the case of the Hwarang, discussed later in this chapter.

Queen Sŏndŏk's rule was further bolstered by such Buddhist vinculum or ties, and in particular, her support from Monk Chajang (590–658) fostered favour for her rule among the many supporters of Buddhism, which also benefitted from the prestige of its affiliation and alliance with the powerful and prestigious Tang dynasty (618–907) where he had studied (Mohan 2005: 131–144). Indeed, during Queen Sŏndŏk's reign, at the bequest of Chajang, Silla's dress code was transformed to reflect that of Tang. Chajang also traced the queen's sacred lineage back to the warrior caste of the Buddha's own clan, enabling her to take advantage of its masculine attributes and symbolic power, which was further embellished by the building of a nine-story pagoda that would ensure the allegiance of the entire population of *Haedong* 海東 [East of the Sea, a term used for Korea in China] (Mohan 2007: 51–64). It was also during the reign of this important queen that the astronomical observatory known as the Ch'ŏmsŏngdae was constructed, and can been seen in the historically rich city of Kyŏngju, Silla's ancient capital. Grayson (2001: 42–43) accentuates Chajang's contributions to Buddhism in Korea during this period, suggesting he standardised it, especially through his focus on rigorous monastic discipline and assessments of monks adherence to their precepts, as well as the study of the sutras and the introduction of a sweeping examination process. Hence, he reinforced the beginnings of Korea's intellectual tradition, where textual analysis was a focal point of one's Buddhist training. He would also found his own monastery at T'ongdosa, which remains today a head temple of the Republic of Korea's Jogye Order (or Chogye Order). He also wrote commentaries on certain sutras, foreshadowing a tradition that would distinguish Korean Buddhists in East Asia, outlined later in this chapter. Queen Chindŏk (r.647–654) continued the reign of queens in Silla, maintaining excellent diplomatic relations with Tang China and demonstrating the ability of women to rule as well as men, something that would be diminished with the rise of Neo-Confucianism on the Korean peninsula, though Silla would have one last female regent, Queen Chinsŏng (r.887–897), before the fall of Unified Silla, which led to the Latter Three Kingdoms period.

In Korea, Buddhism as a religion spread, while at the same time the government drew on Confucian ideas of statecraft. King Sosurim (r.371–384) of Koguryŏ, a supporter of Buddhism, established a National Confucian Academy in 372, as well as initiated the construction of smaller academies, or *kyŏngdang* (經堂), 'Classics' Halls', in the more rural areas where the classics were studied by elite males, bolstering a Confucian social ethos which was patriarchal, and which still reverberates in modern Korea. Note that this too highlights the hierarchy created in society though an elitist education – also palpable in Korea today.

Later interactions: *from the Hwarang to Daoism and indigenous beliefs*

The idea that Buddhism offered some sort of spiritual protection for the state is definitely one of the reasons attributed to its promotion by the royal family, but this also meant that the leaders were individuals who (at least in theory) followed Buddhist precepts and morality in order for its prestige to further validate their rule. Religious and state matters were inextricably intertwined. It would then be no surprise that military figures would also have been expected to be Buddhist, but the fact that armies kill other human beings would clearly contradict the very important Buddhist teaching which forbids taking life. In such a context there seems to also have grown a relationship between monks and military figures, and armies may have been accompanied by Buddhists to perform rituals for the dead and so on, in the same way that Catholic priests would accompany the Japanese armies which would invade Korea in the sixteenth century, as discussed later. There also seems to have been some groups which formed based on special skills, but also based on their looks – an ideal band of warriors – so to speak. *The Legends and History of the Three Kingdoms* and the *Lives of Eminent Korean Monks* both give accounts of the 'Original Flowers', or *Wonhwa* (源花), referring to bands of women, but after two leaders' rivalry ended in the murder of one, it appears they were disbanded and the attention turned to men, or youths to be more precise. Both previously mentioned texts also give accounts of these' Hwarang' (花郎), or Flower Youths. The more factual, *History of the Three Kingdoms*, by Kim Pusik, also gives an account of the Hwarang, but these accounts are all brief and have been greatly embellished and dramatised in modern Korea and their importance greatly exaggerated in TV dramas and movies, which suggest that there is lots of detailed information known about the Hwarang, which is not so. This has been further compounded by the 'discovery' in 1986 of manuscripts of the *Annals of the Hwarang* (花郎世記, K. *Hwarang Segi*), generally considered to be fake – the last mention of this original text appears in the *Lives of Eminent Korean Monks*, from the mid-Koryŏ period (McBride 2010, 2007).

The *Lives of Eminent Monks* (1969: 66) gives the details of the Wonhwa which were disbanded after one of the women drowned another member after getting her drunk. It gives no details of the role of these women, other than to mention that they were selected based on their 'talent' which is also not explained, but that they competed against each other while watched by a crowd. Additionally, in relation to the Hwarang, the same text (66–67), writes that the men of the Hwarang:

> powdered their faces, wore ornamented dresses, and [. . .] men of various sorts gathered around them. They instructed one another in the Way and in righteousness, entertained each other with songs and music, or went sightseeing to famous mountains and rivers, no matter how far away [. . .] and the good were recommended at court.
>
> (see also: *Samguk yusa*, ch. 82)

The text goes on to describe that from these men "brave generals and brave soldiers are born", developing the military theme for which they have become famous in modern Korea, but the text goes on to highlight that from 576 until the end of Silla there were only some two hundred knights chosen, and that they "respected and served their countrymen" (68). This '*Way* of the Hwarang' is actually attributed to King Chinhŭng, praised for his worship of Buddhism. Hence, there is a link between Hwarang morality and Buddhism, which is also reinforced by linking the Hwarang with monk Wŏn'gwang (541–630) – though this is not recounted in the *Lives of Eminent Korean Monks*. Wŏn'gwang is, however, discussed in a separate chapter of the text at some length, noted for his knowledge of Confucianism as well as 'Mysterious Learning', or *Xuanxue* (玄學), another term for Neo-Daoism, and also renowned for his period of study in China (74–82). This illustrates how the scholars of the time were instructed in the teachings of more than one school, and that these teachings did not necessarily clash with one another. Wŏn'gwang's biography also tells how two soldiers (Kwisan and Ch'wihang) sought instruction from him and that he listed five secular commandments for them (79):

Five Commandments for Laypeople

1   Serve your sovereign with loyalty.
2   Tend your parents with filial piety.
3   Treat your friends with sincerity.
4   Do not retreat from the battlefield.
5   Be discriminating about the taking of life.

These commandments reflect a very Korean synthesis of Buddhist virtues with mainly Confucian ones: the first three are directly related to the Five Cardinal Relationships, discussed in Chapter 1. It is only the last commandment which can be described as specifically Buddhist, reminding laypeople that the taking of life is not something to be taken lightly, and that one should refrain from killing when it provides no benefit. This may also be applied to the killing of animals – killing animals for food due to necessity is one thing, however, killing animals to mount on one's wall as a trophy is clearly breaking this commandment! The fourth commandment highlights the importance of these rules for military men, which is why it has been later suggested that these were the oaths or pledges of the Hwarang, though this is nowhere stated or implied in the text. This latter addition appears in the *Legends and History of the Three Kingdoms,* by Iryŏn (2004: ch. 82), where the role of the Hwarang has been embellished and linked with the Maitreya (K. *mirŭk*) cult in Korea – Maitreya referring to a reincarnation of the Buddha in the future, which the Hwarang hoped would be one of them. Indeed, the important military figure, General Kim Yusin (595–673), was considered a Hwarang leader, and his group of warriors were called the 'Band of the Dragon Flower Tree', alluding to the tree under which the Maitreya Buddha would eventually give his teachings. Such noteworthy generals are considered to have been Hwarang as well as loyal followers of Buddhism, clearly excused from taking life by adherence to the commandments of Wŏn'gwang.

There is, however, also a Daoist flavour to the tales related to the Hwarang, and even to Kim Yusin himself in the *Legends and History of the Three Kingdoms*, which has an entire chapter on the great military figure who finds himself caught up in a supernatural Daoist tale (ch. 33). The title given to such a Hwarang leader was *Kuksŏn* (國仙), meaning state (國) immortal (仙), the latter being a term usually used to refer to Daoist mystics. In Iryŏn's text, as he is trying his best to present Buddhism as the true religion of the Korean peninsula, he has generally negative descriptions of Daoism, linked with wondrous tales of fairies and immortal beings. Ch. 64, titled 'Daoism and the Downfall of Koguryŏ', explains how a Daoist priest had been sent from the Tang Emperor with images of Laozi to expound on the teachings of the *Dao De Ching* during the reign of King Yŏngnyu (r.618–642). This tale also suggests that information on Daoism was received into Korea after Buddhism had already become well established, already described as 'orthodox' teachings, while Daoism is described as 'mysterious', alluding to its 'dark' arts and practices. This exoticised tradition, which emphasised the cult of immortality associated with religious Daoism, teaching that people would become immortal spirits (神仙, K. *Sinsŏn*), seems to have blended in more with Korean folk beliefs and existing indigenous shamanistic traditions, especially those relating to spirits of mountains and rivers, where these Daoist monks travelled to. This passage also highlights that through following the teachings of Daoism and not Buddhism, Koguryŏ finally collapsed, reaffirming a widespread belief in the potential powers of Buddhism to protect the state. Korean Daoist sources are far from plentiful, but Koreans surely must have studied Daoism in China, just as they had studied Buddhism, but without widespread and continuous royal patronage it was certain not to become a dominant mainstream tradition in Korea, but rather became subsumed within the indigenous traditions where it clearly had a natural synergy, while its ideas on yin and yang would eventually be incorporated into Neo-Confucian thought. Daoist teachings for prognostication, and the important concept of *feng shui* (*p'ungsu* in Korean) were adapted by Korean Buddhists, who would also fulfil many Daoist roles, thereby obstructing the need for a separate Daoist priesthood. Meanwhile, Korean Buddhists had become interested in the very sophisticated developments in Buddhism which were starting to flow into Korea with native monks returning from study in China, and so the more superstitious Daoist ideas may not have fitted the intellectual milieu of the Korean peninsula at this time.

Intellectual development of Buddhism: *Sino-Korean interactions*

Just as Buddhist ideas were spread in Korea by travelling monks, mainly from China, soon Korean monks, such as Chajang and Wŏn'gwang, would assist in the transmission of developments in this missionary religion, initially by travelling to China. There they would study and practice with the great Chinese masters of Buddhism, but later some of them would also exert their own influence, playing important roles in the embryonic stage of 'intellectual' Buddhism, which arose to interpret and explain the Buddha's teachings and to resolve what seemed to be inconsistencies in the texts being diffused and studied by different groups. Korean Buddhist masters, particularly from Silla, would quickly and energetically absorb all the major developments of Sinitic Mahāyāna, which itself was influenced by Daoism. With the emergence of different doctrinal schools within Mahāyāna, there arose conflict between some of their key tenets, which would seem to suggest inherent contradictions in the Buddha's teachings, especially between the Mādhyamaka, Middle View School (中觀派, K. *Chunggwan-pa*), also known as the Three Treatise School (三論宗, K. *samnon-jong*) in contradistinction to the Yogācāra School (瑜伽行派, K. *Yogahaeng-pa*), more commonly known as the Consciousness Only School (唯識宗, K. *Yusik-jong*). The Mādhyamaka emphasised *Śūnyatā*, or emptiness (previously blurred with the nothingness of Daoism), but as Choi (2007: 103; emphasis added) correctly highlights, in this case "emptiness signifies that everything we encounter in our lives is empty of soul, permanence and innate nature. *It does not mean that things do not exist*", but that they are mutually interdependent, possessing no inherent nature of their own.

Meanwhile, the Yogācāra School, which was influenced by the texts translated by Xuanzang (602–664), who had studied in India, inspiring the Ming dynasty novel of Wu Cheng'en, *Journey to the West* (as well as many recent movies and TV series on 'The Monkey King'), emphasised the idea that things exist in 'consciousness only'. The result was an exposition of an elaborate system of human consciousness into eight levels, whereby things only exist in our consciousness, seemingly at variance with the emptiness described above (106–107). The Fāxiang school (法相宗) or Dharma-Character School, known in Korean as the *Pŏpsang-jong*, developed from the Yogācāra school, and was spread in Korea by the disciples of the Sillan monk Wŏnch'ŭk (613–696), who never returned from China where he went to study with the famous Xuanzang. It also affirms the centrality of the mind, or more significantly, consciousness, in relation to our inherently illusory perceptions of all things. Wŏnch'ŭk, an important translator of texts into Chinese, also left several commentaries, including one on the influential 'Heart Sutra', and his writings were also known among Tibetan Buddhists (Choo 2006).

Attempting to draw together the different strands of Buddhist thought at this time were the metaphysically sophisticated Tiantai (天台, K. *Ch'ŏnt'ae*) and Huayan (華嚴, K. *Hwaŏm*) schools which directly impacted on the history of ideas in Korea, examined in the next part of this study. These schools were collectively known as the doctrinal (or textual) schools, though already teaching about the importance of meditation, which would soon influence the emergence of one of the most prominent schools of Buddhism in East Asia, known as Chan Buddhism (禪, K. *Sŏn*; J. *Zen*), which focuses on meditation as a tool to achieve 'sudden enlightenment', discussed in the next chapter. One thing that cannot be overlooked in any investigation into

Buddhist traditions is the importance of the Huayan and Tiantai traditions in China, which subsequently influenced Korean Buddhism and bolstered its intellectual underpinnings. Both schools focus on the mind and advocate great concentration and insight, ideas developed further by the Chan schools, while their metaphysics greatly influenced the more sophisticated trajectory of later Confucianism, known in the West as Neo-Confucianism. These developments are also regarded as the beginning of a truly Sinitic form of Buddhism, which moved beyond its Indian roots. The Tiantai school got its name from the mountain on which its fourth patriarch, the great master Zhiyi (538–597), lived. The salient feature of the Tiantai School and its doctrinal basis is shaped by its reliance on the Lotus Sutra, one of the most important texts for the Mahāyāna tradition (see H. Kern translation online). A central tenet of this sutra is that everyone has the potential to be a Buddha, hence the ability to free themselves from suffering and engender their own salvation; in other words, universal salvation was possible, "Since everything involves everything else, it follows that all beings possess Buddha-Nature, and are therefore capable of salvation" (Chan 1973: 397).

But what exactly is Buddha-Nature or tathāgatagarbha (佛性, K. *Pulsŏng*)? It may be described as the potential for attaining Buddhahood, hence, one already 'innately' possesses the seeds of Buddha-Nature or the potential for Buddhahood in one's mind. This is clearly comparable to the Confucian teachings on one possessing the four seeds of one's innate good nature which corresponds to the four cardinal virtues of Confucianism: humanity, propriety, righteousness and wisdom. Therefore, just as the Confucians sought to create a path*way* to concretely actualise their innate potential for human goodness, the Buddhists needed a guiding discourse to enable them to attain Buddhahood. In Tiantai philosophy, the method for the attainment of Buddhahood can be found in Zhiyi's text, *The Method of Concentration and Insight*, which would obviously influence the Chan Buddhists, given its focus on meditation techniques (Chan 1973: 398–405). According to this discourse, the "mind's nature" is originally pure, therefore the work of concentration and insight involves striving to recover this "originally" pure mind. The Tiantai School also emphasised the 'Threefold Truth' (Chan 1973: 396):

The Threefold Truth

1 'The truth of emptiness', which taught that even the dharmas are empty being dependent on causes for their production, but that
2 'The temporary truth' of the dharmas should not be ignored as they have been produced, and so have a dependent, though provisory existence, which meant that
3 'The truth of the mean', or middle way, should balance any analysis of the previous two truths and the relationships between all things.

The intellectual impetus of the Huayan, or 'Flower Garland' School, was the *Avatamsaka*, or *Flower Garland Sūtra* (法華經, K. *Pŏphwagyŏng*), giving the school its very name, so central was its study and importance. The *Flower Garland Sūtra* is the second longest in the Buddhist canon and is concerned with a single theme, enlightenment. The school developed the "all-in-one and one-in-all theory" emphasising the interpenetration of all things/realities/views and so on, including the dharma, and therefore also implying their mutual containment, despite multifarious interpretations which may sometimes seem contradictory or paradoxical. It identifies *Principle* (理, C. *li*; K. *i*) with the mind, or rather, the 'One-Mind' (一心, K. *ilsim*), which permeates and connects all things through one's perceptions of them generated by consciousness, which is ultimately illusory and lacking independent origination, known in Korean by the term *t'ongdal* (通達). Following on from this, understanding *Principle* leads to a greater insight into the polymorphous understandings of the dharma, aiding the Buddhist to attain wisdom and eventually achieve Nirvāna (Muller 1995). An important image used to describe this complex idea was that of Indra's Net: Indra (帝釋天, K. *Chesŏkch'ŏn*) being a deity in Hinduism, a guardian deity in Buddhism. Francis Cooke (1973: 2) summarises the tale as follows:

Indra's Net

Far away in the heavenly abode of the great god Indra, there is a wonderful net which has been hung by some cunning artificer in such a manner that it stretches out infinitely in all directions. In accordance with the extravagant tastes of deities, the artificer has hung a single glittering jewel in each "eye" of the net, and since the net itself is infinite in dimension, the jewels are infinite in number. There hang the jewels, glittering "like" stars in the first magnitude, a wonderful sight to behold. If we now arbitrarily select one of these jewels for inspection and look closely at it, we will discover that in its polished surface there are reflected *all* the other jewels in the net, infinite in number. Not only that, but each of the jewels reflected in this one jewel is also reflecting all the other jewels, so that there is an infinite reflecting process occurring.

Cooke (1973) highlights how this image symbolises both "mutual identity" and "mutual inter-causality". The image is referred to repeatedly in Huayan literature, incorporated into many of the texts produced by some of the great Buddhist masters, such as Fazang (643–712), who is considered the great intellectual pioneer of this school. He incorporates the tale into his own work titled *Treatise on the Golden Lion*; however, the ultimate goal of this rather metaphysical text is undoubtedly practical, culminating in sections titled, "Achieving perfect wisdom (bodhi)" and finally, "Entering Nirvāna" (Chan 1973: 409–414). Ultimately, the mind holds the potential for achieving its own liberation, but unfortunately, also its own suffering. A central part of the *Flower Garland Sūtra* (ch. 26 of the text) focuses on the 'ten stages for Boddhisatvas', which again provides a 'path*way*' to achieve enlightenment, whereby the sometimes abstract metaphysical, speculative side of the philosophy becomes an active practice, an idea that is reinforced in Korea.

Fazang is considered to be the most significant exponent of Huayan philosophy that "represents the highest development of Chinese Buddhist thought" (Chan 1973: 406). Yet, a centrifugal part of this development of Chinese thought remains often overlooked: certain aspects of Fazang's intellectual profundity can be unquestionably traced to the Silla monk Ŭisang (625–702), his older friend and greatly esteemed colleague, who studied together with him in China under the great Huayan master Zhiyan (602–688). But more indirectly, there is another intersecting lineage of ideas, those which had influenced Ŭisang himself, those of his friend Wŏnhyo (617–686), who never left Silla and was one of the greatest intellectuals in East Asian history. This juncture really brings us to the point where Korea's own religious and philosophical traditions start to flourish and when scholars did not merely receive ideas from China, but they also helped to fashion the intellectual animus at the very centre of East Asia.

Korean Buddhist pioneers: *Wŏnhyo and Ŭisang*

All Koreans have heard the famous story of the monks Wŏnhyo and Ŭisang, whose initial journey to study in Tang China was derailed by a terrible storm, probably a typhoon, which are not uncommon in Korea. The story seems to be an amalgamation of two early extant accounts of the tale: (1) the *Biography of Ŭisang*, and (2) the *Biography of Wŏnhyo*, which are both easily accessible in English translation with the original in Volume One of *Collected Works of Korean Buddhism: Wonhyo, Selected Works* (Muller 2012: 302–307). The two monks seeking shelter from the storm, found refuge in what appeared to be an earthen shrine. Being thirsty, they drank water in a smooth vessel which tasted fresh, and then had a peaceful sleep. However, when they awoke the next morning and saw where they had spent the night, they were shocked. It turned out that they had slept in a tomb and they had been surrounded by skeletons, and the 'muddy' water that had refreshed them the night before had been scooped up in a human skull. Despite clearly having slept well the first night, due to the continued infelicitous weather they were obliged to stay a second night – this time ghosts appeared! This experience led to what can be described as Wŏnhyo's 'sudden enlightenment'. In this biography (305), Wŏnhyo reflects upon this pivotal experience which left an indelible mark of his ideas, and says:

When a thought arises, the myriad dharmas arise. When thoughts sub-
side [a cup and] a skull are not different. The Tathāgata thus said: 'The
three worlds are only mind; how can I be deceived!' Then he gave up on
seeking a master, and immediately returned to his country.

Ŭisang, we know, continued on his journey to Tang, bringing with him the
great influence of his elder friend: both would transform Korea's Buddhist
trajectory and its intellectual direction.

Wŏnhyo: *one-mind (il-sim) and the singular plurality*

While Wŏnhyo remained behind in Silla, he did not become the understudy
of any renowned Buddhist scholar, but studied under several, which makes
his incredible originality and vast amount of insightful commentaries on
Buddhist scriptures all the more impressive. To pick up the point made by
Wŏnhyo above, how we think about things shape how we perceive them
and hence also shapes their very existence and in turn, our own existence,
which is constructed and patterned according to our thoughts. We interpret
our lives through our encounter with a stream of thoughts, hence we become
what we think, or rather how we think, and rightly so our mental health
is an extremely important thing, and is improved when we rid ourselves of
unwanted mental detritus. Our daily lives are shaped by these thoughts, and
so our experience of this reality is either good or bad – depending on our
thoughts – which make things 'appear' good or bad, because in 'reality',
things in and of themselves are devoid of their own independent nature, and
so this reality only has a temporary existence as long as the thoughts and
perceptions shaping it remain. In short, if you change the patterns that have
become engrained in how you think, you will begin to live differently – to
do this you need to change your 'mental' habits. Many 'modern' gurus have
published books on this very theme, as if it were something new, or as if they
have some particularly original insights. Wŏnhyo might argue that there
are no 'original' insights as thoughts already depend on other thoughts and
interpreting ideas already depends on interpreting other ideas, so at best we
have only ever a provisory *rapprochement* to things in themselves. In this
sense, Wŏnhyo's ideas may be seen as not dissimilar to those associated
with Jacques Derrida's texts on 'deconstruction', which attempt to trace
and expose how traditions and ideas have been structured and organised,
while taught and accepted to be 'natural' or 'normal', but ultimately shaped
by previous traditions and ideas, which have sometimes been forgotten or
suppressed. It is important to note that the first time Derrida (1976: 49)
uses the term, he hyphenates it, hence, "de-construction". This emphasises
the contrastive nature of the morphemes. Cai Zongqi (1993: 389) illustrates
through morphological deconstruction that "the word deconstruct results
from a combination of two *opposing* morphemes: 'de' (to undo, to destroy)
and 'construct' (to do, to build)". This term comes into existence through

the opposition in the very morphemes which create its meaning(s), and so different traditions were shaped by different contexts, where ideas sometimes took on new meanings.

Derrida himself repeatedly argued that the only thing that matters is 'context', as each context is different, ideas and interpretations about those ideas will also be different as one is never able to access the thing in itself, but rather a 'differed' representation (through a sort of temporal and mental suspension) and therefore leads to different appropriations and experiences. Wŏnhyo himself was very wary of how ideas become bound up together and cause frictions between different groups of monks who considered their own interpretations of texts as 'correct' and sometimes the final word, ironically, becoming attached to their own ideas, rejecting other interpretations as 'incorrect', and one could argue (as the Daoists had done), beginning to sound more Confucian. In this regards, we can link together some important and recurrent themes in Wŏnhyo's writings, which expose the error in such dichotomous thinking, namely *Ilsim*, or 'One Mind', and 'Boundless' (無寐, K. *muae*), which considered together can facilitate a reconciliation between ideas and thoughts that 'appear' to be at odds with each other, known as *Hwajaeng* (和諍) – literally, 'harmonisation of disputes', ideas which are particularly relevant to us in the world we live in today.

An Ok-sun (2002: 140) writes that:

> [*Ilsim*] "One-Mind" is an inclusive concept explaining all beings and their interconnection in a single system. *Ilsim* indicates both human subjectivity of mind and the world that is reflected through it.

This One-Mind contains enlightenment (and therefore Nirvana) and non-enlightenment (and therefore Samsara), not as mutually exclusive entities, but as different aspects of the One-Mind which can become overshadowed by subjectivity, falling for the illusion of some apparently inherent and independent identity or 'self-nature'. One of the goals of the Buddhist should be to overcome the ego and one's subjectivity and realise that all beings and all things are interconnected; this is the ultimate truth, sometimes referred to as the mind of 'Suchness', an 'awakened' mind, consciously aware of causal distinctions, which have no existence of their own. This would then allow the individual to overlook and dismantle discriminations by un-binding oneself from them, hence, *mu-ae*, or "not being bound by any fixed thought or convention" (ibid.). Eventually one would become aware of, expose and then to overturn mental constructions shaping traditions and customs, but also ideas about gender and identity, which can then be viewed as more fluid and multiplicitous, yet contained within *Ilsim*. This was already something Wŏnhyo realised after spending the night in the tomb and drinking muddy water from a skull – only his thoughts had made the experience different – and so having grasped the Suchness of the 'mind', he had discovered that this was the hinge of all Buddhist ideas/schools/texts/practices, which are all mere reflections of *ilsim*, depending on each new (and thereby) different context. Understanding these intersecting ideas, at certain different and differed points, can then reconcile disputes, as they simply reflect alternative aspects and impressions of *ilsim*.

Wŏnhyo was greatly influenced by the *Awakening of Faith in the Mahāyāna* (大乘起信論, K. *Taesŭng kisillon*). This sutra had gained much prominence in China, with some scholars suggesting it may have originally have been Chinese, though it is often attributed to Aśvaghoṣa (c.80–150), the Indian Buddhist philosopher. This syncretic scripture is considered to bring together all the teachings of the Buddha, and treat together certain theories that 'appeared' to be contradictory, something that inspired some of Wŏnhyo's greatest ideas, which were transmitted and recorded in China and Japan. Wŏnhyo's openness, non-attachment to views, and cherishing freedom of thought are indeed the very basis of his *hwajaeng* approach, which also revolves around *muae*, which rejects conformity and gestures towards openness and an understanding of the 'other', that requires equality, something very contradictory to Confucianism. His multiple commentaries on the *Awakening of Faith* reconcile different points of view of the Mādhyamaka and Yogacārā schools as "each of the two aspects can completely explain all events, and the two are inseparable" if seen from the position of One-Mind (Ko 2004: 195). This insight must surely have been informed by his own enlightenment experience, whereby caves and graves are merely manifestations of thoughts coming and going (arising and ceasing), leading to the ultimate realisation that "outside the mind there are no dharmas, there is no use in searching elsewhere" reinforced by the centrality of the *ilsim*, which already contains the source of the ultimate truth, which is never separate from us (Muller 2012: 303). Muller (1995) accentuates Wŏnhyo's engagement with another hermeneutical of inter-relatedness in his commentary on *The Awakening of Faith: Essence-Function* (體用, K. *ch'e-yong*). Muller (1995) explains this feature of East Asian Philosophical traditions, which is of particular significance to Korea's own history of ideas, as follows:

> [*Che*] (體) refers to the deeper, hidden, relatively permanent and more fundamental aspects of something, while [yong] (用) indicates its more manifest, visible or superficial aspects. [. . .] The most important application of *t'i-yung* thought, however, is to the human being, where the human mind is seen as "essence", and one's words, thoughts and actions are seen as "function".

The inter-relatedness between correct (awakened) thought and good (compassionate) action is something which is repeated throughout Wŏnhyo's works, and a salient feature of later Korean scholars as well, outlined throughout this book. Wŏnhyo's insightful commentary on this text was considered to have indirectly influenced Fazang through his discussions with

Ŭisang, who was intellectually indebted to his older friend who remained behind in Silla.

Not satisfied with reconciling the textual complexities of the *Awakening of Faith*, Wŏnhyo also set out to overcome multiple doctrinal controversies in his very ambitious, and once again syncretic text, *Ten Approaches to the Harmonization of Doctrinal Disputes* (十門和諍論, K. *Simmun hwajaeng non*) (available online, see Muller 2016). Muller (2016) describes *hwajaeng* as a methodological approach which consists "of taking ostensibly variant or conflicting Buddhist doctrinal positions, investigating them exhaustively until identifying the precise point at which their variance occurs, and then showing how differences in fundamental background, motivation, or sectarian bias have led to the creation of such variances". This demonstrates Wŏnhyo's role as an intellectual bridge-builder, who rather than categorise in terms of 'inferior' and 'superior', saw the benefits of harmoniously drawing together the different threads that ultimately bound together and linked a vast interpenetrating Buddhist tapestry, leading twentieth century Korean scholar and historian Ch'oe Namsŏn (1890–1957) to describe Wŏnhyo's approach as *'tong bulgyo'* (通佛教), or 'integrated Buddhism' (Muller 2012: 21–22). Wŏnhyo's integrated and harmonious approach can also be considered a tool that is not limited to textual disputes found in ancient Buddhist texts, but as a valuable means to assist in our 'being-with' 'others' in our daily life in a more compassionate *way*, bringing us closer to the truth of *ilsim*, where distinctions dissipate. Rather than considering ourselves as individuals, we should celebrate our inter-relatedness which shapes the many manifestations of who we are as singular-interconnected entities: as a child, sibling, parent, friend, teacher, artist and so on. This is not entirely different to the ideas of Jean-Luc Nancy in *Being Singular Plural* (2000), which considers that our 'being' is only really capable of being understood when it is considered as 'being-with', always a part of a greater whole, as paradoxically, meaning means nothing in and of itself, something Wŏnhyo himself might add. This 'being-with' already connotes an 'interbeing-ness', highlighted by the famous Vietnamese monk Thích Nhất Hạnh, who created the Order of Interbeing in 1966, again which emphasises compassion, but which encompasses ideas that are central to Wŏnhyo: openess, non-attachment to views, as well as freedom of thought, which make up the first three 'mindfulness trainings' of the order (see Thích 1993). The focus on the mind is not something new or revolutionary, but from a Buddhist point of view, something inescapable given the importance of *ilsim*, which though not unique to Wŏnhyo's teachings, is championed in them just as they challenge us to recognise the singular plurality of our interconnected thoughts and realities which bind us all ultimately together: there is no 'I' without an 'us'.

Conscious of getting lost in metaphysical complexities, Wŏnhyo was sure to advocate 'practice' and indeed his *Awaken your Mind and Practice* (發心修行章, K. *Palsim suhaeng-jang*) is an explicit call to younger adherents to put Buddhist ideas into practice: an indirect warning not to get lost in

Figure 2.2 Inside the eighth century Sŏkkuram Grotto at Pulguk-sa Temple in Gyeo-
ngju (Kyŏngju) – A UNESCO World Cultural Heritage site since 1995

contemplation alone or in the study of texts, or to become overly embroiled
in disputes (Muller 2012: 261–268) The term for practice, '*suhaeng*' (修行),
is similar to the Confucian idea of *sugi* (修己), or self-cultivation, a con-
crete path*way* to transform oneself (and one's habits) that requires ongoing persistence and dedication, discussed in Chapter 1. Wŏnhyo warns
against procrastinating one's spiritual cultivation until tomorrow, next year
and so forth, reinforcing the transitory and impermanent nature of this life
and of this body, ending with a very sober message: "This body will cer-
tainly perish – what body will you have afterward? Isn't it urgent?! Isn't
it urgent?!" (268). This text is one of the first studied by Korean Buddhist
novitiates today, and it represents "Wŏnhyo's most edifying work and one
of the strongest admonitions about the urgency of religious practice to be
found in all of Buddhist literature" (Lee & DeBary 1997: 87).

But how did Wŏnhyo actualise his own ideas? In other words, how did he
live this thought? Interestingly, he himself transgressed many of the teachings he urged others to adhere to, and he appears not to have been able to
free himself from carnal desires or other 'vices' relating to the mundane
world. However, given Wŏnhyo's radical temperament, it is not entirely
shocking that he would have broken free of the bonds imposed by monastic

life, to have enjoyed alcohol, sex, and shared the company of those disenfranchised and marginalised in the heavily hierarchical society in which he found himself. Eventually, these bonds may have been considered by Wŏnhyo as limiting and segregating, while he still espoused the morality encompassed by his holistic and syncretic view of Buddhism, while proactively seeking to enlighten as many others as possible. This would become a conscious goal that reflects who he was as a human being, interconnected with other human beings from all walks of life.

The *Legends and History of the Three Kingdoms* (Iryŏn 2004: 305–308) recounts the tale of Wŏnhyo the 'unbridled monk', who married a princess and had a son, Sŏl Ch'ong. Sŏl Ch'ong became the great Confucian scholar who invented the 'Idu' writing system, which manipulated Chinese characters to reflect Korean pronunciation, which differs greatly from Chinese pronunciation. However, what matters most in this account is that Wŏnhyo stopped wearing the Buddhist monk robes, and then performed a mask dance, beating a drum, which he called '*muae*', imagery related to Shaman rituals, symbolically breaking down the barriers in his society, as well as the artificial rules that segregated monks, and thereby the teachings of the Buddha from the laypeople, preventing them from reaching enlightenment. To remedy this situation Wŏnhyo reportedly travelled around meeting with the common and marginalised people, similar to Jesus in the Bible, not textual scholars, offering them an alternate path to enlightenment, free from the boundaries of skilled, yet elitist, scriptural exegesis. This he achieved by bringing the teachings of another form of Buddhism, the Pure Land School (淨土宗, K. *Chŏngt'o-jong*), to the masses.

Pure Land Buddhism had grown in popularity in China and was considered as a vehicle of salvation for the generally uneducated secular masses (see DeBary 1963: 374–386). Wŏnhyo himself also wrote commentaries on Pure Land scriptures (for one example, see Muller 2012: 215–218). This further informs us of the broad insight and the prolific scope of his knowledge of the various schools of Buddhism and their texts. This school did not require the ability to read, only to have faith in the Amitābha Buddha, and thereby recourse to a simple invocation, often heard in Buddhist temples today in Korea – *namu-amitabul* (나무아미타불) – paying homage to the Amitābha Buddha. This invocation is supposed to grant salvation to those who repeat and meditate on it, even once before dying, whereby they are promised to be reborn in the Pure Land, *Sukhāvatī* (or Western Paradise), where the Amitābha Buddha teaches and leads them to break the circle of Samsara. This clearly links Amitābha with the Buddhist ideal of the Boddhisatva. Additionally, there is also a form of meditation practiced by this school focusing on visualisations of the Buddha and the Buddhist heaven, ideas which would be more concretely be channelled by later meditational sects of Buddhism. While Wŏnhyo is undoubtedly one of the greatest intellectuals of Korean and East Asian history, it was nevertheless Ŭisang who was responsible for the growth and development of Huayan or Hwaŏm Buddhism in

Unified Silla (668–935), and, despite his death in 702, was responsible for founding many monasteries and gained a substantial following.

Ŭisang and the growth of Hwaŏm schools

While Wŏnhyo remained behind in Silla, Ŭisang continued on his way to Tang, studying with some of the greatest intellectuals of the time, as mentioned above. He was not only a key player in the shaping of Huayan Buddhism in China, but he is generally considered to be the founding patriarch of the Hwaŏm lineage in Korea. While overshadowed by the writings of Wŏnhyo, it should be underscored that he too was a great intellectual, but few of his works are extant, and his influence on Wŏnhyo should not be considered insignificant. His 'Seal-diagram Symbolizing the Dharma Realm of the One Vehicle' (一乘法界圖合, K. *Ilsŭng pŏpkye to*), throws some light onto the meticulous and concise nature of Ŭisang's thought (for a full translation of the poem and Ŭisang's explanation, see McBride II 2012: 101–188). This insightful text is described as (5):

> "[a] Great Poem" (*pansi*槃詩) that combines the "Gāthā on the Dharma Nature" (*Pŏpsŏng ke*法性偈), which is a poem of two hundred ten logographs in thirty lines of seven logographs each, with a "Seal-diagram Symbolizing the Dharma Realm" (*Pŏpkye toin* 法界圖印). In other words, it is a combined poem in the shape of a seal-diagram symbolizing the dharma realm of the one vehicle (*Ilsŭng pŏpkye to hapsi irin* 一乘法界圖合詩一印).

This poem-cum-seal has itself been very important in Korea, influencing monks from both the Koryŏ the Chosŏn periods, who wrote their own commentaries on it, with some of these translated in *The Collected Works of Korean Buddhism, Vol 4. Hwaŏm I: The Mainstream Tradition*. The original 'poem' is short and concise, summarising and explaining the main teachings of the Hwaŏm School: "True nature [. . .] is not attached to self-nature, and is achieved in accordance with conditions. Within one, there is all, and within many, there is one, the one precisely all, and the many are precisely the one" (104). It also includes a line which sounds almost Daoist, writing that all dharmas "have no names and characteristics; all distinctions are severed", not entirely different from the opening lines of Laozi's *Dao De Ching*, discussed in Chapter 1, but this may also have been inspired by the emergence of Chan/Sŏn Buddhism and its growing influence at the time. This then also relates to one's own practice which should also benefit others, embodying the mutually inclusive nature of 'you' and 'I' related through a single all-pervasive *Principle*.

Indeed, to have an overview of the teachings of the Huayan/Hwaŏm schools, dedicated scholars would study the writings of Ŭisang and Fazang, as well as Zhiyan. Nevertheless, Ŭisang is mainly known for being an outstanding teacher, receiving the posthumous title of "State Preceptor of Perfect Teaching" (圓教國師, K. *Wŏn'gyo kuksa*). The practice of the Buddhist teachings were his primary concern and he also composed a text advocating 'practice', rather than mere exegetical analysis. Though most of his writings have been lost, one feature of these appears to have been a question and answer format, such as those used in his explanation of his famous seal-poem, something not very different from a Catholic Catechism, which consists of questions and answers on the main teachings and doctrines.

The *Legends and History of the Three Kingdoms* (Iryŏn 2004: 308–312) also contains a biography of Ŭisang (different from the one mentioned previously), that acknowledges his contributions to spreading the teachings of the Hwaŏm school in Silla, and which also includes a letter from Fazang, praising his insights and asking Ŭisang to correct a commentary on the Flower Garland Sutra that he sent to him in Silla. This version also recounts how the Tang Emperor Gaozung (r.649–683) was planning a surprise attack on Silla (despite their alliance used to help Silla take over Paekche and Koguryŏ). Ŭisang returned home to warn King Munmu (r.661–681), who was then able to maintain his sovereignty, being ready to confront the Tang forces occupying Paekche with the assistance of Koguryŏ soldiers, leading to the Unified Silla period. In this instance, a Buddhist monk had potentially saved the fate of his country. Ŭisang's reward – being able to set up monasteries all over the peninsula, such as Pusŏk-sa temple, founded in 676 – allowed him to spread ideas to a new generation of Silla monks. The Hwaŏm-sa temple on Chiri Mountain contains the remains of Ŭisang's stone inscription of the Flower Garland Sutra, which he carved there, recognised as a National Treasure today, but again reflecting the importance of this sutra to the Hwaŏm sect.

Conclusion

This chapter has provided an overview of the transmission of early Buddhism into the Three Kingdoms, which took root relatively quickly and soon produced a number of important missionaries who spread these ideas to Japan. But as transmitters of Sinic culture, these monks, in particular those from Paekche, also transmitted Chinese writing, Confucianism and Daoism to Japan, as well as the art and architecture associated with Buddhist temples at the time, clearly shaping Japan's intellectual history and cultural identity. Though adopted later to Silla, and not without the blood of martyrs, Buddhism there would be incorporated into the state apparatus at various levels. Monks such as Chajang would return from China, bringing first-hand accounts of the latest developments, acting as mediators and a bridge between Silla and Tang China and its impressive cultural exuberance. Some of those Korean monks would never return, such as Wŏnch'ŭk, whose dedication to translating Buddhist texts into Chinese contributed to the intellectual development of Buddhism in the Middle Kingdom.

At the same time Confucianism was also integrated into the state structure with sons of the elite studying Confucian Classics, and by 372, King Sosurim of Koguryŏ, a Buddhist, had already established a centralised National Confucian Academy as well as smaller schools around the country in more rural areas. Clearly Confucianism and Buddhism, which had both defined and separate spaces and functions, were considered as compatible and complementary systems of thought. This is particularly evident in the 'Five Commandments for Laypeople' by Wŏn'gwang, which were adopted by the Hwarang, who were loyal to the king, but who had a particular reverence for the Maitreya Buddha. Additionally, Daoism had made its ways into Korea, and though not etching out a clearly defined school, it interacted with the pre-existing folk traditions in a more effervescent and elastic manner, also influencing Hwarang lore, but more so in matters of geomancy (*p'ungsu*) and fortune-telling, which would in turn influence and shape some Buddhist practices related to Shamanism. Intellectual Buddhism was the next step in the evolution of Buddhism in China, but also in Korea, and indeed monks such as Ŭisang shaped these developments on the continental mainland, praised by the great masters there, such as Fazang. Different strands of Buddhism expounded teachings on the 'Buddha Nature' and 'Principle' respectively, sharpening their investigations into the illusory nature of reality, shaped by individual contexts.

Korea's intellectual dynamism matured with Wŏnhyo, who never left his motherland. But, what is original and revolutionary is the way in which this Sillan and (to a large degree) self-taught monk sought to reconcile problematic doctrinal disputes between different Buddhist schools, challenging dogma and the illusory boundaries of the artificial structures of one's existence. An (2012: 137–157) argues that such ideas in Wŏnhyo's texts identify concepts regarded by us today as fundamental human rights, such as equality and liberty, fuelled by an engaged practice of compassion, which is evinced through *hwajaeng*, moving beyond mere textual analysis, but rather practiced with sincerity (as a Confucian might say). The *Journal of Korean Religions* had a special edition on "The 1,400th Anniversary of Wŏnhyo's Birth", which illustrates the singular importance of this extraordinary and iconoclastic monk, who would abandon clergical norms to bring Pure Land Buddhism to the masses, and father a son, Sŏl Ch'ong, a Confucian who created Idu to facilitate clearer representation of Korean ideas expressed in written Chinese (Buswell & Cho 2017).

Ŭisang, also a great intellectual, is probably better remembered for the dissemination and growth of the Hwaŏm teachings in Korea. His ideas, like those of Wŏnhyo, also reflect this *t'ong pulgyo*, integrated Buddhism. Ch'oe Ch'iwŏn (857–?) is emblematic of the syncretic tendencies of Unified Silla and of this axial age in Korea's intellectual history. Though many of his writings have been lost, what remains are writings on and/or influenced by Confucianism, Buddhism and Daoism, garnering acclaim in China and fame for his poetry. Such a scholar could only have existed before the great conflict that started to arise between Buddhism and Confucianism in Tang China would eventually prompt the rise of Neo-Confucianism, an ideology that would transform and shape Korea's intellectual and social system right down until the present day.

References and further reading

An, Ok-sun. 2002. "The Fundamental Ideals of Human Rights in the Thought of Wonhyo". *Korea Journal*, 42(4): 137–157.

Best, Jonathan W. 2007. "King Mu and the Making and Meanings of Mirŭksa". *Religions of Korea in Practice*, ed. Robert E. Buswell Jr. Princeton University Press: Princeton, NJ. 35–50.

Buswell, Robert E. Jr and Cho Eun su. (eds). 2017. "The 1,400th Anniversary of Wŏnhyo's Birth: A Special Issue". *Journal of Korean Religions*. University of Hawai'i Press: Honolulu.

Cai, Zongqi. 1993. "Derrida and Seng-Zhao: Linguistic and Philosophical Deconstruction". *Philosophy East and West*, 43(3): 389–404.

Chan, Wing-Tsit. 1973. *A Sourcebook in Chinese Philosophy*. Princeton University Press: Princeton, NJ.

Ch'oe, Yŏngho, Peter H. Lee and Wm Theodore De Bary. 1997. *Sources of the Korean Tradition: From the Sixteenth to the Twentieth Century*. Columbia University Press: Columbia.

Choi, Joon-sik. 2007. *Buddhism: Religion in Korea*. Translated by Lee Kyong-hee. Ewha Women's University Press: Seoul.

Choo, B. Hyun. 2006. "An English Translation of the Banya Paramilda Simgyeong Chan: Wonch'uk's Commentary on the Heart Sutra (Prajnaparamita-hrdaya-sutra)". *International Journal of Buddhist Thought & Culture*, 6: 121–205.

Cooke, Francis. 1973. *Hua-Yen Buddhism: The Jewel Net of Indra*. Pennsylvania State University Press: Pennsylvania.

DeBary, Wm. Theodore. (ed.). 1963. *Sources of Chinese Tradition*. Columbia University Press: New York.

Derrida, Jacques. 1976. *Of Grammatology*. Translated by Gayatari Chakravorty Spivak. The John Hopkins University Press: Baltimore and London.

Eckert, Carter J. *et al.* 1990. *Korea Old and New: A History*. Ilchokak Publishers: Seoul. Chapter Two.

Gale, James Scarth. 1972. *History of the Korean People* (Reprint). Taewon Publishing Company: Seoul.

Grayson, James H. 2001. *Myths and Legends from Korea*. Routledge Curzon: Richmond. ChapterTwo.

———. 2002. *Korea: A Religious History*. Revised Edition. Routledge Curzon: New York. Chapter 5.

Hulbert, Homer B. 1906. *The Passing of Korea*. Doubleday, Page & Company: New York.

Iryŏn. 2004. *Samguk Yusa: Legends and History of the Three Kingdoms*. Translated by Tae-Hung Ha and Grafton K. Mintz. Yonsei University Press: Seoul.

Kang, Jae-eun. 2006. *The Land of Scholars: Two Thousand Years of Confucianism*. Translated by Suzanne Lee. Homa and Sekey Books: Paramus, NJ.

Kern, H. (trans.). 1884. *The Lotus Sutra*. Available at: www.sacred-texts.com/bud/lotus/index.htm [accessed on 13 June 2018].

Kim, C.S. 1971. "The Kolp'um System: Basis for Sillan Social Stratification". *Journal of Korean Studies*, 1(2): 43–69.

Ko, Ik-chin. 2004. "Wonhyo and the Foundation of Korean Buddhism". *Korean Philosophy: Its Tradition and Modern Transformation*, ed. Korean National Commission for UNESCO. Hollym: Seoul. 185–200.

Lee, Ki-dong. 1987. "The Silla Society and Hwarang Corps". *Journal of Social Sciences and Humanities*, 65: 1–16.

Lee, Peter H. (trans.). 1969. *Lives of Eminent Korean Monks: The Haedong Kosŭng Chŏn*. Harvard University Press: Cambridge, MA.

McBride II, Richard D. (ed.). 2007. "Silla Buddhism and the Hwarang Segi Manuscripts". *Korean Studies*, 31(1): 19–38.

———. 2010. "Silla Buddhism and the Hwarang". *Korean Studies*, 34(1): 54–89.

———. 2012. *Collected Works of Korean Buddhism, Vol 4. Hwaŏm I: The Mainstream Tradition*. Translated by Richard McBride II and Sem Vermeersch. Jogye Order of Korean Buddhism: Seoul.

Mohan, Pankaj N. 2001. "Maitreya Cult in Early Shilla: Focusing on Hwarang in Maitreya-Dynasty". *Seoul Journal of Korean Studies*, 14: 149–174.

———. 2005. "The Uses of Buddhist and Shamanistic Symbolism in the Empowerment of Queen Sŏndŏk". *International Journal of Buddhist Thought and Culture*, 5: 131–144.

———. 2007. "Wŏn'gwang and Chajang in the Formation of Early Silla Buddhism". *Religions of Korea in Practice*, ed. Robert E. Buswell Jr. Princeton University Press: Princeton, NJ. 51–64.

Muller, Charles. (trans.). 1995. "The Key Operative Concepts in Korean Buddhist Syncretic Philosophy; Interpenetration and Essence-Function in Wŏnhyo, Chinul and Kihwa". Available at: http://www.acmuller.net/articles/1995-03-kiyo-wonhyo-chinul-kihwa.html [accessed on 13 June 2018].

———. 2012. *Collected Works of Korean Buddhism, Vol.1: Wonhyo, Selected Works*. Translated by Charles Muller, Sem Vermeersch and Jin Y. Park. Jogye Order of Korean Buddhism: Seoul.

———. 2016. *Ten Approaches to the Harmonization of Doctrinal Disputes by Wŏnhyo*. Available at: www.acmuller.net/kor-bud/simmun_hwajaeng_non.html [accessed on 26 June 2018].

Nancy, Jean-Luc. 2000. *Being Singular Plural*. Translated by Robert Richardson and Anne O' Byrne. Stanford University Press: Stanford.

Park, Sung-bae. 2003. "Wonhyo's Faith System, as Seen in His Commentaries on the Awakening of Mahayana Faith". *International Journal of Buddhist Thought and Culture*, 2(2): 25–45.

Rutt, Richard. 1961. "The Flower Boys of Silla (Hwarang), Notes on the Sources". *Transactions of the Korea Branch of the Royal Asiatic Society*, 38: 1–66.

Song, Hang-Nyong. 1986. "A Short History of Taoism in Korea". *Korea Journal*, 26(5): 13–18.

Thích Nhất Hạnh. 1993. *Interbeing: Precepts for Everyday Living*. Parallax Press: London.

Tikhonov, Vladimir. 1998. "Hwarang Organization: Its Functions and Ethics". *Korea Journal*, 38(2): 318–338.

3 From Buddhism to Neo-Confucianism
Hegemony and metaphysics

Introduction

While the Three Kingdoms had been consolidated under Unified Silla, Korea had lost a significant portion of Koguryŏ's territory, and north of the Tae-dong River (which today forms a natural border between North Korea and China), a new, much smaller state emerged known as Parhae (渤海), which lacks any thorough textual history. Towards the end of Unified Silla, the Chan tradition, which had gained prominence in China during the Tang dynasty, was transplanted to the Korean peninsula, where it was known as Sŏn, outlined at the start of this chapter. This meditative school would run into conflict with the doctrinal schools discussed in the previous chapter, but their eventual interaction and amalgamation shaped the form of Buddhism that is found in Korea today, and this unique form of Korean Buddhism would, along with Confucianism, help shape the subsequent Koryŏ dynasty (918–1392), inaugurated by King T'aejo (877–943), its first ruler. In this chapter, King T'aejo's 'Ten Injunctions', or guidelines for ruling a successful state are examined, demonstrating the compatibility of both Confucianism and Buddhism, as well as other folk beliefs and practices. While Buddhism was considered to provide spiritual protection to the state, it also bolstered its prestige, asserting Korea's place as an intellectual hub in East Asia where writing and printing were advanced and promoted.

The rise of Sŏn schools which steadily absorbed the doctrinal schools was helped by monks such as Ŭich'ŏn (1055–1101), who collected Buddhist scriptures and commentaries, eventually leading to the carving of the Tripitaka Koreana on over 80,000 woodblocks. Of particular importance, and examined in detail is Monk Chinul (1158–1210), who set about to renovate the degeneration of the Buddhist clergy, leaving a hugely important collection of texts, but who also is responsible for the particular brand of Korean Buddhism known as *Kanhwa Sŏn*. Chinul would attempt to resolve the divide between different schools, by turning more towards meditational practices, cementing the Sŏn tradition in Korea, while not neglecting the textual practices that had garnered Korean monks such acclaim throughout the Sinic world and beyond.

More invasions by the Mongols during the thirteenth century led to a deeply fractured society and a threat to sovereignty and identity, clearly motivating Monk Iryŏn to write the *Legends and History of the Three Kingdoms* (K. *Samguk yusa*), to highlight and protect Korea's rich culture and Buddhist past. But it appeared that the time had come for a new philosophy to develop a different type of kingship to lead Korea into a new era. This new philosophy would again come from China, brought by Koreans who had studied with the first generation of scholars who had heralded the growth of Neo-Confucianism, based on the ideas of Chinese philosophers from the Song dynasty (宋朝; 860–1279), and on, most importantly, the ideas of Zhu Xi (1130–1200), whose influence on the history of ideas in East Asia cannot be underestimated (summarised in this chapter). This philosophy, which was a more metaphysical recalibration of earlier Confucianism, still reinforced Confucian virtues, and emphasised the moral leadership role of the king. The time had come for a new dynasty, which would be called Chosŏn (1392–1910), founded on Neo-Confucian principles that the elite would use to maintain a patriarchal society where they wielded utmost power, eradicating the sway previously held by the Buddhists, who along with Shamans were rejected and repressed. The final parts of this chapter examine the important Confucian-Buddhist debate uncovered in the writings of Chŏng Tojŏn (1342–1398) and the Kihwa (1376–1433).

The emergence of the Sŏn Buddhism in Silla

Tradition has it that the Indian monk Bodhidharma (c.470–543) transmitted the Chan teachings to China, and this meditative school owes its name to the Chinese phonetic transliteration of the Sanskrit term dhyāna, which means 'meditation', and as mentioned before, this is pronounced Sŏn in Korean, Zen in Japanese. It also traces its lineage back to the figure of Kasyapa, a disciple of the Buddha who in one tale understood his master when he held up a flower without uttering a word: while the other disciples were confused, he alone smiled, having understood without direct communication, hence it denotes a teaching that passes from one-mind to another. Though little is known about the historical Bodhidharma, he is considered the first patriarch of the school in China, who, according to legend, meditated in front of a wall for nine years, but he is still frequently depicted by Chinese, Korean and Japanese Buddhist masters of the meditational schools in their ink paintings (Adler 2002: 86–87).

However, it was the sixth patriarch of Chan Buddhism, Huineng (638–713), whose ideas would be transmitted into the Korean peninsula, shaping the Sŏn tradition there. Nevertheless, the teachings of the earliest Chan schools had already made their way to the peninsula with the Silla Monk Pŏmnang (632–?), who had studied in China, returning during the reign of Queen Sŏndŏk (Grayson 2002: 69–70). Once again, there is little authentic information known about Huineng, but different sources recount that he was an illiterate young monk who succeeded his master Hongren (601–674) who was impressed by his belief that anyone could have a 'sudden enlightenment' experience of the mind that could transform one's understanding of the reality of the universe – recalling the experience of Wŏnhyo, discussed in the previous chapter. This teaching emphasised that the mind could 'spontaneously' achieve enlightenment given the right experience, without the need for doctrinal study, as the mind alone holds the key to achieving its own liberation from the mundane reality. Such ideas do not diverge far from the Daoist teachings of Laozi and Zhuangzi, and partly explain why this form of Buddhism is sometimes described as an indigenous form of 'Chinese' Buddhism, diverging from the Indian traditions. Huineng's selection as successor to the fifth patriarch of Chan, Hongren (601–674), rather than an elder disciple Shenxiu (c.606–706), who taught that the mind needed to be well-prepared for an enlightenment experience, led to a split into two different schools of Chan: Southern Chan, following Huineng, and Northern Chan, following Shenxiu (Ching 1993: 140). As is often the case, many diverging schools of the tradition formed, but two were of great importance and influence, the Caodong School and the Linji School. The Caodong line advocated silent meditation under the guidance of a master, which is what many people associate with seated-meditation. On the other hand, the Linji School, as described by Ching (141), "aims at sudden enlightenment through the use of shouting, beating, and riddles called *kung-an* [*kong'an* in Korean, *koan* in Japanese] to provoke an experience of enlightenment", adding that the *kung-an*, "by posing an insoluble [seemingly illogical and idiosyncratic] problem to reason and the intellect [. . .] is supposed to lead to the dissolution of the boundary between the conscious and the unconscious in the human psyche" ultimately revealing the true nature of the mind. This form of Buddhism clearly moved away from textual analysis of scriptures and commentaries on them – opening a new path*way* for those seeking enlightenment who no longer needed to be elite intellectuals with great proficiency in Classical Chinese (at least in theory). The fact that Chan did not rely on texts meant that it shared this trait with Pure Land Buddhism and so could attract individuals from all backgrounds.

In periods of turmoil, societies are more open to assimilate new ideas, and so, these new Buddhist ideas gained prominence towards the end of the Tang dynasty, which was in decline, just as they would at the end of the Unified Silla period during the ninth century, which also experienced political and social degeneration and decline. In 821, monk To'ŭi (d.844) returned after a period of thirty-seven years study and practice in China, and set up one of the first temples which expounded the teachings of the Southern Chan tradition at Chinjŏn-sa temple on the impressive Sŏrak mountain near the East Sea. As Cho (1977: 208) explains, "After this time, [monks] of Silla who studied in China brought back Southern Chan in successive journeys while domestically, a group of nine large temples came to occupy a focal position in the promulgation of the Chan sect". These are known as the Nine Mountains of Korean Sŏn. Japanese Zen, so well-known by westerners, did not develop there as a separate school until the twelfth century, and only after that would Japan develop its Five Mountain System. Proponents of Sŏn in Korea were also often followers of Hwaŏm Buddhism and were deeply intellectual. It is this form of Sŏn Buddhism, infused with Hwaŏm doctrinal interests, which had gained in popularity and which would develop and shape Buddhism in Korea during the subsequent Koryŏ period, and shape its great Sŏn masters, both Ŭich'ŏn (1055–1101) and Chinul, who would, in different ways, attempt to unify

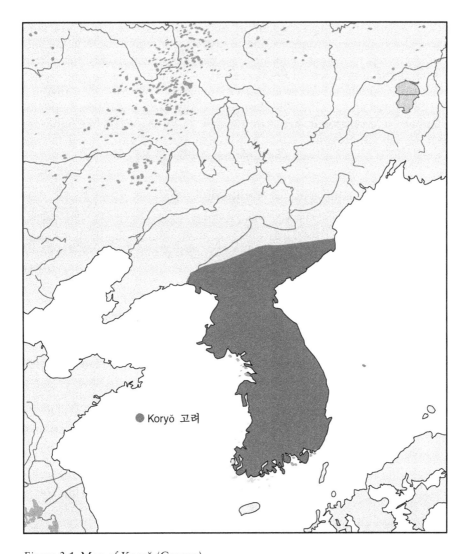

Figure 3.1 Map of Koryŏ (Goryeo)

the doctrinal and Sŏn schools. But Buddhism was already in decline in China by this point.

By the end of the Tang dynasty Buddhism had lost its patronage from the emperor. During the eighth and ninth centuries the power of the Buddhist clergy had grown immensely and by the middle of the ninth century the number of monasteries amounted to some 44,600. Needless to say, the growth of this "alien" religion did not please the Confucian scholars. They criticised the economic impact of such a large number of monasteries and nunneries draining revenue from the state, and also their political and economic abuses, as well as their failure to adhere to their own moral codes. Influenced by Daoist priests, Emperor Wuzong (r.841–847) issued a decree that dramatically reduced the number of monasteries. The aristocratic families who had been promoted due to social connections were in decline, and were replaced by an educated, trained bureaucracy. This meant that the emperor himself would need counsellors from this new bureaucracy to advise him, and hence their role had a more practical function than anything the Buddhists had to offer. Buddhism, especially Chan Buddhism, could not compete on a pragmatic level with the new surge of interest in Confucianism, which its proponents boasted, could remedy socio-political failings (Creel 1971: 203; Fairbank and Goldman 1999: 83–85).

Koryŏ and the confluence of traditions

On the Korean peninsula, the socio-political cohesion of the Silla period was also in decline as warlords sought control, diminishing the power and validity of the throne. For a time, the Three Kingdoms re-emerged (known as the Later Three Kingdoms Period), and eventually there was a power struggle between two Silla figures, Kim Kungye (d.918) and Yi Kyŏnhwŏn (d.936), with the latter finally declaring himself King of Later Paekche in 900. Yi would eventually sack the Silla capital itself before being forced to seek refuge with a descendent of Koguryŏ refugees, Wang Kŏn (877–943), before being killed in battle. Kungye, though born into the royal family, narrowly survived an order to have him killed as an infant, and later declared himself a reincarnation of the Buddha, having spent time in a monastery. He would later reject his vows, turning to a disturbingly violent path, murdering members of his own family, including his children. He was eventually killed during a coup by one of his own lieutenants who sought to remove the 'mandate' of a 'morally corrupt' leader, adhering to Confucian ideology. This mandate would pass from the last king of Silla, King Kyŏngsun (r. 927–935) to Wang Kŏn and would assure the legitimacy of his rule and his desired dynastic change, reflected in his posthumous title of King T'aejo 太祖, literally, 'The Great Ancestor' (Lee & De Bary 1997: 144–151).

King T'aejo, the first ruler of the new unified Koryŏ dynasty (918–1392), issued Ten Injunctions (訓要十條, K. *Hunyo sipcho*) as his final testament to provide guidance to future rulers (Lee & De Bary 1997: 154–156). This is a pivotal document in regards to the theme of this book, as it recognises the intersecting trajectories of both religious and philosophical traditions. The king clearly hoped to reinforce the state ideology which emphasised, as well as recognised, the compatibility of Buddhism and Confucianism, but the Ten Injunctions also reflect the respectful and forward-thinking nature of the King who recognised and esteemed the polymorphous practices of the general population, practices which still reverberate in modern Korea in the twenty-first century. The first two injunctions recognised the prestigious place of Buddhism by (1) highlighting the belief that Buddhism protected the state, also recognising the importance of supporting the doctrinal and meditational schools and (2) acknowledging the role of Buddhist monks in regards to geomancy, especially when deciding where temples should be built. He highlights Sŏn master Tosŏn (826–898) in particular, who, like many Buddhists of this era, had clearly absorbed Daoist practices. This links humans and their natural environment, which has the potential to be recalibrated in the modern era of environmental vulnerability, where we need to be more respectful of nature, something also reiterated in the fifth injunction which states that the dynasty was founded "with the help of the elements of mountain and river of *our country*" (155; emphasis added). In regards to succession, if the legitimate male heirs were deemed unworthy, T'aejo suggests in the third injunction to choose someone else who is worthy, following the example of the sage kings of China. However, though in the fourth injunction he communicates his awareness of the ties and influence from China, he asserts (155; emphasis added) that "*our country* occupies a different geographical location and our people's character is different from that of the Chinese [way]", possibly an early suggestion of some sort of proto-nationalism, an argument developed further by John Duncan (1988). In this regards, it is important to underline the contribution of the Confucian scholar Kim Pusik (1075–1151), who composed the earliest extant history of Korea, the *History of the Three Kingdoms* (三國史記, K. *Samguk sagi*), showing us how seriously the peninsular people considered the study and compilation of historical records, but also of the fact that, while maintaining close links with China, they clearly saw themselves as a distinctive people with their own rich cultural identity and history.

The final five injunctions (Lee & De Bary 1997: 155–156) also incorporate and link the different traditions that make up this uniquely Korean heterogeneous *way*, with the sixth injunction mentioning two particular festivals considered important: (1) *Yŏndŭnghoe*, to worship the Buddha, and (2) *P'algwanhoe*, to celebrate the various spirits associated with heaven, the sacred mountains and rivers, and of course, the dragon god, blending folk beliefs with Daoist imagery that gives Korean religious art such a range of symbols and figures to draw from. The seventh injunction reminds future kings to be humane as a way to "win over the people", and to avoid over taxation and over-working people, to assure balance of yin and yang. The eighth injunction reflects a biased distrust of people from

Kongju, suggesting they are treacherous because they were originally a part of Paekche, indicating that even a few centuries later there must still have existed significant animosity between the former kingdoms – yet regional discrimination is still rife even today. The final two injunctions relay ideas from the Confucian Classics on the social responsibility of state officials and the importance of military (especially in a state which shares borders), noting that salary should depend on merit (something still problematic today), but lastly, also the need to study and read the classics and history, adding to "take the past as a warning to the present". Such ideas may reflect the influence of the king's close confidante, the influential Confucian scholar Ch'oe Sǔngno (927–989), who, while critical of Buddhism, was aware of its spiritual importance to the masses.

Buddhism continued, as it had done during Silla, to be a source of protection for the nation, and known as *"hoguk-bulgyo"* (state-protecting Buddhism), from a political, social and also spiritual point of view (for an extensive examination of this, see Vermeersch 2008). Whilst the Confucian scholars had their own state civil examination system, the Buddhists were soon to have one of their own under King Kwangjong (949–975). Senior monks could also occupy two very important posts: *kuksa* (國師) or "State Preceptor"; and *wangsa* (王師), meaning "Royal Preceptor". This also clearly created competition between monks, who were now also vying for positions of authority and power, ideas eschewed by their very teachings. Needless to add, such close proximity to the king upset the Confucian scholars who felt their realm was that of education, especially that of the monarch, highlighted in their own teachings. In addition, the conflict existing between the different schools of Buddhism was a major issue facing the monks of the new dynasty (Keel 1984: 2).

From Ǔich'ǒn to Chinul and the consolidation of Sǒn

One of the most important monks of this period was Ǔich'ǒn (1055–1101), who was the fourth son of King Munjong (r.1046–83). Ǔich'ǒn had been to China during the Song Dynasty and had the opportunity to meet many of the masters of the Tiantai school, known as *Ch'ǒntae* in Korea. He believed in the compatibility of the doctrines of both the major doctrinal schools, which Wǒnhyo had been eager to reconcile, as well as acknowledge the importance of the meditational schools. This inspired him to revive the *Ch'ǒntae* order in Korea in order to absorb the meditational *Sǒn* lineages into the textual *Kyo* lineages. This serious issue of disunity among the different Buddhist schools distracted monks from developing the philosophical views initiated in China, and could have escalated out of control (think Protestants and Catholics) (Grayson 2002: 85–86; Keel 2004: 172–173). Ǔich'ǒn made Kukch'ǒng monastery the centre of this new consolidated Buddhism, clearly supported with generous royal patronage. Ǔich'ǒn hoped to encourage other leading monks from the Nine Mountain Schools of Sǒn to join and to help him achieve his vision of "*kyokwan kyŏmsu*"(教觀兼修) – concurrent cultivation through doctrinal study and meditation – drawing on both traditions to form a new path*way* of self-cultivation (Keel 1984: 4). Though Ŭich'ŏn died at a young age, unable to see his dream realised, nevertheless, he considered his new development as a Sŏn school – not a doctrinal one – and this is something that would continue to shape the tradition in Korea. His influence led several schools to converge to become known as the *Chogye* order. Readers should at this point note that 'Chogye' is the name of the largest order of Korean Buddhism today, founded in the twentieth century (now usually written as Jogye). Ŭich'ŏn was also interested in collecting the various Buddhist scriptures in order to compile a comprehensive collection which would be a precursor to the *Tripitaka Koreana*, discussed below.

After Ŭich'ŏn, the most significant monk of this era who again tried to unify the different schools was Chinul, known also by his posthumous title State [National] Preceptor (*kuksa*) Puril Pojo 佛日普照. It must not go unrecognised that Chinul was "very much indebted to Zonmgmi (780–841), the ninth century Chinese Huayan and Chan patriarch who wanted to harmonise Chan with doctrinal Buddhism" (Keel 1984: vii). Chinul sought to unite both schools, but unlike Ŭich'ŏn, who was a doctrinal school patriarch, Chinul gave primacy to *Sŏn*. Chinul came to a conclusion much like that of Zongmi who said "Sūtras are the word of the Buddha, whereas Ch'an is the mind of the Buddha; the mind and the mouth of the Buddha should not be divergent" (60–61). For both scholars, while *Kyo* represents what the Buddha said, what is transmitted to the mind is *Sŏn*, therefore they interpenetrated each other. Chinul's focus on *Sŏn* "permeated the subsequent development of the Korean *Sŏn* tradition" (Sim 2004: 221).

This was a turbulent time domestically, with the Ch'oe military family taking control away from the king and his close bureaucrats, and a time, Chinul asserted, for self-reflection: while the country may degenerate, he believed adamantly that one's Buddha-Nature did not. He therefore focused on the mind and believed that the master was *Sŏn*, while the servant was *Kyo*. For Chinul, the internal machinations of the mind should be one's major concern, and this is reflected in his guiding discourse, an intellectually internalised one, which was coupled with very practical advice and guidance. Chinul was also deeply aware of the negative reputation that the Buddhist monastic community had acquired, and realised that unless this was changed, Buddhism would face an inevitable crisis, which he saw in no small way linked to state sponsorship. This may also reflect the fact that there had been a military coup in 1170 and some of the military leaders, such as Ch'oe Ch'unghŏn, actually supported the meditation monasteries, as they had previously been in conflict with the doctrinal schools and their link with the aristocrats whose authority had greatly reduced (Lee & DeBary 1997: 224–226; Keel 2004: 174). These ideas are reflected in the writings Chinul left behind and his emphasis on a retreat community, away from the luxuries of life, with insistence on the necessity of practice (an idea also emphasised by the Confucians and Wŏnhyo), outlined in his first work written in 1190, *Encouragement to Practice: The Compact of the Concertration* [Samadhi] *and Wisdom* [*Prajñā*] *Society* (勸修定慧結社文, K. *Kwŏnsu Chŏnghye kyŏlsa mun*), composed shortly after he had established his retreat community at Kŏjo-sa temple. He reached out to leading monks to join his new community, and criticised the search of certain monks for riches and fame, as well as the degenerate state of Buddhism where he felt some followers overly relied on chanting the Buddha's name, a slight at Pure Land Buddhism, which he felt could lead people to externalise their practice, rather than look into their own minds to recover their Buddha Nature in their own lifetime (Buswell Jr. 2012: 90–93).

Chinul: from textuality to *Kanhwa Sŏn*

Though an emphasis was placed on meditation by the Sŏn masters, they nonetheless collected and composed a huge body of literature. In 1205, Chinul composed his influential text *Admonitions to Beginning Students* (誡初心學人文, K. *Kyech'osim haginmun*), which coincided with his latest attempt to consolidate Sŏn in Koryŏ, his 'Society for Cultivating Sŏn' (修禪社, K. *Susŏnsa*), changing the name of the Meditation and Wisdom Society. It was also established at Chogye Mountain – one of the reasons why Chinul is considered the founder of the order of the same name today, the Chogye (Jogye) Order. Chinul's text resonates with some of Wonhyo's writings, but it was greatly influenced by Changlu Zongze's (?–ca. 1107) *Rules of Purity for the Chan Monastery* (禪苑清規, C. *Chanyuan qinggui*), which was composed in 1103. This 'rulebook' emphasises the rules of conduct monks were expected to adhere to, and highlights the seriousness of this undertaking. The great Neo-Confucian scholar Zhu Xi would similarly draw up a set of rules for his White Deer Grotto Confucian Academy (which would be emulated in Korea), requesting students to learn them and, more importantly, to keep them, possibly showing the influence of Buddhist order (and discipline) on later Neo-Confucian developments outlined in more detailed in the next section. Robert Buswell Jr. (2012: 93) emphasises the importance of Chinul's *Admonitions* in Korea:

> *Admonitions* came to be adopted by Korean Buddhists as the standard of conduct at almost every major monastery, helping to ensure uniformity of conduct and decorum across the Korean Sŏn monastic tradition. It was so popular that an early Korean vernacular translation into the *Han'gŭl* writing system was made in 1612. [It]was so widely used in Korean Buddhism, in fact, that during the middle of the Chosŏn dynasty (1392–1910) it was included in a primer of three short texts used to train Korean postulants and novices in the basics of Buddhist morality and daily practice.

This primer, *Personal Admonitions to Neophytes Who Have First Aroused the Mind* (初發心自警文, K. *Ch'obalsim chagyŏngmun*), consists of only three texts, the first of which is Chinul's, followed (unsurprisingly) by Wonhyo's *Awaken your Mind and Practice.* Both texts are still studied by novice monks in Korean temples today, and only the third text in this primer, called *Personal Admonitions,* was composed during the Chosŏn dynasty, by Yaun Kagu (fl. ca. 1376) (自警文, K. *Chagyŏngmun*).

Despite the ubiquitous importance of Chinul's texts, mentioned above, probably his greatest contribution to Sŏn thought in general, but in particular within the Korean context, is his text *On Cultivating the Mind* (修心訣, K. *Susim kyŏl*). This outlines his teachings on sudden awakening followed by gradual cultivation, as well as the practice of meditation and its cardinal focus on wisdom. Buswell (2012: 94) describes how this 'sudden' (swift and sharp, known as 'subitism') enlightenment experience makes students lucidly and incontestably aware of their inherent Buddha Nature (*Pulsŏng* in Korean), which he describes as "tracing the radiance emanating from the mind back to its source", which helps them to lift the clouds that have hidden even unto themselves that they are already enlightened beings. This is a powerful message and metaphor, leading Buswell (1991) to call his collection of translations of Chinul's texts, *Tracing Back the Radiance: Chinul's Way of Korean Zen.*

One's own "mind" needs to be clarified of impurities, which cloud ones Buddha Nature, and enlightenment is necessary before attempting to lead others to their own salvation. This required a path*way* of cultivation to recover one's original Buddha-Nature, which is already contained in one's mind, though people search for it outside themselves, even in the sages from the past, detailed by Chinul in *On Cultivating the Mind* (Buswell Jr. 2012: 205–246). Chinul (Buswell Jr. 2012: 206–207) writes:

> It is so tragic. People have been deluded for so long. They do not recognize that their own minds are the true buddhas. They do not recognize that their own natures are the true dharma. Wanting to search for the dharma, they still look in the distance for all the sages. Wanting to search for the Buddha, they will not observe their own minds. [. . .] I hope all of you who cultivate the path will never search outside. "The nature of the mind is untainted; it is originally consummate and complete in and of itself. If you will only leave behind false conditioning, you will be a 'such-like' buddha".

This idea also leads to another salient feature of Chinul's thought, that of 'sudden enlightenment and gradual cultivation', also discussed in the same text. This method, he suggests, is much more accessible than 'sudden enlightenment and sudden cultivation', which was only "for people of extraordinary spiritual faculties" (213). But why the need for gradual cultivation if one is enlightened? Buswell (2012: 95) astutely answers this:

"just because students understand that they are inherently Buddhas does not mean that they will be able to act as buddhas", an idea (and lesson) that could easily be transferred to Confucians, Daoists, Christians, Muslims and so on – practice what you preach, but *practice it every day*. This may explain why Chinul had an ambivalent attitude towards "radical subitism", that a singular awakening experience was enough to make you permanently act in an enlightened manner (Buswell 1989).

Chinul's approach recognises the mind as the essence (*che*) of one's Buddha Nature, while continual practice and cultivation aids in refining its function (*yong*), again bringing together the important essence-function (*che-yong*) feature of Korea's Buddhist tradition, discussed in the previous chapter. While also encouraging students to study texts as a precursor to a successful introduction to the practice of meditation, this synthesises both strands of Buddhism, *Kyo* and *Sŏn*, into a holistic guide and practice. It is not some ideal 'out there', but something which emanates from within, where it already exists perfectly (though clouded), and which requires practice to transform our (heart and) mind so that we *become* our own truth. This idea resembles the idea of truth which the American philosopher John D. Caputo discusses in his text *Truth* (2013: 52–53), where truth is an 'event' that can transform (us/everything), which he describes as "the process of trying to *become*-true". When considered in regards to religion, he notes that it "is the passionate search for the things we most care about, the restlessness of our heart [and mind] in the midst of a mysterious world". Unlocking this 'mystery' requires us to think of the world and ourselves in a dramatically different way, not based on knowledge predicated through 'reason', or based on what is rational. It requires us to suspend all conceptual understanding, which brings us to a discussion of Chinul's engagement with the study of *kong'an* (J. *koan*).

Chinul only engaged with the *kong'an* and the meditational techniques related to them in his final years. Nevertheless, his teachings and writings on the subject would greatly impact his disciples, and Korean Buddhism in general, right down until the present through the technique known as Kanhwa Sŏn 看話禪. This study of the *kong'an* developed from the great Chinese Chan master Dahui Zonggao (1089–1163) of the Linji School:

Kanhwa Sŏn

Chinul advocated Master Dahui's practice developed from the study of *kong'an*, literally meaning 'public cases', open for all to examine, and hence not some secretive or private transmission between a master and a student. *Kong'an* were generally discussions or dialogues between a master and student with subsequent commentaries and explanations of renowned Sŏn masters that could also include poetic verses, often collected and published in editions which were studied by monks. But more than that, it emphasised a meditational practice focused on the keyword in the *kong'an*, known as *hwadu* in Korean (*hua tou* in Chinese) from two Chinese characters: *hwa*話, meaning speech or spoken words/conversation, and *du* 頭, meaning head or lead/boss, which may be interpreted as the key phrase, or in more colloquial terms – the punchline. Often the *hwadu* involves a shocking, yet probing, enigmatic question, which challenges any rational or doctrinal resolution, such as 'does a dog have a Buddha Nature or not?' or 'Is the Buddha a dried shit stick?' (yes, you read correctly!). Continual concentration or meditation (*sŏn*) on the *hwadu* is known as *kanhwa*, from *kan*看, meaning to study or examine (but could also mean 'to depend on'), and it ties together the idea of contemplation of the keyword, with the goal of a sudden epiphany of one's Buddha Nature.

* (For an in-depth discussion see: Buswell 2012: 75–88; Masters Gou *et al.* 2014).

Buswell (1991: 68–69) describes how in Korea, "Hwadu is the predominant technique cultivated in meditation halls, and almost all masters advocate its use for students at all levels". It is important to point out that this practice, carried out today in temples all over Korea, developed on the peninsula before the *koan* achieved its iconic importance within the Japanese Rinzai Zen tradition. Chinul collected various *kong'an*, publishing them in *On the Resolution of Doubts in Kanhwa* (看話決疑論, K. *Kanhwa kyŏrŭiron*). The title itself highlights an integral part of the practice, which revolves around generating doubt – or challenging our general perceptions of things, even Buddhist ideas and teachings, then, even doubting the teachings in the Buddhist texts and sutras. Great doubt, it was believed, was necessary for great enlightenment, clearly reflected in a recent publication on *Kanhwa Sŏn* in English: *Great Doubt, Great Enlightenment: The Tradition and Practice of Ganhwa Seon in Korean Buddhism* (Master Gou *et al.* 2014).

Interestingly, within the Christian tradition in the Middle Ages there emerged a radical contemplative tradition, which also moved away from a reliance on scripture and fixed ideas about God, arguing that this could mislead people into thinking they actually understood God through 'knowledge' (which continues to fuel divisiveness today). One of the most famous of such texts is *The Cloud of Unknowing* (Anonymous 2001), dating from the fourteenth century, whose author remains unknown. This unusual book opens describing itself as "a book of contemplation", suggesting that readers empty or "overthrow" all the conceptual knowledge they have about God, "who is beyond the reach of all created faculties", where the Divine or God is not understood as a man/being in a cloud, but an intense mystical experience generated through intense love, and utterly inexpressible through language, which actually sounds quite Daoist (23). Just as *Kanhwa* meditation focuses on a phrase or word from the *kong'an*, so too does the author of *The Cloud* (28) urge readers to take a short word or phrase close to their heart [and mind] and to focus on it at all times in order to "pierce that darkness [. . .] that thick cloud of unknowing", urging them: "do not give up, whatever happens". The goal of this meditation is to achieve a sharp communion or inexplicable epiphany of this unknowable God who "sends out a beam of spiritual light, piercing this cloud of unknowing". Such 'negative' contemplative techniques of 'un-knowing' contrast greatly with the complicated Catholic doctrine, especially the *Summa Theologica* of Thomas Aquinas (1225–1274), who attempts to answer everything about this 'unknowable' Deity. Both techniques, that of *Kanhwa Sŏn* and the practice of 'contemplation' of *The Cloud*, de-emphasise the scriptures in their traditions and overturn the centrality of the text. For the Buddhists in East Asia, this move away from dependence on the textual tradition led Neo-Confucians contemporaneous with Chinul in China to criticise it as something esoteric and too abstract to be effective, and before too long, this negative attitude would reach the peninsula itself, foreshadowing an extended period of decline.

Before this crisis would reach its peak due to the new intellectual influence of Yuan China, some influential monks did emerge. Hyesim (1178–1234), an important disciple of Chinul, would carry on and develop his master's ideas, especially the meditational *kanhwa* practice, collecting well over a thousand *kong'an* published in his *Collection of the Meditation School's Explanatory Verses* (禪門拈頌集, K. *Sŏnmunyŏmsong-chip*), one of the largest collections in East Asia, highlighting how seriously their study became for the Korean Buddhist tradition. Hyesim also believed in the compatibility of Confucianism and Buddhism, noting that they had similar teachings, and that many Confucians had become Buddhists, like Kihwa discussed later in this chapter. Of incontestable importance is Iryŏn (1206–1289), author of the *Legends and History of the Three Kingdoms*, already discussed earlier in this book, whose text is of tantamount cultural importance for his collection of myths and legends, but also as a source of information on the contributions of Korea's early outstanding Buddhist monks, as well as documented evidence of material Buddhist culture from pagodas to relics stored in specific temples. Po'u (1301–1382), who was ordained at the age of 12, travelled to Yüan China in 1346 and mastered the Sŏn teaching of the Linji School there. When he returned to Korea he was made Royal Preceptor, in 1356. Hyegŭn (1320–1376), like Po'u, travelled to China and studied meditation. When he returned from his travels, he too was made Royal Preceptor, but also received another noble honour as he was made head of the *Chogye-jong*. Another very important figure also emerged at this time, Muhak (1327–1405), who studied in Yanjing (now Beijing) for three years, returned to Korea where he was a close associate of Hyegŭn. He also developed a close friendship with the future King of the new dynasty that was soon to come and represents a transition stage between governing ideologies (Lee & De Bary 1997: 230–237; Grayson 2002: 8–99; Su 1995: 160–161).

Printing achievements of Koryŏ Buddhists

Buddhists during this period also contributed to Korean literature in terms of their Sŏn poetry, used to reflect on their teachings, but creating a uniquely Korean approach while doing so (Pihl 1995). Additionally, Koryŏ monks contributed to the development of writing and printing culture, which deserves special recognition globally for their mammoth and exemplary undertakings in this field, all too often associated with Europe and 'the West'. Firstly, the *Koryŏ Tripitaka*, also known as the *Koryŏ Kyojang*, completed in 1087, was one of the most comprehensive collection of Buddhist texts in East Asia in the eleventh century, emulating prominent versions published in the newly emerged Song dynasty (960–1279). 'Tripitaka' from the Sanskrit word *Pitaka*, literally means 'the three baskets', describing how the Buddhist teachings had been divided into three parts: (1) the sutras (經, K. *kyŏng*); (2) the vinayas (律, K. *yul*), which consisted of the commandments and rules of the Buddhist order, and (3) the sastras (論, K. *non*), commentaries on sutras. With the carving of the Tripitaka underway, Ŭich'ŏn, Chinul's influential precursor, masterminded the collection of a comprehensive selection of supplementary commentaries on the Tripitaka, compiled over 20 years and known as the *Supplement to the Tripitaka* (續藏經, K. *Sokchanggyŏng*). He was interested in collecting all the available commentaries in the region, from the Chinese, but also from the Khitan, and most importantly, from his Korean predecessors, such as Wŏnhyo and Ŭisang, cementing their reputation by bestowing on them the same importance as earlier revered Chinese masters, reflecting Ŭich'ŏn's indiscriminative genius. Unfortunately, both the original *Koryŏ Kyojang* and Ŭich'ŏn's vast supplemental collection to it were destroyed by fire, along with many other temples and their treasures, with the arrival of the Mongol invaders in 1232 (Ahn 1982: 81–87; Hyewon & Mason 2014: 233–234).

Soon the mammoth task of recarving the Tripitaka and its supplemental texts onto birch-wood blocks had begun. This undertaking was completed in 1251, by monks from the doctrinal and Sŏn orders, resulting in the now worldwide acclaimed *Tripitaka Koreana*. This also demonstrates the level of state-sponsored Buddhism at the time, and the money invested in the carving of these scriptures must have been immense. This also clearly reflected the leadership's belief in the power of the Buddha to intervene on behalf of the nation, though Confucians may have argued that reinforcing the military would have been wiser and more effective, especially during subsequent invasions and military threats. Nevertheless, as Hyewon and Mason (2014: 230) point out, "This is the largest, most-complete compilation of

Buddhist Scriptures from ancient times extant in the world [. . .] one of Korea's greatest National Treasures and globally recognised as a precious and landmark religious heritage". This is known to Koreans as the *Koryŏ Taejanggyŏng* (高麗大藏經), where *Taejanggyŏng* is the term for Tripitaka (or Great Buddhist Scriptures); or *P'alman Taejanggyŏng* 八萬大藏經, whereby *P'alman* (80,000) refers to the number of woodblocks carved for the collection rounded off (though there were actually over 81,000 blocks), and these woodblocks contain some 52 million Chinese characters – carved backwards – in order to print the right way around! (Ahn 1982: 87–91). The blocks are currently housed at Haein-sa temple and its depository there is designated as a UNESCO World Heritage Site, reflecting the scientific ingenuity of the monks and builders who managed to create the perfect environment to house the woodblocks which remain in pristine condition today. What is also impressive is the precision with which the characters were carved, evidenced by the prints still produced today. In 2007, the *Tripitaka Koreana* was also inscribed in the UNESCO Memory of the World Register, which celebrates the world's documentary heritage (see UNESCO.org).

The next technological advancement after printing with wood would be texts published with movable metal characters. Though the *Jikji* (shortened title of *Paegun hwasang ch'orok pulcho chikchi simch'e yojŏl*, 白雲和尚抄錄佛祖直指心體要節, Anthology of Great Buddhist Monks' Sŏn Teachings), a Sŏn Buddhist text compiled in 1377, at Hŭngdŏk-sa temple by Paegun (1298–1374), is generally considered as the first text published in this

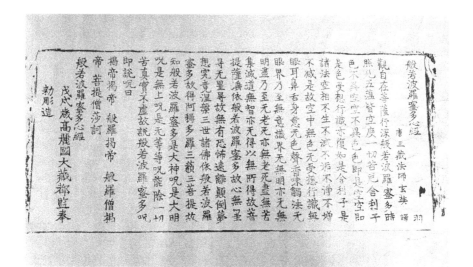

Figure 3.2 Author's copy of the *Heart Sutra* made from the Koryŏ Taejanggyŏng

manner, Ahn (1982) suggests that there were actually other texts printed using this method in the previous century. However, the *Jikji* (of which only the second volume is extant of the movable print version) has been inscribed into UNESCO's Memory of the World Programme as the world's earliest example of metal type printing. It is currently stored in the Bibliothèque Nationale de la France in Paris, much to the chagrin of the Koreans who would, quite understandably, like it returned to the country of its creation, as it is part of its cultural heritage.

The rise of (Neo) Confucianism

The demise of Buddhism that ensued during the thirteenth and fourteenth century continued towards the end of the Koryŏ Dynasty, and the Buddhist hierarchy was the only thing standing in the way of the rising Neo-Confucian elite, and it still wielded substantial power. The Buddhist church had become rich, but this excessive wealth, combined with political power, led to severe corruption, and a movement to remove the Buddhist predominance had begun well before the collapse of the Koryŏ dynasty. During this period, state and society were indeed lamentable: there was conflict between the growing powerful *yangban* and the local officials known as *hyangni*, the Mongol Dynasty collapsed, Yellow turbans' invasions (1359–1362), raids by Japanese *Wāko* pirates, and the kings were virtually powerless pawns. However, during this period of confusion and change, Korean scholars in China managed to assist the transmission of Neo-Confucian ideas to Korea, something that would shape its entire future and undermine Buddhism (Duncan 2000: 155; Su 1995: 168).

Ironically, often scholars who were interested in Buddhism, also had an interest in Confucianism and Daoism (The Three Teachings), and they would open a new path*way* for Confucians to revitalise their own tradition by engaging with Buddhist and Daoist ideas – which they would then turn against and attack vehemently, lacking the inclusivistic approach of the Buddhists. For example, Liang Su (753–793), though a proponent of the Tiantai school and a practitioner of Chan, he was also an erudite scholar (and sometimes still referred to as a Confucian) and outstanding prose writer. Nienhauser (1986: 562) points out that Liang Su:

> re-affirmed the schools basic eclectic and syncretistic tendencies, which made it possible for thinkers to interpret certain passages in Confucian texts as rudimentary expositions of Buddhist metaphysical principles, thus laying the ground for Neo-Confucian philosophy.

Confucian scholars, accused of having a rudimentary metaphysical basis for their ethical codes, sought to "offer a cosmology that could compete with the Buddhists", leading them to construct a more sophisticated hermeneutical approach to their own tradition (Creel 1971: 205).

It is generally agreed that Han Yu (768–824) is responsible for the "rejuvenated traditionalism" which was Confucianism (Nienhauser 1986: 397). He, however, is also responsible for the initial attacks against Buddhism, whilst at the same time his writing has been influenced by both Buddhism and Daoism, but re-appropriated to reflect Confucian ideas. His work relies deeply on *The Great Learning* and reflects its call for sincerity and self-cultivation. There is also an influence from *The Mencius* (outlined in Chapter 1) in his essay *An Inquiry on Human Nature*, and he has helped shape a guiding discourse that encapsulates the Confucian one of a moral being and the interrelationship with a moral society. In his essay *An Inquiry on the Way* (*Dao*), he has even further highlighted the unseen *way* and its inextricable link with Humanity (仁), which can be followed. He rejects the Buddhists as they "insist on discarding the relationship between ruler and ministers, doing away with the relationship between ruler and ministers", a version of which would be adapted later to criticise the Catholics (Chan 1973: 452–455).

One of Han's disciples was Li Ao (died ca. 844) and whereas the great Buddhist master Xuanzang had described five stages to guide the Bodhisattva towards enlightenment, Li Ao's essay '*Returning to the Nature*', consists of three components to become a sage: "(1) a general discussion on the nature (性, K. *sŏng*), the feelings (情, K. *chŏng*), and the sage (聖, K. *sŏng*); (2) the process of self-cultivations whereby one may become a sage; (3) the necessity for self-exertion in this process" (Fung 1983: 414). What we can notice is the attempt at formulating a guiding discourse to enable one "to become a sage" to recover the original mind, which urges one to continuously practice as part of a gradual process (echoing Chinul). His writings are more indebted to Buddhist ideas about the recovery of the inherent good nature or Buddha-Nature, although he has used Buddhist notions of self-cultivation and self-exertion in order to lead one to 'sagehood', and that is inextricably linked with the Confucian *way*. Li Ao's discussions on 'nature' remind us of *The Mencius*, and that would fuel a much later debate between Korean Neo-Confucians, outlined in the next chapter.

However, the greatest elaboration of Neo-Confucianism appeared during China's Song Dynasty (960–1279). The development of this new ideology was a southern Song phenomenon and initiated by the writings of 'The Five Sages of Song': Shao Yong (1011–1077), Zhou Dunyi (1017–1073), Zhang Zai (1020–1077), and two brothers, Cheng Hao (1032–1085) and Cheng Yi (1033–1107). However these five thinkers were "acclaimed only later when their various contributions were synthesised by the impressive scholar Zhu Xi (1130–1200)", particularly the ideas of the Cheng brothers (Fairbank & Goldman 1999: 98). These contributions were particularly interested in the question of human nature, developed its own intricate metaphysics, and was centred around Zhu Xi's interpretation of 'Principle' (理, C. *li*, K. *i*) and material force (氣, C. *chi*, K. *ki*). The important question was, "Can sagehood be learned?" (De Bary 1997: 687). These ideas would incite the minds of some of Korea's greatest intellectuals, who would also contribute greatly to these developments, but with a particular focus on sagehood.

Though Koryŏ had declined into a state of disarray, and although the prestige of the Buddhists had declined and left an opening for a new philosophy to remedy the situation, a solution for both these problems was to be found in the transmission of Neo-Confucianism to Korea. What had initially started as a Southern Song (1127–1279) phenomenon, due to the unified Mongol kingdom (1271–1368), would gradually be used to construct a new dynasty, with Neo-Confucianism as its guiding ideology. As previously mentioned, Zhu Xi had reanimated an unprecedented interest in Confucianism, which had greatly influenced all Chinese socio-political spheres through his intertextual reappraisal of the works of the Song scholars. However, a divided China made the interchange of ideas problematic. Additionally, issues with the Jurcheds and Khitans (peoples from Northeast Asia) also severed contact with China from within Koryŏ, along with military regimes started by General Chŏng Chung-bu in 1170, and consequently leading to a Ch'oe clan military dictatorship forcing scholars from the capital. Many Confucian scholars actually fled to Buddhist temples where they encountered the intricate Buddhist doctrines. Such a symbiotic relationship would leave its imprint on late Koryŏ Confucianism and inspire scholars to develop a moral discourse that could rival such intricate issues as the metaphysics of Buddhism (Deuchler 1992: 16; Nahm 1996: 86–90).

Whilst the Mongols caused much chaos and destruction, "though hardly dedicated to the propagation of Chinese culture, [they] became the unpremeditated sponsors and purveyors of Neo-Confucianism" (De Bary 1985: 2). It is also worth noting, as stated by Li (1965: 262), "Foremost among Yüan's achievements was its transportation system", which provided the internal framework that made gradual transference of ideas possible from Southern China to the Yuan capital. This transmission is mainly attributed to the scholar Zhao Fu (c.1206–1299) who brought the teachings with him to the capital in 1235. It was further developed Zhao Fu's disciple Xu Heng (1209–1281) who "absorbed the teachings of the Ch'eng Chu School and made them the basis of Confucianism in Yüan China" (Deuchler 1992: 16).

In 1259, Korea became a vassal to the Mongols and connections were strengthened through the intermarriage of the Korean royal clan with Mongol princesses. There was also much interaction between the Korean literati and the Chinese literati at the Mongol capital. The most important Korean scholar of this era was An Hyang (1243–1306), inspired by Zhu Xi's texts, "he copied them by hand, drew (Zhu Xi's) likeness and brought them back home" (Deuchler 1992: 17). Paek I-jŏng (1247–1323) also helped transmit the new ideology to Korea as he was acquainted with many Chinese scholars at the Man'gwŏndang library (the Hall of Ten Thousand Scrolls), founded by King Ch'ungsŏn (1308–1313). Many of the direct successors of the Cheng-Zhu tradition also met here (19). Yi Che-hyŏn (1287–1367) endorsed the printing of The *Four Books* and believed that a king should indeed be a "sage" and interpreted the relationship between government and Neo-Confucianism as essential. Yi Saek (1328–1396), son of Yi Che-hyŏn, was responsible for the dissemination of the texts in Korea where Neo-Confucian prestige was increasing rapidly and he was "appointed educational intendant for the Yuan in Korea" (De Bary 1985: 41). These ideas would redefine the moral guiding discourse of the emerging dynasty.

Accordingly, the philosophy of the Confucian scholars defined their society and also defined all relationships within that society. The final years of the Koryŏ Dynasty had been a time of upheaval, but the final insult for the Confucian scholars at the time was the role played by Buddhist monk Sin Ton (d.1371), who had virtually usurped the full authority of King Kongmin (1330–1374). Though he was soon removed and eventually beheaded, this contributed to the continuous attacks by the Neo-Confucian scholars in an attempt to assert their dominance at the expense of Buddhism. This was definitely an aim of the great Confucian scholar Chŏng Tojŏn (1342–1398) who was strategic in successfully accomplishing "the transition from Buddhist Koryŏ to Confucian Yi [Chosŏn dynasty]" (Hong 1983: 163). The decaying Koryŏ royal household had no realistic way of regaining prestige. Chŏng Tojŏn would help General Yi Sŏnggye, following his monumental decision to oust the king and his commander-in-chief from power in 1388, to establish the Chosŏn Dynasty (Eckert 1990: 101). Yi Sŏnggye was well aware that he needed more than military power alone to rule, and his reign would be legitimated by Neo-Confucian socio-political ideology.

Dynastic change: towards a Confucian *Modus Vivendi*

The underpinnings of the new king's reign was masterminded by Chŏng Tojŏn, the "architect" of this new dynasty (Chung 1985: 59–88). It would reject Buddhism and adopt Neo-Confucianism as the state ideology. The goal of Chosŏn politics was not to "govern by law" but to "purify" though, "not by punishment" (Yi 1983: 115). It had a deep respect for ethics and morality, and guiding moral principles translated themselves into law. Boehm (2002: 96) remarks that whilst moral communities engage in social control, morality is a political phenomenon as well as a social one. Accordingly, Chŏng Tojŏn would instigate a moral polity that would culminate with the Confucianisation of the state, and that would commence with the renewal of society on the whole through the use of rites, which shape social norms in a more cohesive manner than the use of laws with the threat of punishment. These social norms were guided through adherence to The Five Relationships, which advocated loyalty (忠, K. *ch'ung*) towards the higher ranks in social relationships, and within the family, *hyo* (孝), or filial piety underpinned this ideology. These patterns of behaviour were inculcated through *ritual* sourcebooks, especially *Zhu Xi's Family Rites*, which fostered the development of propriety, or *ye* (禮), through four specific rites (none of which were related to God or Heaven): capping (or coming-of-age), wedding, mourning and ancestor memorial rites. The most important of these rites are the memorial rites, known as *Chesa* (祭祀) in Korea, and they are conducted by many Korean families even today, but they were made obligatory by law during the early Chosŏn period. They had great significance, as (1) they reinforced patrilineality, and (2) they further denigrated the rights of women from the previous Koryŏ dynasty, as women could no longer perform these rituals (Deuchler 1992: 110–111). From this point, a hierarchical metamorphosis of both living and dying would be guided by a meticulously prescribed socio-cultural Neo-Confucian order.

Although the Chosŏn Dynasty was founded according to Neo-Confucian principles, Yi Sŏng-gye was in fact a devoted Buddhist and had a close relationship with the monk Muhak. After Yi became king, he appointed Muhak as his Royal Preceptor. Though he was urged to reduce the number of temples and monks, he never openly engaged in severe oppression of the Buddhists. The new king consulted Muhak for advice, and it is he who was responsible for choosing the site of the new capital, Hanyang (modern-day Seoul) based upon his highly developed geomantic knowledge of *p'ungsu*. The oppression of Buddhism and Shamanism was very severe during the reign of King T'aejong (r.1400–1418) with the result that both groups were subject to much discrimination, and were reduced to the rank of the lowest échelon of Chosŏn society (Cho 1992: 5; Kwon 1995: 172–173).

One of the first texts critical of the Buddhists was that of Paek mun-bo (1303–1374) whose text *In Rejection of Buddhism* (斥佛疏, K. *Ch'ŏkpulso*) used Shao Yung's Daoist inspired cyclical cosmological philosophy to ratiocinate that it was again time for restoration of the 'way' of the sage Confucian rulers Yao and Shun (Deuchler 1992: 23). Chŏng To-jŏn played a focal role attempting to wipe out Buddhism and "made the elucidation of the Learning of the Way and the repulsion of heterodox teachings [i.e. Buddhism] his own responsibility", where 'Learning of the Way', or *Dohak* (道學), was one of the titles given to Neo-Confucian studies at that time (Deuchler 1992: 101). Chŏng's arguments are encapsulated in his final treatise, *Array of Critiques of Mr. Buddha* (佛氏雜辨, K. *Pulssi Chappyŏn*), along with his shorter text, *On Mind, Material Force and Principle* (心氣理篇, K. *Simgiri p'yŏn*). The most comprehensive rebuttal to the Neo-Confucian critiques came from the first disciple of Muhak, a Sŏn monk by the name of Hamhŏ Kihwa (1376–1433), who had coincidently studied at the Confucian university, the Sŏngyun'gwan (成均館), at the same time as Chŏng. His treatise entitled *The Exposition of the Correct* (顯正論, K. *Hyŏnjŏng-non*) sought to illuminate the Confucian scholars with a correct understanding of Buddhism, something he felt they lacked. These important texts represent a conflicting hermeneutics of the moral *way* of Chosŏn and have been translated and annotated (along with the original Chinese characters) by Charles A. Muller (2015) in *Korea's Great Buddhist-Confucian Debate.*

Simgiri p'yŏn and *Pulssi Chappyŏn*: critique of Buddhism or appraisal of the Confucian *way*

In discussing Chŏng To-jŏn's concept of the Confucian *way*, it is worth pointing out that the Chinese characters of his first names "To-jŏn" (道傳) translate as *Transmitter of the way*. Indeed, he was predominantly predisposed to transmitting the *way* of the Neo-Confucian sages of Song, and similarly, he was unwilling to acknowledge any conceptual dependence on Buddhist doctrines. However, he does begin to investigate some fundamental philosophical issues, primarily the phenomenological issues concerning man's nature and their ethical implications (see Muller 2015: introduction). Chŏng's shorter treatise, *On Mind, Material Force and Principle* (see Muller 2015: 45–53), examines the main metaphysical issues that were of great importance at this time: the mind (and-heart), 心; the material force, 氣; and *Principle*, 理. Here, it is important to add that there was not any agreement or unanimity of opinion in these matters between Confucians themselves, something that would cause great debates and attacks between different Confucian factions. Chŏng, nevertheless, insists that only the Confucians have understood these ideas correctly, reflecting his very unilateral approach, which then forces him to disown any links with competing intellectual traditions, despite *the fact* that Confucians had clearly drawn on and developed ideas from Buddhism and Daoism. Chŏng highlights the main areas of conflict in the teachings of the Buddhists and Daoists, culminating in his justification of Confucianism as the one true "accurate" *way*. These represent the three parts of Chŏng's text, translated by Muller (2015) under the following headings:

On Mind, Material Force and Principle

1   [The Buddhists'] Conflation of the Mind with the Material Force
2   The Material Force Conflated with the Mind [the Daoist Teachings]
3   Principle Clarifying Mind and Material Force [the Confucian Teachings]

The first part critiques Buddhist ideas from the *Diamond Sutra* and the *Sutra of Perfect Enlightenment*; the second part mainly critiques ideas from the *Dao De Ching* and the *Zhuangzi*; while his rebuttal rests mainly with quotes from the *Mencius*, the *Analects*, and Zhu Xi, as well as the *Book of Rites*. Chong's main point at the end of his critique is that it is impossible to follow 'two *ways*', that there is only one way that "does not have two destinations" (53). Buddhists and Daoists would clearly disagree with this radical exclusivistic approach, the source of conflict with other religious and philosophical path*ways*.

The title of *Pulssi Chappyŏn* which Muller (2015) has translated as *An Array of Critiques of Buddhism*, literally translates as 'an array of critiques against *Mr Buddha*' – scathing and degrading from the onset. The text opens with a list of 19 critiques which Chŏng goes through systematically, but unwilling to engage with Buddhism at all, he initially launches into an attack on principle Buddhist doctrines: transmigration and karma. However, these are more than merely philosophical doctrines, they also represent the basic beliefs of religious Buddhism, and highlight the Confucian scholar's lack of respect and tolerance for another tradition. Considering this fact, the author of the critique should have understood that religious beliefs are not meant to be explained logically or rationally. Additionally, the language used to undermine these beliefs does not belong to traditional Confucianism, but is the language of Daoist cosmology, with references to yin (陰, pronounced *ŭm* in Korean), yang (陽) and the Five Elements (五行), ideas later woven by Confucians into a more complex intellectual tapestry, after they had adopted the *Yijing* (Classic of Changes) as a central text of their own. Such ideas were re-appropriated by Neo-Confucianism to enable it to compete metaphysically, as well as ontologically with Buddhism. In fact, dealing with questions and speculating about an afterlife was not something that Confucians had ever been too concerned about, especially as Confucius (*The Analects* 11.12) himself asked, "Not yet understanding life, how could you understand death?" (Ames & Rosemont 1998: 144). The goal of Confucianism was firmly focused on this life, which has been used by some to suggest that it is not a religion. Indeed, the use of the *Yijing* here is somewhat anachronistic: the Confucians had criticised the Buddhists and Daoists for fortune-telling and their 'superstitious beliefs', yet this book is the foundation for many such beliefs in East Asia. Chŏng could be accused of resorting to condemning one superstitious belief system by using another.

The next three sections of the text (Muller 2015: 59–83) cover the Buddhists interpretations of the mind (心, K. *sim*) and of the nature (性, K. *sŏng*), and Chŏng's basic argument is that Buddhist texts contradict each other, castigating Chinul himself of "nebulous supposition", lacking "hard facts", accusing Buddhists of "word play", but lacking a definitive doctrine. If the Buddhists understand that the mind is "the nature" and outside of it there is no Buddha, subsequently "outside of the Nature there is no dharma". Chŏng suggests that this shows a distinction, and therefore a contradiction in the "oneness" of nature and mind. This is dangerous territory for a Confucian scholar to criticise, considering the *problematique* of human nature within the Confucian texts. As one of the forerunners to Neo-Confucianism, Han Yu recognised:

> In discussing human nature, Mencius said, "Man's nature is good". Hsün Tzu said, "Man's nature is evil". And Yang Hsiung said, "Man's nature is a mixture of good and evil".
>
> (Chan 1973: 452)

Han Yu, a Confucian himself, speaks of three grades of nature: superior, medium and inferior. The apparent disunity of the Buddhist minds was merely phenomenological and was comprehensible considering the interpenetration of all things (known as *t'ondal*, mentioned before). For the Confucians, the question about various aspects of nature was not resolved until Zhang Zai (one of the Five Sages of Song) enunciated his doctrine of the "physical nature" that should be distinguished from the "original nature" (511). These 'anomalies' will be discussed in more detail in Chapter 4 as it is integral to the intellectual discourse of the great Chosŏn scholar, T'oegye, but they show that Chŏng's claims that the Confucian teachings were consistent are not substantiated.

Contrarily, Chŏng is quite in control when illuminating Confucian values that function in reality, in the external world, which the Buddhists consider completely illusory (in *his* opinion). He recalls the important story from Mencius (Book II, Part I) where a child falls into a well and inspires a spontaneous reaction (which is an external reaction to an internal one) to help the child, showing human nature is inherently good and displays the "nature of humanity" (仁之性, K. *injisŏng*), or "altruistic nature" as Muller translates it (2015: 62–63). Here the concept of humanity reflects the external manifestation of internal goodness. The argument, therefore, is that the Buddhist's path*way* is one-sided through its deeply focused internalisation, and lacks any method to guide its externalisation process. Chŏng refers to Cheng I and states, "The study of the Buddhists includes reverence to correct the internal, but does not include justice to straighten the external" (63). Similarities exist in passages by Zhu Xi, as well as Cheng Hao who adds that "the Buddhist way of internal and external life is incomplete" (Chan 1973: 538). This argument also supports the "Critique of the Buddhists' Abandonment of the Basic Human Relationships" and the "Buddhist Notion of Compassion", initiating his discourse (64–67) on humanity "仁" enacted through social interactions. Again Mencius is quoted, "[The Superior Man] loves his parents intimately and loves people as people. He loves people as people and cares about creatures" (66). Therefore, the goodness within oneself should be cultivated in order to produce honourable external actions. Hence, righteousness and propriety are externalised representations of the nature of humanity. This can be manifested through 'The Five Relationships', but especially through filial piety, which Chŏng denounces as something absent in Buddhist teachings. Sakyamuni Buddha himself is criticised for having abandoned his parents and neglecting to do practical work of any kind. From a Confucian point of view, the love for our parents should be distinguished, as they share the same material force (*ki* energy), and this is one of the strongest criticisms against the Buddhists who, Chŏng asserts, reject work and who "regard their most intimate family members like passers-by on the street".

Chŏng believed Confucianism was intrinsically more profound than Buddhism as it attempts to investigate *Principle* and create a harmonious society based on reciprocal obligations reflected in relationships: the basis of *The Four Books*. The Confucian *way*, he argues, is one of natural goodness that seeks to lead man to fulfil his innate potential, both mentally, and functionally, as part of society. Chŏng accuses the Buddhists of being motivated by fear, and not by natural goodness, which for Confucians, he suggests, is spontaneous. This fear is engendered through the "Buddhist Notion of Hells" (69–70), which is used to intimidate them into good behaviour. This is, in Chŏng's opinion, diametrically opposed to the Confucian concept of sincerity (誠, K. *sŏng*). The "sincerity of the will" is fundamental in *The Great Learning* and was central to the philosophy of Zhu Xi and subsequent Korean Neo-Confucian scholars. From this point of view, its contribution to the Confucian diatribe is to furnish it with a more noble praxis. The "superior person" (君子, K. *kunja*), according to Confucians, simply likes goodness and his cultivation and behaviour, which lead to his fortune, or misfortune are entirely his own responsibility, hence the need for constant 'seriousness' (敬, K. *kyŏng*), explained in detail in the next chapter, where it has a specific meaning and function for T'oegye. For the Buddhists, one can take refuge in the Buddha and thereby rely on something external, which by their own admission, does not exist, further excoriated in his critique of Sŏn Buddhist teachings (72–73), which he adds, "took nothingness as their cardinal teaching and abandoned the obligations of society", further summarising its teachings as "voidness, which does not produce real results", contrasted greatly with the 'way' of Confucianism that is expounded in the next section, 'Critique of the Equivalence and Differences between Confucianism and Buddhism' (73–77).

The teachings of the sage are a guide to "fully develop the mind's functions", reflecting the essence-function (*che-yong*) complementarity. These functions are internal, as well as external. The problem with the Buddhists, according to this idea, is that they do not act in accordance with how they are supposed to, and hence Chŏng accuses them of being "masters of glibness, lewdness, trickiness, and evasiveness" (77). The role of the Confucian

'Sage' is also acutely heralded as a pragmatic path*way* that has use for governing, and hence the three sages Yu, the Duke of Zhou, and Confucius are revered. The role of the sage is not merely one of learning, but a practical one, to plan for the welfare of the people and to "avoid activities that would bring harm to [them]" (81). People themselves also have to act morally towards each other as they live within a social context. They are conscious, and are conscious of this consciousness, therefore, they *should* act responsibly. Therefore, they are attributed the responsibility of assuring order in society, and as a result, all are provided for, and no one is reduced to begging, unlike the Buddhists, who have no practical guidance in their discourse to ameliorate their existence within society, chides Chŏng.

The final critiques assume that the causal transmission of Buddhism as a foreign *barbaric* doctrine, i.e., not from China, was responsible for a shortened reign. Such deductions are extremely weak: one should recall that the Middle Kingdom, China, was not 'China' when Confucius was alive, and the whole of 'China' was not unified linguistically. Many of these ideas echo Han Yu's *Memorial on the Bone of Buddha* (see: De Bary 1999: 583–585) and indeed Chŏng quotes him at length in *Critique 18*. Chŏng's text draws together multiple quotes by Confucius, Mencius, Zhu Xi, the Cheng brothers, as well as other renowned Confucian scholars. Their ideas fuel his arguments most succinctly and support his overall view that Buddhism had no practical social worth. By sharp contrast, his criticism of the actual Buddhist texts sometimes leave us wondering if he had completely read and understood their complex and sometimes bewildering metaphysics. This may explain Muller's (2007: 182) summary of Chŏng's view that "the components of Buddhist doctrine are disconnected from each other and incongruous". The most important retort to this diatribe would come from the monk Kihwa, who overturns Chŏng's caustic attack using a bitter tool – Confucian texts.

Kihwa's *Hyŏnjŏng-non* and the *Way of Humanity* (仁之道)

Kihwa (1376–1433) received an education at the Confucian Sŏnggyun-gwan Academy, where he had been a distinguished student. Moved by the death of a friend, and realising the impermanence of life, he became a monk. He also became a prolific writer and was noted for his commentaries on various Sūtra, such as *The Sutra of Perfect Enlightenment* (see: Muller 1999b). He lived during a time of great transition and displacement for the Buddhists. Neo-Confucian scholars had managed to eliminate the title *kuksa* (State Preceptor); however, Kihwa still managed to obtain the honourable title of *wangsa* (Royal Preceptor). As head of the Buddhist *sangha* during this time he took it upon himself to respond to the Neo-Confucian diatribe. Unlike Chŏng To-jŏn, Kihwa was as familiar with Buddhist scriptures as he was with Confucian texts. He uses an inclusivistic approach, in sharp contrast with the exclusivistic approach of Neo-Confucians who were so unwilling to admit any similarities or conceptual dependence at all and who rejected Buddhism vehemently (Kwon 1995; Muller 2007).

Kihwa's text attempts to illuminate (for the Neo-Confucians) the concept of nature and the subsequent "discriminations". He notes that whilst one has originally good nature, due to the confusion caused by the emotions, discriminations arise that can prevent true wisdom. Therefore, the goal is to remove these *discriminations*, resulting from emotions and promote purity. This process is not entirely different from that previously discussed by Li Ao, who focused on the interrelationship between nature, the feelings, and the sage. The enlightenment of the Buddha does not know discriminations, nor does the attainment of sagehood. The goal of sagehood is similar to that of the Buddhists "inducing people to abandon discrimination and manifest their original natures" (Muller 2015: 83).

The disturbance of the original nature by feelings is equated with the image of "clouds appearing in the vast sky". The clearness and purity of the clear sky represent the original nature, but it is sometimes obscured and hidden from us though it is still there. This imagery is similar to that of Cheng I who uses the imagery of water as: "It is the nature of the water to be clear, level and tranquil like a mirror. But, when it strikes a sand and stone, or when the ground underlying it is not level, it immediately begins to move violently" (Chan 1973: 567). However, the original nature is still the same and can be recovered. Indeed, this imagery is not completely unlike that of the natural goodness *p'u* (樸) of virgin blocks of wood found in Lao Tzu's *Tao Te Ching*, mentioned in Chapter 1. This is the stage of all possibility before any corruption takes place, like the child in infancy.

Kihwa rejects any claims that Buddhism cannot be used as an instrument in society and cleverly uses a Buddhist appropriation of the most important passage from *The Great Learning*:

> If you teach people to rely on this teaching and practice it, then their minds can be corrected, and their bodies can be cultivated. You can regulate your family, you can govern the state, and you can bring peace to all the world.
>
> (Muller 2015: 84)

This illustrates that the remarks made about Buddhists rejecting society and the state are ill-founded, and that the goal of all path*ways* is to bring peace to the self, the family, the state and the world. In retaliation to the Confucian attack on the Buddhist doctrine of *karma*, and its use of fear of retribution to engender goodness, Kihwa comments on the use of laws and punishments used by the Confucians. This may be alluding to Xunzi (298–238 BC) whose negative view of humanity inspired the authoritarianism of Legalists like Han Fei (d. 233 BC), discussed in Chapter 1: the Legalist school rejected

Confucian moral standards and sought power to subjugate, not to imbue the people with virtuous behaviour; instead, it used harsh punishments and rewards to support its totalitarian regime. Kihwa admonishes Confucians as they do not teach people "through the example of virtuous action", suggesting they do not practice what they preach, a thinly veiled attack on what he considers their hypocrisy (85).

Kihwa also rejects allegations that Buddhists do not respect filial piety and claims that the teachings of the Buddha brought his parents to "liberation", and argues that this is greater than anything obtainable through external and transitory social principles. He further states that the fact that the Buddha's name has been known by so many later generations and that his parents are praised as the parents of a great sage, he has fulfilled the greatest concept of filial piety, "Did not Confucius say 'Establishing yourself and practicing the Way, your name is known to later generation. This is the full manifestation of filial piety'?" (89). Kihwa also links the Buddhist idea of 'Harming Life' with the Confucian teachings on 'humanity' or 'humaneness', their chief virtue, but turns this against them, suggesting they have miscomprehended the universalistic applications of humanity regarding all sentient beings, meaning that taking 'any' life is inherently wrong. The Buddhist scholar highlights a passage from the *Book of History*, which states that "heaven and earth are the parents of all creatures". Then, quoting Cheng Hao, he reminds Confucians that "the humane man forms a single body with heaven and earth and the myriad things", which also alludes to Zhang Zai's Diagram of the Western Inscription and the idea that *Principle* is one and its manifestations are many, attributed to Cheng Hao – therefore, man and animals share a common *Principle* (89–95). Kihwa's argument for the preservation of life is a clever manipulation of Confucian ideas. If the ten thousand things indeed form one body, then they all share the same '*ki*', vital (material) force (氣) and *Principle* (理). Therefore, it is essentially wrong to destroy or kill life which links heaven and earth. Cheng Hao said, "there is no creature in the world that does not possess sufficient *Principle*", and "the human mind (in essence) is the same as that of plants and trees, birds and animals" (Chan 1973: 527). For Kihwa this means the interpenetration of heaven, earth and the myriad things, and the man of humanity seeks to illuminate the way for the people, and bring salvation to everyone, ultimately by preserving *Principle*, not by destroying it.

Karma and rebirth, which were rejected by Chŏng using examples from the *Yijing,* are substantiated using the same book by Kihwa. He quotes, "When you accumulate virtue you will have abundant good fortune; when you accumulate evil you will have abundant calamity" (96–97). The Confucians, it then appears, interpret only whatever areas in the *Yijing* seem to validate their arguments and ignore the rest. Kihwa also replies directly to another criticism by Chŏng relating to the "two kinds of mind". He simplifies previous Buddhist arguments, and relates them in Confucian terms that are similar to those of Zhang Zai. He discusses the existence of the "intrinsically real mind" and the "corporeal mind". The intrinsically real mind is the seat of real intelligence and contains the "original mind" (97–98). Subsequently, he also relates various stories reflecting on spirits and rebirth, a topic Confucians had neglected to talk about. He criticises the Confucians for not discussing what happens after this life, and notes that like with all things there is a transition, consisting of before, during, and after, known as *the three times*, an idea criticised by the Confucian scholars, who (in his opinion) have once again missed an important point in the *Yijing*, which discusses the past and attempts to "interpret the future", hence implying a division of "before and after" (98–103). Kihwa's knowledge of the *Yijing* is impressive, and used cleverly against Confucian critiques.

In his "Defense of Buddhism as a Foreign Religion", Kihwa consolidates the notion of an eternal *Dao* (道) which deserves the veneration of everyone. This *Dao* cannot be confined to time nor space, and therefore cannot be seen as foreign as it is replete in the myriad things (萬物, K. *manmul*). Therefore, the Buddha and the Sages have all relied on the same *Way* even though they have existed in different places, and at different times: East and West depend on where you are situated only (especially on a round planet which rotates!). Calamities have arisen during the apogée of Buddhism, as well as during the times of the venerated Confucian sages. These calamities were caused by rulers who have not embodied the *Dao* correctly. He further adds, "He who embodies the Way is the one who the people will rely upon" (104). This is the ultimate argument relating to the overall guiding discourse. Kihwa also refutes other negative accusations made by Confucians: that monks are living in decadence, mere parasites, and their teachings nothing but a harbinger of calamity (105–108). The penultimate refutation addresses the Confucian complaint of emptiness and nihilism linked with Buddhism, pointing out that the goal of Buddhists is to practice moral discipline and to illuminate all people, criticising the Confucians (and clearly Chŏng) who seem not to have a wide knowledge of the Buddhist texts. Scolding them, he writes: "If you want to determine a teaching's truth or falsity, you must first examine its texts" (109).

Finally (110–111), Kihwa argues for the "unity of the Three Teachings", giving a valid piece of advice that is useful for us all today: "Holding stubbornly onto one's own opinion while ignoring the positions of others, arbitrarily affirming this and rejecting that [. . .] How could they make determinations of right and wrong based on the positions of self and other or this and that?" He suggests that the person of wisdom would read broadly the writings of different traditions and schools: "the Buddhist, Confucian and Daoist canons". The overall approach of the exposition is syncretic and both Confucianism and Buddhism, along with Daoism, should be seen as vehicles to transport mankind along the proper path*way*, hence, their various moral principles and teachings reflect the interpenetration of one overall guiding reality (which the much later founder of Wŏn Buddhism would agree with, outlined in Chapter 6). The goal of the sage is to put teachings into practice and to cultivate 'humanity' so that (s)he may guide others with it so that they can become more humane, more compassionate to *all* beings. The Confucians ultimately hoped to guide everyone by banning other doctrines they considered a threat, including Buddhism, and later Catholicism, but also Shamanism, which penetrated all levels of society during the Koryŏ period, as well as the Chosŏn period, which attempted to eradicate all alternative religious and philosophical path*ways*.

Critiques of Shamanism

While men have clearly been the centre of both the Buddhist and Confucian traditions, Shaman women held great importance for women from all levels of society, from royalty to slaves. Clearly if Confucians were attacking Buddhists, it was certain they would also try to undermine, discredit and attempt to eradicate the power of the Shaman, especially her links with the royal court. Some of the earliest accounts of Shamans appear in texts written during the Koryŏ period, particularly the (Confucian) *History of the Three Kingdoms* (*Samguk Sagi*) and the (Buddhist) *Legends and History of the Three Kingdoms* (*Samguk Yusa*). The descriptions in these accounts demonstrate the important role of Shamans throughout the peninsula, who also were clearly important figures at court, called upon as professionals who engaged in divination and spirit-mediumship, but, most importantly, to perform various rituals (usually the function of men), including the ancestral rites of the founding king, something that must have greatly displeased later Confucians who saw this as their domain. McBride (2007: 235) notes that in both texts there are only a combined total of 11 references to Shamanesque figures, referred to using '*mu*' denoting the *mudang*, the Korean word used to translate Shaman (outlined in Chapter 1). During the Koryŏ period, Confucian officials had presented multiple petitions to different kings to have Shamans banned and banished – but ultimately to be prevented from performing such rites, which granted them power and authority, something Confucian men wanted to control entirely themselves. The *History of Koryŏ* (高麗史, K. *Koryŏsa*), composed during the Chosŏn period by Chŏng Inji (1398–1498), provides us with a much clearer account of the role of Shamans during the Koryŏ period. It provides details of their important link with the "palace women", their roles at Buddhist ceremonies (such as the P'algwanhoe), as well as their spiritual connections with the various "native Korean gods", especially the mountain god (*sansin*), while at the same time paying their taxes (236–237). It also describes the interrelationships between different traditions, and inadvertently depicts the Confucian attempts to become sole powerbrokers.

Yi Kyubo (1168–1241), a Confucian scholar and poet, leaves us with one of the earliest written descriptions of Shamans, though an ascerbic critique, in the 'Lay of the Old Shaman'. Richard D. McBride II (234) describes it as "the single longest treatment of Shamans prior to the Chosŏn period". Yi's preface to his poem reports how men and women frequented the shaman he depicts in his poem on a daily basis, describing his displeasure at the "licentious songs and absurd chatter", but how a recent edict has ordered them far from the capital, which he celebrates in his poem (2007: 240–241). Yi hopes that now the people will be chaste and that there would be a "return to the customs of high antiquity". Of course, these Shamanic practices the poet berates, and is happy to have censored, echo back to some of the most ancient customs of the peninsular people of Korea – something Confucianism cannot boast of. Additionally, the poem describes Shamanic practices that one could easily find happening in Korea today: spirits descending into the shaman's body, who then speaks in their different voices, with images of her gods/spirits on the wall, as she dances and sings, surrounded by callers, both men and women. One telling verse suggests that the author was hopeful that the days and the songs of the *mudang* were coming to an end (242):

> The shaman in the house to the east is approaching the evening
> of her years.
> Sunrise and sunset, death stalks – how is she able to live so long?
> How could what I am thinking of now be like this?
> My intent is to get rid of [these shaman] completely,
> and wash clean the shelters of the people.

This would never come to pass, and ironically, the *mudang*, their rituals and songs continue to be important and show no signs is diminishing in modern Korea, examined in more detail later in this book. While the Confucians would ultimately rise to power during the Chosŏn dynasty, followed up in the next chapter, their own authority would eventually be challenged by a new religion which drew in women in huge numbers, Catholicism, as would some of the much later 'new' religions.

Conclusion

This chapter has shown the transmission of the Linji School of Chinese Chan to the Korean peninsula by Koreans, leading to the growth of Sŏn Buddhism in the late Silla period to emerge as the defining feature of Koryŏ Buddhism. Many attempts were made to finally draw the doctrinal schools into the quickly emerging Sŏn centres, a confluence that shaped the form Buddhism would take on the Korean peninsula right down until the current day. State support integral to the growth and spread of Buddhism was reciprocated by Buddhists who prayed for the protection of the state, invoked through their writings and artwork. King T'aejo, the first ruler of the Koryŏ dynasty assured the important place Buddhism would have, safely securing its place in his 'Ten Injunctions', which also alluded to the general folk beliefs and practices, highlighting the diverse spiritual resources of the people at that time. The predominance of Sŏn Buddhism was solidified through important monks such as Ŭich'ŏn and Chinul, who strived to overcome opposition and contention between the doctrinal and Sŏn schools, clearly leaning towards the meditative approach. This approach was cemented by Chinul, who founded his own Sŏn society and who also advocated the use of the study of the *hwadu* (keywords) from the collected *kong'an*, which gave rise to *Kanhwa Sŏn*, a salient feature of Korean Buddhism, right down until the twenty-first century. Buddhists contributed to the printing of books in Korea hitherto never seen, cementing their place in the world's intellectual history with the monumental printing of the Tripitaka Koreana, and even creating the first movable metal type.

But, ideas are shaped by the times, and socio-political fragility, further weakened by invasions and the rise of the Confucian literati, firstly in China, soon saw an intellectual transformation in Korea, too, when 'Neo-Confucianism' rose to challenge and critique Buddhism, and all other traditions for that matter. The Chosŏn dynasty emerged along with the rise to power (and legal authority) of the Neo-Confucian elite, aided and abetted by Chŏng Tojŏn who orchestrated a serious blow to Buddhism in the two texts examined in this chapter. Buddhists like Kihwa sought to redress the matter, hoping to illustrate how Buddhists and Confucians had much in common; however, the situation would only get worse. Shamans, too, though not maintaining a literary tradition of their own, had an integral place in Korea's diverse spiritual Weltanschaung. Confucians did not appreciate this either, evident from Yi Kyubo's critical poem, which is an important document for uncovering the history and role of Shamans in Korea, where they have penetrated all levels of society, providing particularly important functions and rituals for women, by women. Though men had positions of power in regards to the government, these women wielded a spiritual power that they dared to use in the face of ongoing repression, something that showed no sign of relenting despite the Confucian attempts to silence them, and women in general.

References and further reading

Adler, Joseph A. 2002. *Chinese Religions*. Routledge: London. Chapter 4.
Ahn, Kai-hyon. 1982. "Publication of Buddhist Scriptures in the Koryo Period". *Buddhist Culture in Korea*, ed. International Cultural Foundation. Si-sa-yong-o-sa Publishers, Inc.: Seoul. 81–95.
Ames, Roger T. and Henry Rosemont, Jr. (trans.). 1998. *The Analects of Confucius: A Philosophical Translation*. Ballantine Books: New York.

Anonymous. 2001. *The Cloud of Unknowing*. Translated by A.C. Spearing. Penguin Books: London.

Boehm, Christopher. 2002. "Conflict and the Evolution of Social Control". *Evolutionary Origins of Morality*, ed. Leonard D. Katz. Imprint Academic: Thorverton. 82–93.

Buswell Jr., Robert. 1983. *The Korean Approach to Zen: The Collected Works of Chinul*. University of Hawai'i Press: Honolulu.

———. 1986. "Chinul's Systematization of Chinese Meditative Techniques in Korean Son Buddhism". *Traditions of Meditation in Chinese Buddhism*, ed. Peter N. Gregory. University of Hawaii Press: Honolulu. 199–242.

———. 1987. "The 'Short-Cut' Approach of K'an-hua Meditation: The Evolution of a Practical Subitism in Chinese Ch'an Buddhism Glossary". *Sudden and Gradual: Approaches to Enlightenment in Chinese Thought*, ed. Peter N. Gregory. University of Hawai'i Press: Honolulu. 321–377.

———. 1989. "Chinul's Ambivalent Critique of Radical Subitism in Korean Sŏn Meditation". *The Journal of the International Association of Buddhist Studies*, 12(2): 20–44.

———. 1991. *Tracing Back the Radiance: Chinul's Way of Korean Zen*. University of Hawai'i Press, Honolulu Press: Honolulu.

———. (ed.). 2012. *Collected Works of Korean Buddhism, Vol.2. Chinul, Selected Works*. Jogye Order of Korean Buddhism: Seoul.

———. 2016. *Numinous Awareness Is Never Dark: The Korean Buddhist Master Chinul's Excerpts on Zen Practice*. University of Hawai'i Press, Honolulu Press: Honolulu.

Caputo, John D. 2013. *Truth: The Search for Wisdom in the Postmodern Age*. Penguin Random House: Milton Keynes.

Chan, Wing-Tsit. 1973. *A Sourcebook in Chinese Philosophy*. Princeton University Press: Princeton, NJ.

Ching, Julia. 1993. *Chinese Religions*. Macmillan Press: London.

Cho, Hŭng-yun (1992) "Le Chamanisme au début de la dynastie Choson". *Cahiers d'Extreme-Asie*, 6: 1–20.

Cho, Myong-gi. 1977. "Ch'an Buddhist Culture in Korea". *Korean and Asian Religious Tradition*, ed. Chai-Shin Yu, trans. Kenneth L. Richard. University Toronto Press: Toronto. 208–224.

Chung, Chai-sik. 1985. "Chŏng Tojŏn: 'Architect'of Yi Dynasty Government and Ideology". *The Rise of Neo-Confucianism in Korea*, eds. Jahyun Kim Haboush and Theodore de Bary. Columbia University Press: New York. 59–88.

Creel, Herrlee. 1971. *Chinese Thought from Confucius to Mao Tse-tung*. University of Chicago Press: Chicago.

De Bary, Wm. Theodore (ed.). 1985. "Introduction". *The Rise of Neo-Confucianism in Korea*. Columbia University Press: New York. 1–58.

———. 1997. *Sources of Korean Tradition*, vol. i. Harvard University Press: Cambridge, MA.

———. 1999. "Ideological Foundations of Late Imperial China". *Sources of Chinese Tradition*, vol. i, eds. Wm Theodore De Bary and Irene Bloom. Columbia University Press: New York. 755–799.

Deuchler, Martina. 1992. *The Confucian Transformation of Korea*. Harvard University Press: Cambridge, MA.

Duncan, John. 1988. "Proto-Nationalism in Pre-Modern Koryŏ". *Perspectives on Korea*, eds. Sang-oak Lee and Duk-soo Park. University of Hawai'i Press: Honolulu.

————. 2000. *The Origins of the Chosŏn Dynasty*. University of Washington Press: Washington.

Eckert, Carter J. *et al.* 1990. *Korea Old and New: A History*. Ilchokak Publishers: Seoul.

Fairbank, J.K. and Merle Goldman. 1999. *China: A New History*. Harvard University Press: Cambridge, MA.

Fung, Yulan. 1983. *A History of Chinese Philosophy*, vol i. Translated by Derk Dodde. Princeton University Press: Princeton, NJ.

Grayson, James H. 2002. *Korea: A Religious History*. Revised Edition. Routledge Curzon: New York. Chapter 3.

Hong I-sŏp. 1983. "Political philosophy of Korean Confucianism". *Main Currents of Korean Thought*, ed. Korean National Commission for UNESCO. Si-sa-o-yong-sa Publishers: Seoul. 162–176.

Hyewon, Ven and David A. Mason. 2014. *An Encyclopedia of Korean Buddhism*. Unjusa Publishing: Seoul.

Jikji Digitised Version. Available at: http://gallica.bnf.fr/ark:/12148/btv1b6300067k/f2.image [accessed on 13 June 2018].

Keel, Hee-sŏng. 1984. *Chinul: The Founder of the Korean Sŏn Tradition*. University of California: Berkeley.

————. 2004. "Word and Wordlessness: The Spirit of Korean Buddhism". *Korean Philosophy: Its Tradition and Its Modern Transformation*, ed. Korean National Commission for UNESCO. Hollym: Seoul. 169–184.

Kwon, Ki-jŏng. 1995. "Buddhism in the Chosŏn Dynasty". *The History and Culture of Buddhism in Korea*, ed. The Korean Buddhist Research Institute. Dongguk University Press: Seoul. 171–218.

Lee, Peter H. and Wm Theodore De Bary. (eds.). 1997. *Sources of the Korean Tradition: From the Sixteenth to the Twentieth Century*. Columbia University Press: Columbia. Part Two: Koryŏ.

Li, Dun J. 1965. *The Ageless Chinese*. Aldine House/J.M. Dent and Sons Ltd: London.

McBride II, Richard D. 2007. "Yi Kyubo's Lay of the Old Shaman". *Religions of Korea in Practice*, ed. Robert E. Buswell Jr. Princeton University Press: Princeton, NJ. 233–243.

Muller, Charles A. 1999a. "The Buddhist-Confucian Conflict in the Early Chosŏn and Kihwa's Syncretic Response: The Hyŏn chŏng non". *The Review of Korean Studies*, 2: 183–200.

————. 1999b. *The Sutra of Perfect Enlightenment: Korean Buddhism's Guide to Meditation (with Commentary by the Sin Monk Kihwa)*. Suny Press: Albany.

————. 2007. "The Great Confucian-Buddhist Debate". *Religions of Korea in Practice*, ed. Robert Buswell Jr. Princeton University Press: Princeton, NJ. 177–204.

————. 2015. *Korea's Great Buddhist-Confucian Debate: The Treatises of Chŏng Tojŏn (Sambong) and Hamhŏ Tŭkt'ong (Kihwa)*. University of Hawai'i Press: Honolulu.

Nahm, Andrew. 1996. *Korea: Tradition and Transformation*. Hollym: Seoul. Chapter Three.

Nienhauser, William H. (ed.). 1986. *The Indiana Companion to Traditional Chinese Literature*. Indiana University Press: Bloomington.

Pihl, Marshall R. 1995. "Koryŏ Sŏn Buddhism and Literature". *Korean Studies*, 10: 62–82.

Seon Masters Gou, Muyeo, Uijeong Hyeguk and Seoru. 2014. *Great Doubt, Great Enlightenment: The Tradition and Practice of Ganhwa Seon in Korean Buddhism.* Jogye Order Publications: Seoul.

Sim, Chae-ryong. 2004. "Seon Buddhist Tradition in Korea as Reflected in Jinul's Seon". *Korean Philosophy: Its Tradition and Its Modern Transformation*, ed. Korean National Commission for UNESCO. Hollym: Seoul. 201–224.

Su, Yun-kil. 1995. "The History & Culture of Buddhism in the Koryŏ Dynasty". *The History and Culture of Buddhism in Korea*, eds. The Korean Buddhist Research Institute, Dongguk University Press: Seoul. 117–168.

Vermeersch, Sem. 2008. *The Power of the Buddhas: The Politics of Buddhism During the Koryŏ Dynasty (918–1392)*. Harvard University Asia Center: Cambridge, MA.

Yi, Sang-ŭn. 1983. "On the Criticism of Confucianism in Korea". *Main Currents of Korean Thought*, ed. Korean National Commission for UNESCO. Si-sa-o-yong-sa Publishers: Seoul. 112–146.

4 Sagehood meets 'Western' learning
From '*Principle*' to 'The Lord of Heaven'

Introduction

Buddhism and Shamanism continued to be marginalised during the Chosŏn dynasty, despite the fact that several kings were in fact adherents of Buddhism, and Shamans were still important ritual specialists for women. Neo-Confucian scholars dominated the social and political scene, even taking over the education of the king. Both the Crown Prince Tutorial Office and the Royal Lecture aimed at establishing the perfection of the monarch (Kim 1985: 161). The most important example of such a sage ruler is considered to be King Sejong the Great (r. 1418–1450), the most revered king in Korean history. However, King Sejong suppressed Buddhism, had Shamans driven out of the capital, and had lesbians punished (even executed) in the palace: this side to his character has been, for the most part, downplayed, as outlined by Han Hee-sook (2004). His greatest achievement was to facilitate the creation of a new phonetic alphabet, *Hunminjŏngŭm* (훈민정음; 訓民正音), which literally means, the correct sounds for the instruction of the people. Originally conceived of as a script so that the poor and 'women' could learn to read easily, it was rejected by the elite, and shunned by Confucian scholars at large – for several hundred years. Often referred to as the vulgar script, *ŏnmun* (언문/諺文), it became associated with 'ignorant' women and lowly men, further inscribing discrimination against them. It was not until the colonial period, when it became known as the *Script of the Han* [i.e., Korean people], that *Han'gŭl* (한글) was designated a great scientific 'national' script. Some basic Confucian texts were translated from Chinese characters to *Han'gŭl* for women, but ironically, it would become the script used by the early Catholic Church in Korea, and employed by 'heterodox' Confucian scholars to convert the women and the poor – not exactly what King Sejong had in mind.

Later kings merely acted as reminders of the fact that the Confucian ideal of a sage king was still only that, an ideal, and so it is hardly surprising that the role of the king was championed by two of the greatest Neo-Confucian scholars of the Chosŏn period: Yi Hwang (1501–1570), known by his penname T'oegye, and Yi I (1536–1584), known by the penname Yulgok.

Their ideas, examined in this chapter, dominated intellectually, especially their ideas concerning sagehood. In this regards, Oh Kangnam (1993: 313) describes the concept of sagehood as "one of the essential components, if not the essence, of Korean Confucianism [. . .] and Neo-Confucianism's hallmark was its emphasis on sage-learning". This encounter reveals how Neo-Confucianism had been shaped by earlier intellectual developments within Buddhist schools, as well as by blending important ideas from Daoism. But as Neo-Confucianism was reaching it pinnacle, Catholic missionaries had already been sent to Japan, then China.

This chapter then outlines the Confucian encounter of the Italian Jesuit Matteo Ricci (1552–1610), whose text *The True Meaning of the Lord of Heaven* (天主實義, C. *Tianzhu shiyi*) exerted a great influence later in Korea. By the early seventeenth century, Western scientific ideas started to infiltrate Korea in the aftermath of Japanese invasions of the late sixteenth century, where Korean philosophy is often described as taking a more practical turn, known as *Sirhak* (實學), or Practical Learning, though this appellation only comes into play, once again, later during the colonial period. However, Ricci's catechism had a huge impact on Korean intellectuals who initially rejected it, such as Yi Sugwang and Yi Ik (1682–1763), and the latter's disciples Sin Hudam (1702–1761) and An Chŏngbok (1712–1783). Later, scholars from the same intellectual lineage and Southern '*Namin*' faction converted to Catholicism, and their evangelisation soon lead to brutal persecutions by Confucian authorities. This leads to a discussion of the early Catholics and their texts, such as, the first "*Han'gŭl Catechism*", written by Chŏng Yakchong (1760–1801). This text, though one of the most widely read texts of this entire period, especially by women and poorer classes, has not been recognised for its seminal role in Korea's history of ideas, and its author's important contribution has been eclipsed by the fame of his younger brother, Chŏng Yagyong, known by the penname Tasan (also written as Dasan). Tasan is generally considered one of the greatest figures of Korea's intellectual history, and hailed in modern accounts as a synthesiser of '*Sirhak*' ideas. Though initially deeply involved with the early Catholic Church, Tasan later renounced his association with Catholicism, when his own life was in danger, and when some of his closest friends and family members were executed. His 'Christo-Confucian' writings, clearly intellectual products shaped by the socio-political and religious violence of their time, are examined at the end of this chapter.

Understanding Chosŏn Confucian ideology: T'oegye, Yulgok and sagehood

During the sixteenth century, works by T'oegye and Yulgok on sagehood, represented the maturation of early Chosŏn Dynasty Neo-Confucian philosophy and were heavily influenced by the orthodoxy of Zhu Xi-ism, due to the fact that Zhu's *Reflections on Things at Hand* (近思錄, C. *Jinsilu*), "played a leading role" among Korean Neo-Confucian scholars (Keum 2000: 83). A lot of literature on Korean Neo-Confucianism links the ideas of T'oegye and Yulgok. In Korea, the ideas of both these philosophers have been inextricably intertwined for almost 500 years, with a special focus on how they disagreed on certain metaphysical points, in particular the 'four-seven debate', referred to below. I would argue that the sometimes singular focus on this issue, which was only a small part of their writings, and mainly through correspondences, has distracted from their overall ideas, and hence, their voluminous contributions to the history of ideas in Korea. In particular, Keum Changtae (2000: 40) selects Toegye's *Ten Diagrams on Sage Learning* (聖學十圖, K. *Sŏnghak sipto*), written in 1568, and Yi I's *Essentials of the Learning of the Sages* (聖學輯要, K. *Sŏnghak chibyo*), written in 1575, as "the two main classical works epitomizing Neo-Confucian learning in the Chosŏn era".

From the late fifteenth century until the mid-sixteenth century, whilst there had been a rise of Confucian elitism, there had also been a series of purges of scholar officials known as the *Sarim*. The monarchy sometimes felt undermined by the power of the scholars, who were even in charge of the personal conduct of the king and able to criticise him. This divisiveness was most disastrous during the reign of the Yŏngsan-gun (r.1494–1506), and he himself oversaw two of the four bloody purges known as *sahwa* in Korean. The following two kings were each responsible for a literary purge. During this time, it is also important to note that Buddhism had a brief revival led by the influential monk Pou (1515–1565). During the reign of King Myŏngjong (r.1545–1567), the government was actually controlled by his mother, Queen Regent Munjong (r.1546–1553), a devout Buddhist follower. Not only was the Buddhist examination system revived, but the monk Hyujŏng (1520–1604) was an adviser to the royal family and the anti-Buddhist policy of the previous reigns was reversed for a period. These facts must have directly influenced T'oegye and in retrospect we can now perceive a sense of urgency in the *Ten Diagrams on Sage Learning* (Deuchler 1985: 384; Grayson 2002: 122; U 1983).

T'oegye: ten diagrams on sagehood and the Four-Seven debate

The great Japanese Neo-Confucian scholar Yamazaki Ansai (1618–1682), described T'oegye as "the greatest Confucian in Korea", on a par with Zhu Xi himself (Pak 1983: 69). T'oegye's most influential work, *Ten Diagrams on Sage Learning*, composed in 1568 towards the end of his life, represents the synthesis of Neo-Confucian thought in Korea and is one of the most reproduced texts of the entire Chosŏn dynasty. It is one of the few texts by a Chosŏn dynasty scholar to be translated into English. Michael Kalton has translated it under the title *To Become a Sage* (1985: also available online), reflecting the goal of T'oegye's text. It is a collection of diagrams by Neo-Confucian scholars from China and Korea (including three by T'oegye himself) that elucidate Zhu Xi's main teachings, as well as T'oegye's own development of them, especially through his focus on the mind. Each diagram is followed by Zhu's commentaries on certain key teachings, which are then further clarified by T'oegye's commentaries. In his address presenting the "Ten Diagrams" to the king, T'oegye (Kalton1988: 36) suggests that if the king masters the application of the diagrams in his daily life he will govern properly and "then great will be the joy of the nation, great the joy of the people!" Therefore we must recognise that T'oegye did seek 'practical' (實, K. *sil*) results, and as Tu Weiming (2004: 77) explains, "he was an active participant of the *realpolitik* of his time [who] wanted his ideas to work in the court, to reform bureaucracy and to exert a shaping influence on the political culture", and this refutes the sometimes one-dimensional depiction of him as an abstract and idealistic metaphysician. Metaphysics were nevertheless important for him – but they always had practical implications and applications.

The first two diagrams in T'oegye's work are (1) Zhou Dunyi's *Diagram of the Supreme Ultimate* (太極之圖, K. *T'aegŭk chido*), and (2) Zhang Zai's *Western Inscription* (西銘圖, K. *Sŏmyŏngdo*), providing us with the metaphysical underpinnings of Neo-Confucianism. The first diagram identifies the Supreme Ultimate as *Principle*, which generates yin and yang, which then materialise through the Five Elements, while the second diagram describes Heaven as the father and Earth as the mother of all things (drawing on the first two trigrams of the *Book of Changes*), unified through a universal organising principle that is most perfect in humans, where humanity reflects an interdependent and interrelated microcosmic reflection of the macrocosmic universe, differing greatly from European dualism.

The next three diagrams are all concerned with Confucian education: The *Diagram of Elementary Learning*, the *Diagram of the Great Learning*, and the *Diagram of Rules of the White Deer Hollow Academy*. This education embodies Confucian morality, which is the basis for understanding more complex issues of the mind and the nature. *The Elementary Learning* is an original diagram by T'oegye himself and reflects Zhi Xi's conceptual framework of the learning process and focuses on 'The Five Relationships'. T'oegye informs us that the *Diagram of the Great Learning* was by Kwŏn Kŭn (1352–1409), an influential Neo-Confucian who supervised editions of the Confucian Classics and who had also published a diagrammatic treatise in the early Chosŏn Dynasty. He had influenced T'oegye through his diagram entitled *Heaven and Man, Mind and Nature, Combine as One*, (天人心性合一圖, K. *Ch'ŏnin simsŏng hap'ildo*) (Kalton 1985). By including Zhu Xi's *Rules of the White Deer Hollow Academy*, T'oegye was undoubtedly, indirectly, requesting the king's endorsement of such academies (known as *sŏwŏn*書院) in Korea. At the end of King Sŏnjo's reign, there were more than one hundred *sŏwŏn*, which had become renowned places of learning, occupying a similar place of esteem as had the Buddhist temples during the Koryŏ dynasty (Kalton 1988: 117).

The previous diagrams may be perceived as propaedeutic instructions that represent the basic steps of a much more complicated process. The complexities of this process are encompassed in the meta-psychological theories concerning the mind (K. *sim*) and nature (K. *sŏng*), and the sixth diagram elaborates this theoretical framework. This may be interpreted as the fruit of the 'Four-Seven Debate', which Kalton refers to as "the single most important intellectual controversy of the Yi dynasty" (Kalton 1988: 119). I would suggest that the greatest metaphysical debate was actually between Confucians who encountered Catholic ideas, discussed later in this chapter, between *Principle* (K. *i*) and a monotheistic creator God, which finally lead to the spread of a new 'Western' religion in Korea. The Four-Seven Debate originated from two cycles of correspondences between T'oegye and Ki Taesŭng (1527–1572), and later between Yulgok and Sŏng Hon (1536–1598) – and not directly between T'oegye and Yulgok.

The Four-Seven Debate

The 'Four Beginnings' are referred to by Mencius (2A:6) as humanity, righteousness, propriety and wisdom, while the 'Seven Feelings' are referred to in the ninth chapter of the *Book of Rites*: joy, anger, sadness, fear, love, dislike and liking. These separate passages were only linked together much later by Neo-Confucian scholars. But, if human nature is completely good – why do people do things that are 'not good'? Where does this disparity come from? From *Principle* or the material force? This was a conundrum for Neo-Confucians just as good and evil was for the Scholastics in Europe trying to explain why there was evil if their God was good! T'oegye originally suggested that the Four Beginnings and Seven Feelings had different origins and this instigated the original debate with Ki Taesŭng, who did not agree with T'oegye's dualistic approach: that *Principle*, or *i* was the source of the Four Beginnings and that the material force, *ki*, was the source of the Seven Feelings. However, T'oegye revised his theory but still gave primacy to *i* and saw it as preceding *ki*. Hence, things could be less than perfect/less than good, when activated by the material force, which was T'oegye's way of solving this issue, whereby *Principle* still remained pure and 'good', as did the Four Beginnings. Yulgok, by contrast, noted that *ki* was the activating factor of both the Seven Feelings and Four Beginnings; in this sense, he is less idealistic than T'oegye in relation to *Principle*. However, he also noted that while the Seven Feelings included the Four Beginnings, the Four Beginnings did not contain the Seven Feelings – keeping human nature 'innately' good and intact. T'oegye saw *i* as the substance of the mind and *ki* as the function (on which *i* mounts), again *che-yong*. Substance (*che*) represented natural goodness, whereas function (*yong*) included the potential to actualise good behaviour, as well as the possibility for digression due to the negative aspect of feelings that could disturb or alter one's mind, and thereby one's habits, which explains the 'seriousness of mindfulness', highlighted in T'oegye's diagrammatic text, outlined below (see Chung 1995; Ro 1989).

The Sixth diagram corresponds with T'oegye's final evaluation of the Four-Seven debate consisting of three sections: Diagrams A, B and C, relating to the saying *The Mind Combines and Governs the Nature and the Feelings* (心統性情圖). The first of the three diagrams was by Cheng Fuxin (1279–1368), a Yuan dynasty scholar, whilst the other two diagrams are by T'oegye himself, summarising his views of *i* and *ki* in relation to the Four Beginnings and the Seven Feelings. Diagram A describes two aspects of the mind and presents human nature "as the not yet aroused state", linked to the Four Beginnings, and the Seven Feelings linked to "the aroused state" and interaction with the material force. Diagrams B and C then develop these meta-psychologies; however, it is important to note that the relationship between the different aspects of the mind does not encompass dualism as they are inter-related and only phenomenologically exclusive (Ro 1989: 50). T'oegye has in fact incorporated Zhang Zai's notion of the combination of "physical nature" with "original nature", and it is this physical nature that gives rise to the occasion for evil (Chan 1973: 511).

Though an explanation of the Four-Seven debate is a fundamental step in comprehending T'oegye's meta-psychological theory, his work is much more comprehensive, as highlighted in the *Ten Diagrams*. The seventh diagram is entitled *Diagram of the Explanation of Humanity* (仁說圖, K. *Inrondo*) and represents a focal point of Zhu Xi's teachings. The inborn tendency for goodness may be reduced to passivity, but through seeking to become a person of Humanity we aspire to activate it, and allow the unhampered operation of the original mind manifest itself through our character in action. Humanity is then the realisation of our *optimum level of perfection* that already exists in the stage of *potentiality of actualisation*, which depends upon how we think about things and our perceptions of them, ideas heightened in the eighth diagram. The eighth *Diagram of the Study of the Mind* (心學圖, K. *Simhakdo*) was also originally by Cheng Fuxin (1279–1368). In depicts both aspects of the mind: the Mind of Tao/Original Mind and the Physical Mind/Human Mind. Yet, at the centre of the lower part of the diagram is 'Mindfulness' or *Kyŏng*敬: transforming the concept of 'seriousness' needed to control one's feelings and to focus on one's good nature.

T'oegye's ideas have been profoundly influenced by the *Classic of the Heart and Mind* (心經, K. *Simgyŏng*), by Zhen Dexiu (1178–1235), that deals almost exclusively with inward cultivation and emphasises "Mindfulness" (敬, C. *Ching*; K. *Kyŏng*). It also provides the key to understanding T'oegye's ideas on this subject. Often "*kyŏng*" is translated as "seriousness", but in Michael Kalton's (1988) translation of T'oegye's Diagrams, he translates it as 'mindfulness', which emphasises the reverential nature of the term, as well as identifies the need for constant effort to control one's mind. The Buddhist influence, though not entirely repressed, is recalibrated in T'oegye's practical path*way* towards sagehood. Thus, whilst T'oegye depends on Zhu for so much, one must note that his intellectual dynamism is greatly indebted to Zhen Dexiu as his spiritual guide, and for T'oegye, mindfulness is as serious as meditation is for the Buddhists. In fact, the Neo-Confucians had their own meditational practice of 'quiet-sitting' (靜坐, K. *Chŏngjwa*), which focused on recovering the 'original mind' which was calm and not agitated. This idea is carried forward and emphasised in the final two diagrams, which emphasise the 'practice' of mindfulness to transform our thoughts and to guide them towards appropriate 'moral' actions. The final diagrams, the *Diagram of the Admonition of Mindfulness Studio* (敬齋箴圖, K. *Kyŏngjae jamdo*) and the *Diagram of the Admonition on Rising Early and Retiring Late* (夙興夜寐箴, K. *Sukhŭng yamae*

Figure 4.1 Confucian study hall in South Korea

chamdo), reinforce the need for a daily practice of Confucian mindfulness, because practice leads to 'good habit' creating (and maintaining) routines. There is no short-cut provided, no weekend intro to this practice: it is life long and that is what makes it transformative, leading us to become better versions of who were in the beginning.

Yulgok: sagehood and community compacts

As mentioned at the beginning of this chapter, alongside T'oegye, Yulgok was the other most influential philosophical figure in the first half of the Chosŏn dynasty. T'oegye's influence is most noticeable in Yulgok's *Essentials of the Learning of the Sages*, written in 1575. Although there is not yet an English translation of this text, there is a French one by Philippe Thiébault (2009), *Anthologie de la sagesse extrême-orientale: Yi I Yulgok*. Yulgok's text on sagehood was also presented to King Sŏnjo and while the largest section of it treats "Self-Cultivation" (修己, K. *Sugi*), there are two other significant sections dealing with how to "Rectify [Regulate] the Family" (正家, K. *Chŏng'ga*), as well as on "How to Govern" (爲政, K. *Wijŏng*). Keum (2000: 110) emphasises that Yulgok, believing that "policies had to be based on a realistic evaluation of contemporary conditions", was more reform minded and practical, somewhat undervaluing T'oegye's own "practical" ethos. Yulgok's focus on the ordering of the family and on good governance does seem to confirm this practical side, but it also reveals his reliance on *The Great Learning*, and the important passage, which exhorts one to "regulate" oneself and one's family, which in turn "orders" the state. However, his practical focus must not be seen as advancement along a trajectory other than Neo-Confucianism, or as some great metaphysical leap forward. Indeed, if we investigate briefly some of Yulgok's other "reform-minded" texts, dramatic change was far from his mind. But, as Keum (2000: 107) highlights, for Yulgok, "political reform for the benefit of the people's livelihood was seen as the most urgent requirement".

This "urgent requirement" can be seen in Yulgok's *Community Compacts*, also known as "village contracts" or *hyangyak* (鄉約) sought to improve rural communities by dividing them into groups who were responsible for their own members, influenced by Zhu Xi, who also advocated community compacts (see Ch'oe *et al.* 2001: 145–157). Nevertheless, these compacts reinforced a hierarchically organised social order, which distinguished between different grades of people. *Hyangyak* depended on these enforced distinctions to create the illusion of harmony and balance, modelled on a male-centred interpretation of yin (distorted to mean female passivity) and yang (redefined as masculine activity), allowing metaphysics to affect all aspects of life, and to exert an invisible yoke of control. At the top of this social ladder were the *yangban*, to which the literati belonged, followed by the *chungin* (middle-people) who had more technical professions, such as translators. Next were the commoners or *sangin*, like merchants and craftsmen who represented the largest percentage of the population. Below all these groups were the *ch'onmin* (low-born) who were slaves, as well as Shamans and Buddhist monks and nuns (Nahm 1996: 100–101). Slavery was a serious problem in Chosŏn which "deserves to be called a slave society", with up to 30 percent of the population in slavery up until the late eighteenth century, by which time Catholicism had started to become accepted by some *yangban* scholars (Ch'oe *et al.* 2001: 157). With no religious sects able to compete with the Neo-Confucians, one can anticipate the difficulties and dangers that a new religion would face trying to infiltrate this highly stratified web of control; this would have been especially true for Catholicism, with its inherent (though often ignored) boundary-dissolving doctrine of equality for all – including women, even slaves – something that would attract the attention of both these groups in Korea.

Undoubtedly, these compacts provided a mechanism of assistance for those in need in particular communities. For example, Yulgok's *Community Compact for Sŏwŏn County* (145) describes how people within the "same" community should help each other in times of need. The strong sense of duty draws on teachings from the *Four Books*, admonishing the Five Relationships, while emphasising respect for elders and filial piety. Yulgok (152) advises against "inappropriate companions [. . .] who are not accepted by the people". His definition of acting virtuously "means to investigate principle through reading, learning proper decorum, and learning how to calculate clearly so as to be able to manage one's household [to] respect the law, and to be scrupulous with regard to taxes" (150). Incorporated into Yulgok's text is an overlooked rhetoric that illustrates how 'virtue' was studied by the wealthy and educated, and in reality most of the population could never be considered "cultivated", simply because they couldn't read classical Chinese. With *Han'gŭl* holding a minor, inferior place, the poor had no access to the great Neo-Confucian ideal that Yulgok himself wrote about, sagehood. In addition, power relations were inscribed into the very language Koreans used (and still use) to address each other, highlighting important factors influencing power relations reflected in speech level, which reflect "age, kinship relation, social status, or other ranks" (Park 1992: 26).

Both T'oegye and Yulgok wrote on the importance of rites (禮學, K. *yehak*), which inculcated ethical norms and standards of behaviour. Rites crystallised the social ideals into strict formats that could easily be transmitted for generations, for example, ancestor memorial rites, still performed by many Koreans today. Nevertheless, the art of sagehood was T'oegye's *pièce de résistance*. On the other hand, Yulgok's discourse revealed practical attempts to redress some of the social ills of his time, and to amend the legal system, both issues taken up later by Tasan (Song 1984). In the eighteenth century, proponents of Yulgok's metaphysical ideas would get involved in another metaphysical controversy known as the Horak Debate, relating to the heart-and-mind, one's nature and tendencies, as well as the intricate complexities of 'original nature' and 'physical nature', and how they related to humans and other animals (for a discussion of this debate, see Ivanhoe 2016). In time, the anthropocentric metaphysical preoccupations of Chosŏn would be challenged due to new 'religious' and intellectual encounters from beyond China.

Matteo Ricci and early Catholic traces in Korea

Matteo Ricci (1552–1610) is largely unknown to Westerners, including in his native Italy. Yet, he remains a highly respected intellectual and admired figure even today in China and Korea. Ricci was a member of The Society of Jesus, better known as the Jesuits, founded in 1534 by Saint Ignatius of Loyola (1494–1556). The Society introduced Catholicism to China at the end of the sixteenth century with a clear objective, "to recover in Asia the influence of Catholicism that had deteriorated in Europe" (Choi 2006: 14). The mission to China had learned from "mission mishaps" in Japan, where their lack of linguistic preparation or proper knowledge and respect for the native people and Buddhism had caused some major problems. Alexandro Valignano (1539–1606), head of the missions in the East visited Japan in 1579, and sought to accommodate to Japanese ways insisting "that the foreign missionaries learn the Japanese language and have a deep understanding of the mores, national traits, thought and customs of Japan" (Mullins 2003: 8). Valignano's respectful approach would shape the missions as they attempted to spread their religion in China. Handpicked by Valignano himself, Ricci would translate Western ideas for the Chinese, as well as translate Chinese ideas for Europeans, with all benefiting from his translational apostolate (Cawley 2013: 294–296).

Ricci mastered Chinese in quite a short time and forged important friendships with the Confucian literati, even dressing like them – this was after a brief flirtation with the Buddhists, until he realised they did not hold the same political sway or influence in China as they had in Japan – in fact, they were held in disdain. Ricci soon started to study the Confucian Classics, even translating them into Latin. Hence, thanks to such Catholic missionaries Latinised names for Confuc*ius* and Menc*ius* are used! Ricci advocated a re-reading of the "original" Confucian texts, the *Five Classics*, rejecting the philosophical developments of the Neo-Confucian Song philosophers, because, as Mungello (1982: 254) explains, Ricci "found the interpretations of [Song] Neo-Confucians to be filled with philosophic materialism, polytheism, or even atheism, which were irreconcilable with the proposed Confucian-Christian synthesis". Hence, the "original" texts could more easily be related to Christianity: Ricci redirected Confucians back towards *Shangdi* 上帝 (the Lord on High) of the *Five Classics*, suggesting this was another name for the Catholic *Tianzhu* 天主 (the Lord of Heaven), the term he adopted to designate his Catholic god. If Thomas Aquinas had attempted to Christianise Aristotle in the thirteenth century, then Matteo Ricci would attempt the same with Confucianism in the early seventeenth century. Ricci felt that the philosophical anthropocentrism of Confucius, who refused to discuss the spirits (*Analects* 11:11) meant that he could weave certain threads of his own religious tradition, especially ideas about god, into what he considered to be Confucius' unfinished latticework (Cawley 2013: 302–303).

Ricci (1985) achieved this in his masterpiece, *The True Meaning of the Lord of Heaven* (天主實義, C. *Tianzhu zhiyi*; K. *Ch'ŏnju sirŭi*). This influential text was first published in 1603, and consisted of a discussion in the form of questions and answers between a Chinese scholar and a Western scholar. It was an apologetic Christian text, which Ricci referred to as his *Catechism*, attempting to draw his Confucian audience to 'gradually' discover the finer points of Catholic doctrine: the text omits the Crucifixion and the Resurrection. Of course, Ricci was also attempting to present his religion as a sophisticated doctrine with a great civilising influence – the idea that 'Westerners' had tortured and executed their Messiah (the very son of their god) would not have helped his 'mission' at this early stage. Instead, Ricci had manifold references to the Confucian classics, praising their moral teachings as a path*way* for self-cultivation, but he was extremely critical of Daoist "nothingness" (無, K. *mu*) and Buddhist "emptiness" (空, K. *kong*), clearly further aligning himself with the Confucians. He focused his discussion on the idea that *Shangdi* was also the creator, further describing this figure as the original ancestor/original father, accommodating his *ways* to Confucian teachings on filial piety. Ricci also asserted that ancestor rites were civil, not religious, rites, and therefore not idolatrous. This issue would cause a rift between the Jesuits and the Dominicans and Franciscans, who disagreed with him (and who were also jealous of his success), eventually leading the pope to forbid newly converted Confucians from performing the rites, and even for a time disbanding the Jesuits entirely. (For an overview of the rites controversy, see Latourette 1966: 131–152.) The fact that Ricci permitted his new converts to perform ancestor memorial rites clearly led many to convert as they could maintain this important Confucian ritual, and so he managed to avoid conflict between both traditions to some degree. After it was banned, things became difficult for the missions and hampered their ability to have their religion taken seriously as it undermined the basis of filial piety. This would have serious implications in Korea later.

Missions never made their way to Korea during this period. Unfortunately, an unsettling period in East Asian history had erupted with the rise of Toyotomi Hideyoshi (1536–1598), who issued the first edict of persecution of Christians in Japan in 1587, crucifying Japanese Christians and Jesuits together in Nagasaki. The end of the sixteenth century also brought war and turmoil to Korea. The Japanese invasions in 1592 and again in 1597 were orchestrated by Hideyoshi, who had unified Japan and who now sought to conquer Korea as a stepping-stone on his way to conquering Ming (明朝) China. Both plans failed, but not without great destruction on mainland Korea. Villages were wiped out and loss of life was great. In the ensuing chaos, slaves seized the opportunity to burn the registries which had "officially" recorded their inferiority. Ming China sent over 80,000 troops to Korea to help fight against the Japanese to prevent the war spreading to them, recounted in a letter written in 1596 by Matteo Ricci, who described the negative implication of what he referred to as the 'Korean War', and its cost to the state bursary. In 1598, Hideyoshi died and Japan was forced to retreat and abandon the foiled plans of *aggrandisement* after suffering many losses, especially in the naval battles lost to the Korean admiral Yi Sunsin (1545–1598), still revered in Korea today (see Lewis 2017). It should be highlighted that Buddhists also formed an army to fight off the Japanese, with one notable general, the monk Sŏsan Hyujŏng (1520–1604). Hyujŏng is also famous for his Sŏn text, *Models for Sŏn Practitioners* (禪家龜鑑, K. *Sŏn'ga kwigam*), a summary of the main teachings of Sŏn, much needed at a time when Buddhism was oppressed and the Buddhist exam system eliminated. This remains an important text within the Korean Sŏn tradition until the present (for translation and extensive introduction, see Jorgensen 2015).

It appears that the first Christians in Korea came from Japan, along with the Japanese invasions. According to De Mendina (1994), a Spanish Jesuit priest Gregorio de Cespedes (1551–1611) had come to Korea to perform religious rites for Japanese troops and their Catholic *daimyō* Konishi Yukinaga (1556–1600). After the war failed they returned to Japan with numerous Korean slaves, who converted to Catholicism, suggesting that the Korean Church began in Japan. De Mendina (1994: 101) estimates that by 1595 in Kyūshū alone, there were more than 3,000 Korean converts. Additionally, Christianity almost made its way into Korea after the Manchu invasions in the early seventeenth century, when the Crown Prince Sohyŏn (1612–1645) and his brother were both held at the Manchu court as hostages. Towards the end of this period, the Crown Prince and the renowned German Jesuit Adam Schall von Bell (1591–1666), who worked at the astronomical observatory of the Shunzhi Emperor (1638–1661), became friends. Von Bell hoped to convert the Korean prince, who could then transmit his ideas to Korea. A few months later, the prince was sent back to Korea, receiving gifts, including Catholic books from his Jesuit friend. Unfortunately, the Crown Prince died shortly after his return to Korea and the gifts he had received were destroyed following a *mudang*'s claim that they were inauspicious portents (Choi 2006: 17–18).

External factors further compounded internal instability on the peninsula. King Sŏnjo's successor Kwanghae-gun (r.1608–1623), supported by the Northern faction, had started to strengthen Korea's defences, but his court was besieged by further factional struggles. He was overthrown by the Western faction and Sŏnjo's nephew replaced him to become King Injo (r.1623–1649). One of the military leaders among the Westerners, Yi Kwal (1587–1624), who had assisted in King Injo's ascension, but who felt unfairly recompensed, carried out a revolt of his own and forced the king to flee. Soon Yi's rebellion dwindled and he fled with his supporters to Manchuria, requested assistance from another enemy, the Manchus, and asked them to intervene. The Manchus seized this opportunity to invade Korea in 1627 and a peace deal was soon brokered. When the Manchu had taken over China as part of the Qing dynasty (清朝), they invaded Korea again in 1636. This time, the peace terms were severe and Korea was forced to become a vassal of Qing. This vassalage required that envoys were regularly sent to Beijing, and it so happened that a certain envoy brought, among other things, Christian ideas via Matteo Ricci's *True Meaning of the Lord of Heaven* into Korea (Eckert *et al.* 1990: 149–150). Andrew Ross (1994: 146) draws attention to the influence of Ricci's *Catechism* in Korea:

> Perhaps most striking was its impact on a group of Korean intellectuals which led to the beginning of Catholic Christianity in Korea before the arrival of any missionaries in the country.

Western learning (*Sŏhak*) and early Confucian reactions

The first Western writings to enter Korea made their way via China and were initially all grouped together as Western Learning (西學, K. *Sŏhak*), which consisted of anything from science and cartography to their religious treatises. Koreans encountered Western knowledge through their envoys in Beijing who probably met with Catholic Jesuits. Yi Sugwang (1563–1627), a *Namin* scholar whose penname was Chibong, is credited with having introduced some of the earliest Western texts ever to make their way to Korea at the beginning of the seventeenth century. Yi is often referred to as one of the as the earliest proponents of so-called *Sirhak* ideas, having written on an extensive range of encyclopaedic material collected in the *Classified Writings of Chibong* (芝峯類說, K. *Chibong yusŏl*). Among the foreign ideas in his text are the earliest Korean references to Matteo Ricci's *Catechism*. Yi provides a short analysis of Ricci's text, rejecting Ricci's idea that *Shangdi* was the same as the Catholic 'Lord of Heaven', who created the world. He also incorrectly indicates that Ricci, like Confucians, asserts that human nature is originally good – Ricci, in fact, pointed out that the Confucians had no unanimity of opinion at all: Mencius thought human nature was good, but Xunzi thought the very opposite. This rejection would continue throughout the seventeenth century, and it seems that Koreans, though writing about Western ideas, did not adopt the Western 'scientific ideas' with great fervour.

One exception was Kim Yuk (1580–1658), who in 1653 advocated the adoption of the Western calendrical system developed by Jesuits in China such as Xu Guangqi (1562–1633), a Confucian converted by Matteo Ricci; Johann Schrek Terrenz (1576–1630), whose pulley system diagrams were used much later by Tasan; and Adam Schall von Bell (1591–1666), who attempted to spread Catholicism to Korea. The calendar was named the *Sihŏn* (時憲, C. *Shixian*) calendar in Korea, and though it dated back to the end of the Ming dynasty, it was first used from the start of the Qing dynasty in China, also discussed by Yi Ik a century later (Ch'oe *et al.* 2001: 118–121). Practical ideas were less pressing concerns for some of Chosŏn's ritual-obsessed Neo-Confucians. Ritualistic interpretations fuelled prominent rifts among the factions in power. For example, Yun Hyu (1617–1680), who was taught by Yi Sugwang's son Yi Min'gu (1589–1670), disagreed with Zhu Xi's interpretation of the *Doctrine of the Mean*, among other texts, but these interpretations were regarded as the "correct" and "orthodox" interpretation in Korea. This put Yun, who was a member of the *Namin* or Southern faction, in direct conflict with an elder scholar Song Siyŏl (1607–1689), who was a member of the Western faction and an influential follower of T'oegye. Matters intensified over mourning rites in 1659 and again in 1674. Yun's appraisal of royal lineage above all others (an idea pleasing to the king) almost presented an opportunity for the *Namin* to gain some political power. Song was exiled for apparently denigrating royalty and almost executed, but later Yun was forced to kill himself! Pak Sedang (1629–1703), in a work entitled *Records of Clarifying Thoughts* (思辨錄, K. *Sabyŏn-nok*), though critical of Buddhism, also criticised Zhu Xi, and was so bold as to praise Wang Yangming (1472–1529), considered heterodox in Korea. He was inevitably accused of 'heterodoxy' and King Sukchong (r.1674–1720) ordered the text burned, but luckily Pak escaped with his life. This highlights the intellectual horizon that was current during the first century after Catholic ideas first entered Korea. The rejection of any alternative to the orthodox Neo-Confucian socio-cultural framework also explains, to some degree, why, in this cultural climate of Zhu Xi-ism, Catholic ideas were neither discussed, nor accepted. According to this orthodoxy, the image of a strong powerful king represented stability and power, an image that would not easily be overturned (Setton 1997: 26–43).

The intellectual milieu of the eighteenth century retained Zhu Xi's orthodoxy where metaphysical speculation was still prominent. Yi Ik (1681–1763), who became the leader of the *Namin* school, would later be considered as a major exponent of *Sirhak* or "Practical Learning". However, while he did write on ideas considered 'practical', he was also a follower of T'oegye's metaphysics, writing his *New Treaty on the Four-Seven Debate on the Four-Seven Debate* (四七新編, K. *Sach'il sinp'yŏ*). Yi had no problem accepting the advances of Western science, which reflects his practical side. He also examined the moral teachings of Matteo Ricci, as well as those of Diego de Pantoja (1571–1618). In his commentary on Pantoja's *Seven Victories* (七克, K. *ch'ilgŭk*), which described how to overcome the seven deadly sins, Yi argued that if one removed what was written about God and the devil, the morals could almost be considered Confucian. His critique of Ricci is called *Reactions Against Tianzhu zhiyi* (天主實義跋, K. *Ch'ŏnju sirŭi-bal*). Yi suggests there are similarities between *Sangje* (the Korean pronunciation of *Shangdi*; the Sovereign on High) and *Ch'ŏnju* (the Korean pronunciation of *Tianzhu*; The Lord of Heaven) [*Sangje* and *Ch'ŏnju* are used from this point on as this concerns the Korean context]. Yi Ik, nevertheless, criticises the way *Ch'ŏnju* is served and feared, like Sakyamuni is among Buddhists. Yi's reaction is understandable as he upheld T'oegye's metaphysics where *Principle* shaped reality and did not need to be revered. One thing Yi rejects outright is the incarnation of *Ch'ŏnju* in the person of Jesus, called *Yaso* (耶蘇). Yi Ik adopts a somewhat sarcastic tone when he speaks of Jesus, and cannot understand why God would chose to come as a man, to walk around and spread his teachings to the poor, devoid of the distinction of the Five Relationships with the king on top (Cawley 2012: 20–21).

Some of Yi's associate *Namin* scholars were much more critical of Western ideas (*sŏhak*) in general, especially Sin Hudam (1702–1761) and An Chŏngbok (1712–1783). Sin Hudam was particularly scathing of Catholic teachings in his critique entitled *A Critique of Western Learning* (西學辨, K. *Sŏhak pyŏn*). He also criticised Giulio Aleni's (1582–1649) *World Geography* (職方外記, K. *Chikpang oegi*), which was a cultural geography and provided information on Europe and its education system, suggesting that the Western practice of allowing young people to read literature could permanently damage young minds (see Ch'oe *et al.* 2001: 127–130)! In addition, Sin provided an in-depth analysis of Francesco Sambiasi's (1592–1649) *Treatise on the Soul*, as well as Ricci's *Catechism*. Sin argued that there are no traces of *Sangje* as the creative force behind the origin of the universe in the Confucian Classics, and again was critical of the idea that Jesus was the incarnation of *Sangje*, ridiculing this idea, as, in his opinion, Heaven would have been without its ruler (Cawley 2012: 22)

An Chŏngbok provides us with an interesting intellectual and cultural vantage point, as he witnessed the transformation from philosophical curiosity among certain Confucians to religious belief and practices among others, including his own son-in-law, the renowned Confucian scholar Kwŏn Ilsin (1736–1791). Hence, the intensity with which An rejects Catholicism is palpable, hoping to divert persecution from his own doorstep, and attempting to dissuade young scholars from their study of Catholic texts. This led him to write two critiques of Catholicism: *Thoughts on Heavenly Learning* (天學考, K. *Ch'ŏnhakko*) and *Questions and Answers on Heavenly Learning* (天學問答, K. *Ch'ŏnhak mundap*). In *Thoughts on Heavenly Learning* An stresses that the ideas of this religion are not new, and that they have been circulating in Korea since the reign of King Sŏnjo, therefore since around the time of Yulgok and T'oegye. However, the first issue An addresses is that of these young Confucian scholars who have been influenced by Catholic books. But, what is evident is that An is referring to a very specific group of *Namin* scholars, from his own faction, and so his tension is heightened by the fear of political repercussions that he and his friends might (and would) suffer from the political fallout that was an inevitability due to dabbling in heterodoxy: if Yun Hyu (mentioned previously in this chapter) had died as a result of criticising Zhu Xi and for his interpretation of rituals, what dangers lay ahead for Confucians who became Catholics and who abandoned the ancestor memorial rites? Clearly, torture and execution (Cawley 2012: 22–24).

In his *Questions and Answers on Heavenly Learning*, An gives further details of the new practices performed by growing numbers of Christo-Confucians, including the sacrament of baptism and the use of 'holy water', as well as adopting Christian names. He seems most scandalised by the idea of Confucians holding their hands together, praying to and worshipping a 'Catholic' [Western] God. These ideas were probably based on real conversations An had with his own son-in-law, Kwŏn Ilsin, who would soon be martyred (Ch'oe *et al.* 2001: 131). We can discern from An Chŏngbok's text that the information Korean Confucians had read about Catholic ideas had expanded beyond Ricci's text, and for the first time in these critiques, the crucifixion is described and it horrified this staunch Confucian, who recounts how Christians believe that Jesus was the saviour of the world and how he willingly chose to die on the cross taking the burden of our sins upon himself.

Converting Confucians: the early Catholic Church in Korea

Catholic ideas were initially adapted by a most unlikely group of men, all Neo-Confucian scholars who all belonged to the same *Namin* faction in Seoul. More curious is that they met at Chŏnjinam Buddhist hermitage in Kyonggi Province: Confucians at a Buddhist temple, clandestinely studying Catholic texts. The two main leaders of this group were Yi Pyŏk (1754–1786) and Yi Sŭnghun (1756–1801), but most noteworthy among their earliest followers were three brothers from the same family: Chŏng Yakchŏn (1758–1816) and Chŏng Yakchong (1760–1801), and their younger brother, Chŏng Yagyong (1762–1836), now famously known in Korea as Tasan (茶山). Yi Pyŏk is generally recognised as the author of the first lengthy outline of Catholic doctrine in Korea, *The Essence of the Divine Doctrine* (聖教要旨, K. *Sŏnggyo yoji*), written in *Hanmun* (Classical Chinese), hence, appealing to his elite Confucian entourage. More importantly, Chŏng Yakchong wrote the first religious exposition of Catholicism in *Han'gŭl*, called *The Essence of The Lord's Teachings* (주교요지, K. *Chugyo yoji*), which I refer to here as the *Han'gŭl Catechism*. This revolutionary text (which is not to exaggerate) was directed at a growing audience who were not elite men trained in Classical Chinese: most were not men at all, but women who sought the equality Catholicism taught them, as well as equality for their children, even for their slaves. In fact, this text had the greatest impact on the early adherents to Catholicism in Korea, read by thousands, though generally unacknowledged for the significant role it played in this history of ideas in Korea. In reality, this text was more widely read, and its ideas more widely adapted and practiced by those of his much more famous brother Tasan. The older Chŏng brother was considered to be spreading Western ideas, which were unorthodox, while Tasan's ideas are now portrayed as more originally 'Korean' and 'Confucian', with an immense emphasis on him as a '*Sirhak*' scholar, even describing him as head of a '*Sirhak'pa*'

(*Sirhak* faction), which *never* existed. Such appraisals of Tasan's ideas are anachronistically disconnected from the author's life-threatening existence, which shaped the vast majority of his writings – commentaries on Confucian Classics – discussed later in this chapter.

Yi Pyŏk was one of the most important figures from this early period of conversion, but he was also a mentor to Tasan, influencing his earlier Confucian commentaries. The earliest hymn written in *Han'gŭl* is attributed to Yi Pyŏk, and reflects his conversion from a philosophy without God to a theocentric religion. This hymn embodies his "religious" experience, called the *Hymn in Adoration of Ch'ŏnju [God]* (천주공경가, K. *Ch'ŏnju konggyŏng-ga*): it even uses the Riccian term for God in its title. In addition, Tasan's brother, Chŏng Yakchŏn, along with two other participants of the secretive Buddhist temple meetings, wrote the *Hymn in Praise of the Ten Commandments* (십계명가, K. *Sipkyemyŏng-ga*), which also refers to God as *Ch'ŏnju*, but also as *Sangje*, interchangeably. These texts reflect that a new consciousness was emerging, a Catholic one with very practical (*sil*) effects. Yi Sŭnghun is also an extremely important figure in the history of the Catholic Church in Korea, but it should be noted that it was Yi Pyŏk who urged him to seek baptism in Beijing in late 1783 while he accompanied his father there. Yi Sŭnghun was baptised by the French priest Louis de Grammont in early 1784 before returning to his homeland, where he recounted what he had seen and soon others were baptised by these Korean Confucians who had no formal initiation into the Catholic Church. Soon after his return, Yi Sŭnghun and Yi Pyŏk studied the new Catholic texts the former had brought back from China and soon began to spread their religious ideas in an altogether very unusual context. By this stage, Chŏng Yakchong, Tasan's other elder brother, had become deeply involved with the early Church. Christian ideas had spread to different classes, expanding beyond the initial clan-based gatherings (Keum 2000: 190; Choi 2006: 25). Soon they were meeting in the house of the *chungin* (middle-class) Kim Pŏmu (?–1786), whose house was the site of the first Catholic Cathedral in Seoul, situated in Myŏngdong (Myeongdong). There had been regular meetings at his house attended by Tasan and his brothers, Yi Sŭnghun and Yun Chich'ung (1759–1791), a cousin of Tasan's from the countryside. In fact, Yun Chich'ung had been converted by Kim Pŏmu after borrowing and reading his copy of Matteo Ricci's text: *Chungin* converting *yangban* – transgressing the rigid Confucian social order which segregated different classes, becoming involved in evangelising themselves. The strict Confucian social ordering had started to decay, arousing concern from some other *Namin* members and, soon, the state (Choi 2006: 92–93; Cawley 2014).

In 1785 the authorities burst into one of these meetings, which Tasan clearly hid from his friend the king, breaking the Confucian commandment of loyalty to the king above all else. The meeting was held in the home of Kim Pŏmu, and all those present were arrested and their Catholic paraphernalia seized. The *yangban* members received strong admonishments for their un-Confucian behaviour, but the *chungin* was condemned and imprisoned, eventually dying from the wounds inflicted from his torture in prison after being exiled to Tanyang, becoming the first Catholic martyr in Korea. In addition, Catholicism was proscribed by law and the following year the importation of Western books was also prohibited. All subsequent Catholic involvement was punishable by law and this reinforced the fear instilled by Kim Pŏmu's brutal torture and death, which served as a serious warning to the noble *yangban* members of the organisation. This dabbling with heterodoxy left the *Namin* vulnerable to attacks from their rival and more conservative *Noron* faction who had been ousted from power but were eagerly awaiting a chance to return. Leaflets were circulated all over the country in condemnation of the new religion, which ironically led to knowledge of Catholicism in areas that otherwise knew very little about its existence. After an initial period of quiet, and the death of Yi Pyŏk from disease, the Catholic leaders soon regrouped with Yi Sŭnghun still a driving force despite having made an official apostasy, clearly made to save his life. These believers (including former apostates) formed their own pseudo-hierarchy, confessed to each other, were baptised and confirmed, as well as celebrated mass, administering sacerdotal rites despite not having been ordained, soon supplanting Confucian rites (Keum 2000: 190–191; Choi 2006: 93–94).

In 1789, Yi Sŭnghun wrote a letter to Bishop Alexander de Gouvea in Beijing, to clarify such ecclesiastical elements of the faith and to request a priest be sent to Korea. It was delivered to Beijing by Yun Yuil (1758–1795), who (according to his later trial diary) had been taught about Catholicism by Kwŏn Ch'ŏlsin and Tasan (Choi 2006: 84). Tasan was, therefore, a 'practicing' priest in the pseudo order at this stage of the early Church, and at the same time attended the Confucian university, wrote commentaries on Confucian texts, and regularly met with the king. Bishop de Gouvea, though sympathetic towards the Korean church that had no direct leadership from priests, forbade the practice of ancestral rites, which had been banned by the Pope at this point. As a result, when Yun Chich'ung's mother died in 1791, in adherence to the directives received from Church authority in Beijing, Yun and his cousin Kwŏn Sang'yŏn (?–1791), whom Yun had converted, refused to hold the usual Confucian ancestor memorial rites, which were a legal requirement. This news eventually reached King Chŏngjo, who, on December 3, 1791, commanded that Yun Chich'ung and Kwŏn Sang'yŏn be beheaded. On December 8 the order was carried out, and their heads were left exposed for five days to terrify anyone involved with this new outlawed religion. Soon after, Kwŏn Ilsin was arrested for his involvement in the church, and although he was exiled, he died from the wounds inflicted during his imprisonment. Banners were posted all over the country explaining what had happened to Yun and Kwŏn (Cawley 2012: 26; Choi 2006: ch. 3).

It was not until the final days of 1794 that Korea finally had its own priest, a Chinese missionary, Fr Zhou Wenmo (1752–1801), who had arrived under great secrecy from China fulfilling Bishop de Gouvea's earlier promise. This

Figure 4.2 Myeongdong Cathedral in Seoul – at the site of Catholic martyr Kim
　　　　Pŏmu's house

significant event encouraged Catholics and contributed to new growth
within the Church. He had brought with him catechisms and other religious
texts, and soon set about compiling new texts for his Korean congregation
who, for the first time, had the religious doctrine explained to them by a
Catholic priest (Choi 2006: 56). Father Zhou founded the *Myŏngdohoe*
(明道會) [Society for the Illumination of the Way] which organised secret

meetings to instruct Koreans in Catholic doctrine; its members included people of different classes, as well as men and women, actively illustrating Catholic emphasis on equality through friendship, not just familial relations (46–49). Koreans themselves, particularly friends and family of Tasan, had started to become more involved by compiling their own religious books, translating prayers and scripture into the language of the masses, accelerating what Cho Kwang (1996: 126) describes as *"Han'gǔl* culture". These *"Han'gǔl"* writings should be regarded as monumental texts within Korea's rich intellectual history. Unfortunately, they are undervalued, and remain even today rare artefacts from a religiously tumultuous past and a greatly transformative period for Korea's religious and philosophical traditions. Their value is undermined by modern nationalistic narratives, which instead emphasise 'indigenous' and *'original* Korean' ideas.

Early evangelisation: the *Han'gul Catechism* and dangerous women

The infamous "Silk Letter" of 1801 written by Hwang Sayŏng (1775–1801), the son-in-law of Tasan's elder half-brother, Chong Yakhyŏn (1751–1821), depicts the horrifying persecution of Catholics, their violent torture and execution, as well as the work of Koreans to spread the religion despite the situation on the ground. The letter, which was written on silk and intended to be smuggled secretly into China for the bishop there, pleaded for foreign assistance due to the ongoing brutality which he feared might wipe out the Catholic Church entirely. The letter never reached its destination. It was intercepted and was used as ammunition to amplify the persecution of Catholics by Confucians, where Tasan and his brothers and other figures were brought back from where they had already been exiled to face further, more serious charges. Over the next year, several hundred Catholics were executed, several hundred others, who were more fortunate, were exiled: Chŏng Yakchong, his son-in-law and author of the Silk Letter, Hwang Sayŏng, as well and Yi Sŭnghun and many of their immediate circle were further tortured and beheaded. The other two Chŏng brothers were banished to a lonely exile in remote areas, separated, never to meet again. Tasan would remain there for 18 years – an utterly disgraced Confucian (Cawley 2017).

Hwang Sayŏng's 'Silk Letter' is an invaluable first-hand account of the early history of the Catholic Church in Korea from someone who was an influential member, recounting its horrific persecution, which ultimately led to his martyrdom (for an abridged English translation, see Hwang & Kim 2009). It highlights the seminal role of Chŏng Yakchong, president of the male meetings of the *Myŏngdohoe*. It describes the elder Chŏng brother in detail, his noble character and sagacious mind, as well as his profound knowledge, highlighting his catechism, *The Essence of the Lord's Teachings* (K. *Chugyo yoji*), drawing attention to the fact that it was deliberately written in *Han'gŭl* as part of an evangelising strategy, to convert women and members of the poorer masses. In fact, it would be read by thousands of those undervalued by Chosŏn society and ignored by Chosŏn's patriarchal hegemony. It is worth noting that there is one prominent female exponent of Neo-Confucian ideas, Im Yunjidang (1721–1793), who argued about the moral equality of men and women, though she was not in a position to reform the strictly patriarchal society of her time. Her essays, only very recently investigated in English, illustrate that she could read Confucian texts and write in Classical Chinese: she represents the exception to the general rule, whereby women were excluded from more meaningful learning (see Kim 2017). Chŏng Yagchong would fill in this gap, as would the women drawn to the ideas he wrote about.

Chŏng Yagchong's *Essence of the Lord's Teachings* has been translated into English, accompanied by the original *Han'gŭl* text, by Hector Diaz as *A Korean Theology* (1986). The text is divided into two parts with 43 separate headings that are then explained: Part One has 32 sections (Diaz 1986: 275–351), while Part Two has 11 sections (352–434). The first part also reflects the importance and ongoing influence of Ricci's text, from the terms used for God, using *Sangje* and *Ch'ŏnju* interchangeably. In it Chŏng rejects the idea of 'spontaneous origination', the idea that things simply spontaneously 'come into being', asserting that, just as men have parents, even the first man must have had a parent, so he presents God as our first parent, or original ancestor, echoing similar ideas from Yi Pyŏk's *Han'gŭl* hymn, but clearly drawing on Ricci's Catechism. This is significant in Chosŏn's Confucian context where filial piety or *hyo* was the most important virtue, revealing the author's attempt to acculturate his religious ideas into an ethno-relative path*way* that respected Confucianism, and which his readers, including women and children, could relate to. This also reinforced the Catholic monotheistic viewpoint, as well as the Scholastic teachings that God exists originally by [her]himself, without beginning or end. Chŏng provides contextual relativity for his readers, clarifying scholastic theories in simple language for his target audience, a task that further underscores his intellectual dexterity, exemplified in his description of the 'Trinity', with Jesus as the face of God, and God's love embodied in the Holy Spirit. Like Ricci, Chŏng also attacks Buddhism and Daoism in a condescending manner, describing their leaders as mere men, unlike Jesus, who is praised as divine and God himself.

Part Two reflects a deeper knowledge of the Bible. The first verses of this second part outline the *Old Testament*'s account of creation as well as the concept of original sin, and man's fall from "goodness". According to this text, because we all originate from the original parents Adam and Eve, then mankind consists of a single human family, implying inherent equality between people of all races and both sexes. However, the *Bible* (Genesis 2:18) makes it clear that man was created first and that woman was his "helper", an idea that is still sometimes manipulated to undervalue the role of women. In Chŏng's Catechism, man's corruption reflects his inability for correct self-cultivation and this becomes the reason for the incarnation of Jesus – to provide mankind with a new path*way* – and to lead believers away from sin. Hence, Christ's function becomes a Confucian one which is perfected by Catholic supplementation to produce a positive effect: to save man from man, invalidating the Four-Seven debate, as well as any discussions of *Principle* and *ki*, making this, in the author's opinion, the most significant metaphysical conflict of the Chosŏn dynasty.

Chŏng describes the incarnation using the term *kangsaeng* (강생), where *kang* (강) literally means to descend or to surrender, incorporating the idea of God humbling himself to be born among the poor (emptied of his divinity), with details from the *New Testament*, including the 'virgin' birth. Jesus is described as "truly God and truly man", hence, a mediator (거간, K. *kŏgan*) between God and man. He is also described as an elder brother (장형, K. *changhyŏng*) to all people, Confucianising the Catholic Christ, and continuing Ricci's project. Importantly, it is not the supernatural feats of Jesus (such as miracles) that makes Jesus seem such an outstanding sage in this *Han'gŭl* Catechism: it is his words, his teachings and his 'kindhearted' actions. The humiliation of the Crucifixion is depicted in detail, and following the Resurrection, Jesus becomes known as the redeemer (구세주, K. *kuseju*), the lamb (고양; K. *koyang*) who has come to free all mankind, high and low, men and women, from sin and death through his sacrifice. He explains that the incarnation took place in Judea (and not China), simply because the people there had worshipped God, but that now all people could follow the teachings of Christ and be saved: all depended on whether one "practiced" the new path*way* set out by Jesus. Chŏng calls for this change to begin now, calling for his Confucian audience to repent and reform. This new path*way* was adapted and spread mainly by women – subverting Confucian gender norms, where women became 'active practitioners' of Catholic ideas.

The evangelical role of women was detailed in the *Silk Letter* of 1801, which unfortunately led to the arrest and execution of so many. Additionally, the *Edict for the Persecution of Heterodoxy*, which was also published in 1801, and pasted all over Korea, singled out women, describing them as dangerous, having "overturned their moral duty and confused public morals" (Cawley 2015: 83). I have written on this important role of women in the early Catholic Church in detail in an article called "Dangerous Women in the Early Catholic Church in Korea" (2015). It highlights how women, though repressed through Confucian attempts to prevent them from having any public role in Chosŏn society, initiated a religious transformation, becoming missionaries themselves among women. One such brave woman, Kang Wansuk (1760–1801), baptised as Colombe, left her husband, taking their daughter, as well as his mother whom she had converted, as well as his son from a previous marriage, and moved to Seoul to be a part of the Catholic movement, blatantly disregarding the 'Three Bonds' from the

Book of Rites: women were expected to follow their fathers, husbands, even their own sons. There she led the female members of the *Myŏngdohoe* Catholic society, and was clearly intelligent and literate, teaching Catholic theology to women, overturning Confucian norms. Her role becomes even more shocking, considering the rigid Confucian rules which curtailed inter-gender interactions, when learning of her role in bringing Father Zhou to Korea, then hiding him in her house, in the female quarters – for several years. This also exposes the inherent misogyny of the 'Seven Evils' which accused women of being too frivolous and gossipy: women, it turns out, could keep secrets, while the Confucian men informed on each other, afraid of losing their wealth and prestige. Many of these women had nothing to lose, but they had equality and, along with their slaves, freedom to gain, as they challenged the patriarchal bonds that had chained them into a subservient system. Some of these young Catholic women, such as Luthgarde Yi Suni, chose to remain a virgin after marriage, obliging her husband to do the same, guiding him along this new path*way*. They used their wealth to help the poor and took in strangers, further undermining the ideological apparatus of Confucian hierarchy, actively putting their 'dangerous knowledge" into practice, where men and women, rich and poor, those free and slaves, could worship as equals, reflecting a metamorphosis of Confucian values (Cawley 2015: 84–92).

Recalibrating Tasan: from *Sirhak* to *Shepherding the people*

One of the Confucian scholars who eventually renounced the Catholic religion was the youngest Chŏng brother, Tasan. He is one of the most written-about thinkers in Korea's intellectual history and is a complex figure due to his association with Catholicism, but, as mentioned already, he is often studied as a *Sirhak* scholar, and also praised as a synthesiser of *Sirhak* thought (Wŏn 1976; Chon 1984; Shin 2000). However, these depictions reflect a later re-engagement with Tasan's writings and those of other writers, originating during the colonial period when many of them were collected together for the first time. Jung Ok-ja (1992: 166, 168) writes that "studies of *Sirhak* were motivated by the national crisis between late 19th century and early 20th century", but also relates this trend to post-liberation historians who "have essayed positive revaluations of the late Chosŏn period to rediscover and reaffirm national culture". This was as a reaction to Japanese rule and its colonial government's attempts to undermine and devalue Korea's past and humiliate its people.

This is not to say that Tasan and other Confucian writers did not have 'practical' ideas – Confucians were renowned for them – this was not something new. In fact, that was why Confucians were so confident in their criticisms against the Buddhists, whom they felt provided no practical social remedies or solutions for matters of state. Wŏn (1976: 41–48) highlights Tasan's innovative ideas but underscores that due to Catholicism and his shameful exile, "Tasan never participated actively in the administration [. . .] He was always outside the arena and unable to overcome this disability". Yi Hidok (1962: 35) underscores that Tasan's main theme was the Confucian Classics, on which he wrote 230 *kwŏn* (volumes), compared with only 78 *kwŏn* on politics. But what of Catholic influences on Tasan's texts, especially his Confucian writings? Park Seong-rae (2004: 347) suggests that "[Tasan] may have camouflaged his view in the guise of the authority of the [*Yi Jing*] at a time when Catholic followers were being persecuted". Keum (2000: 202; emphasis added) makes an astute observation:

> [T]he severe suppression of the Catholic faith during that era and the life-threatening situation may have forced Tasan to lead a *double-life* in which he outwardly had to hide his religious belief.

The fact is that Tasan's authorial control had been compromised, and he had *no* choice but to write on the Confucian Classics if he wanted to live. This was not only an indispensable strategy for maintaining his own life, but it was also necessary to save his wife and children from being sold as slaves were he to be executed.

Don Baker (2004, 1999) has repeatedly argued that Tasan, though early on interested in Catholicism, eventually rejected it as he was fundamentally a "Confucian" and Catholic ideas finally conflicted with his Confucian values and worldview. He also suggests that the "theism" one finds in Tasan's writings was related to a belief in a "Confucian god". While this is an alternative possibility, many of Tasan's contemporaries did not consider him a particularly convincing Confucian (remember he hid his 'secret' Catholic meetings from his own King!): no small number of them petitioned for his removal and for the extension of his time in exile when appeals were made (Cawley 2014). 'Belief' in a 'Confucian god', in essence, contradicts the very core of Confucianism and the basis of its moral system: even the European *philosophes* (including Voltaire) praised Confucian morality *without* 'belief' in God. In reality, Tasan was exiled and considered a renegade Catholic, not an 'upright' Confucian, and though he wrote copiously on Confucian texts, he still under surveillance, without any political or 'practical' influence.

The recalibration of ideas and motifs that appear throughout Tasan's writings on the Confucian Classics reflect ideas that he had read in Matteo Ricci's text – ideas he had carefully studied and attempted to spread – before his closest friends and cousins had been tortured and persecuted. "Dis-assembling Traditions: Deconstructing Tasan via Matteo Ricci" (Cawley 2014) examines the influence of Matteo Ricci on Tasan's commentaries, which is unquestionable. Tasan was engaging with the constituent ideas of original Confucianism, but redirecting it towards a sort of Post-Confucian recalibration, notably rejecting the Song Neo-Confucian metaphysical developments (i.e., *Principle* and the Supreme Ultimate), while also criticising Buddhism and Daoism, but also the ideas used from those traditions by earlier Neo-Confucians. He reconfigurates this new schema with *Sangje* as central to morality and the overseer of human actions as God, just as it was for Matteo Ricci, also explained in his own brother's *Han'gŭl Catechism*, which was widely read at that time. Song Young-bae (2001) also underlines how Tasan's morality is "similar to the philosophical configuration of *Tianzhu shiyi* [Ricci's catechism]". Considering Tasan's writings without recognising a Christian influence overlooks an important aspect of his sophisticated Christo-Confucian transcultural textuality, influenced by Matteo Ricci, who, himself, though a Catholic, praised Confucian morality. In this context, Confucianism and Catholicism were complementary, and a Confucian philosopher could value Catholic beliefs (even if they were outlawed by the state).

Both Setton (1997: 64–66) and Kim (1996: 243–264) (and many others) single out three texts as representative of Tasan's thought: *Kyŏngse yup'yo* (經世遺表) [Treatise on Government]; *Mongmin simsŏ* (牧民心書) [The Heart Book for Shepherding the People]; and *Hŭmhŭm sinsŏ* (欽欽新書) [New Treatise on the Legal System]. *Mongmin simsŏ* is referred to below as the *Heart Book*, as this is how Tasan referred to it himself in his introduction to the text. It is often considered as Tasan's masterpiece, divided into 12 books (or sections) and each of these sections has a further set of (mostly 6) sub-sections. It is usually discussed in terms of governmental or administrative reforms, though these accounts sometimes overlook Tasan's intent to 'shepherd the people'. Kim Sunghae (1996: 244) translates it as the *Heart Book for Pasturing People*, describing this "heart book" as "a detailed guide for local governors", reflecting the emotional call for change and action made by its author. The entire work has been translated into English by Choi Byonghyon (2010), appearing with the title *Admonitions on Governing the People*. In the preface to the *Heart Book*, written in 1821, a few years after the actual text had been composed while in exile, Tasan (Choi (trans.) 2010: 1) writes that there are two dimensions to being a sage: "half depending on one's own self-cultivation, the other half is nurturing, or 'shepherding' the people". Tasan (Choi (trans.) 2010: 2; emphasis added) contrasts the time of the "shepherds" to the current time of politicians:

> The age of the sages has already passed away, and the influence of their teachings has declined; those who rule the people nowadays do not know how to *shepherd the people*. As a result, the common people are malnourished and harassed; they have become so sick that their dead bodies fill the ditches. The so-called shepherds of the people, on the other hand, indulge in fine clothing and tasty food, busy only making themselves fat. How unfortunate!

Matteo Ricci (1985: sec. 419) also used the image of a shepherd as someone who guides his sheep unlike others who misled people, and Tasan was, as already mentioned, very well acquainted with this text. Tasan does not depict a society benefiting from some revolutionary *Sirhak* movement, rather, his quite negative depiction of the reality of the times, highlights exactly why people would seek an alternative path*way* to guide them, and they clearly would have found solace in the hope of an afterlife. This also echoes the *Silk Letter*, which, more than once, referred to the Church in Korea as sheep without a shepherd, highlighting how the hierarchy was abusing its power, exploiting and punishing the weak and the poor (see: Cawley 2017). Tasan's goal is also to rectify the wrongs of the people in power – the same people who beheaded his brother and friends, and who banished him and his other brother into exile, preventing them from ever meeting again. Tasan (Choi (trans.) 2010) refers to his exile in this text, as well as his in-depth study of the *Confucian Classics* that prepare a man for self-cultivation, not for "shepherding". Tasan (4), writes that this is his "Book from the Heart" lamenting that "my circumstances would not allow me to shepherd the people even though I desire this opportunity".

Lee Eul-ho (2004: 346–349) investigates Tasan's unique view of the ideal man, denoted by what he describes as Tasan's "profound interest in the idea of the *mokja* [*mokcha*, 牧者]", the shepherd, who "has faith in the Ultimate Being". In an essay entitled, "Tasan's View of Man", Lee (349) attempts to consider "the historical conditions in which he [Tasan] lives", but discusses the influence of T'oegye and Yulgok, as well as Zhu Xi and the Song philosophers. He never mentions Yi Pyŏk or Tasan's own brother who composed *Han'gŭl* texts, or a single other person who lived during Tasan's lifetime, thereby overlooking the actual "historical conditions" and social context of the philosopher and his intellectual horizon which was influenced by Catholicism, and compromised by Confucian persecutions. Lee (352) writes that "the moral duty of the *mokja* is not to reign as a political authoritarian, but to devote himself to the cultivation of the people according to the mandate given him by the Ultimate Being", who in Tasan's text is *Sangje*, and not *Principle*. But, how does Tasan implement these ideas in his *Heart Book*?

Tasan overturns the normal idea of the lawmakers "enforcing" the law by reinforcing the needs of the people, while challenging powerful political structures which safeguard those who are at the top of the hierarchy that protects them. Such ideas have very serious social implications. In an attempt to deconstruct the injustice of the time, and thereby criticising Confucianism itself, Tasan encourages people to actively love each other, and not to behave as passive bystanders when we see people in need. The six sub-sections of Book Four, "Love of People", clearly express Tasan's extension of Confucian humanity to the "Other", beyond one's expected duty, but most radically, beyond one's family (Choi (trans.) 2010: 189–212):

1   Caring for the elderly
2   Fostering orphans
3   Saving the poor

4   Commiseration and support for the families of the dead
5   Generous treatment of the ill
6   Saving the victims of natural disasters

Though Tasan has discussed the importance of classes and the importance of the family, he also contradicts their limitations, and he looks beyond them, developing ideas from Yulgok's community compacts. Book Four calls for charity between all human beings, something being put into action by Catholics at this time. The elderly that we should look after need not be our relatives, hence filial piety is extended and transformed. The children we should have compassion for, are those who are abandoned and who no longer have parents of their own blood: this parenting depends on love, not bloodline, and indeed many Koreans today still have an issue with adoption due to bloodline. The poor include widows, widowers, orphans and those without children, who, with the help of "the Other" who is a stranger, can be lifted out of their hardships. Those in hardship should be assisted with funerary expenses through generosity and without equivocation. Taxes should be reduced or annulled for those who are injured and who cannot work. Those who are disabled should be provided with shelter and food. Soldiers who are ill due to hunger and affliction should be assisted and, during times of epidemics, the state should do all possible to assist those affected. Helping people in distress due to fires and floods and assuring their well-being reflects the humanity (仁) of shepherding the people. These ideas also form the basis of a welfare state, but unfortunately were not put into practice by subsequent Confucian governments – things only got worse.

Tasan had authentic experiences of living with poor people, dejected and humiliated, suffering from loneliness and depression after the death of so many of his loved ones in a short space of time. He points out how the lawmakers or law enforcers are the very people who corrupt justice. Tasan paints a starkly contrastive picture between those who abuse power and those who are abused by it, which he and his family were. We do not discover a scholar eulogising Confucianism and its laws, rather, we find a harsh critique of it, comparable to the critiques of the *Silk Letter*. In the *Heart Book*, we discover a distrust of those who wielded power, those responsible for enforcing and spreading the law, magistrates and sub-magistrates, who were also expected to be morally responsible leaders. Nevertheless, these ideas again embody the intersection of traditions (Confucian and Catholic) reflecting Tasan's own context of conflict where the 'law' had transgressed the very justice it should stand for. These are not the writings of an official in power at court, far removed from the people: these are the writings of a neighbour who understands their burden and who wishes to expose the cruelty of abusive local administrators who exploit their positions, which reinforces delusions of superiority based on birth and rank, not good example and virtuous conduct.

People follow by example: this simple idea is repeated throughout the text. Tasan explains how those who are governing with the menace of punitive sanctions alone, do not merit their positions as they contribute to the already deplorable suffering of the people. In addition, he chastises the frivolity of the petty officials and their expensive banquets which magnifies the desperation of the poor, many of whom starved to death. Tasan repeatedly rejects the use of violence, or threats of violence, and even suggests that whipping slaves be banned – quite a radical idea for that time. In these same sections Tasan openly criticises the Korean law, and despite his discussion of a revision of laws including land laws, tax laws, among others, he constantly repeats that they be revised to raise the living standards of the people and to prevent the tyranny and abuse of the poor. Law becomes a call for responsibility, a gesture of "Humane" government actively involved in *loving* the people. This "Humanity" is also reflected in Tasan's suggestions for military reform, accompanied by his critique of the military law in general which he views as out-of-date, resulting in increasingly serious abuses of power which put the lives of the people in danger, discussed in Book Eight (557–654). Tasan depicts the harsh reality and the poverty endured by those in the decaying countryside who are unable to feed their family without the additional burden of the military cloth tax. It is in Book Nine, *Administration of Justice*, that Tasan (655–824) engages in a discussion about Penal Laws where he insists that using one's "heart" (*sim*) when one is making judicial decisions is a sure way to discover the truth. He suggests that people who wish to make an appeal and petition against their grievances should be permitted to do so without erecting barriers to prevent them entry, that they should be welcomed "as if into their parent's houses", displaying the trait of a "good shepherd" (良牧, K. *yangmok*). This good shepherd appearing in Tasan's text, embodies Christian ethos and his post-Confucian *Weltanschauung*: listening to the downtrodden, welcoming them like family, disregarding the codified structures which separates the social classes, refusing to construct barriers to prevent them from approaching him. In Tasan's text, the sheep represented by the poor common people, should be treated with equality, a far cry from their social reality which he laments.

Book Nine is where Tasan's reality filters into and shapes his text. His own personal experiences, and those of his kith and kin who were imprisoned and punished as a result of their Catholic involvement, reverberates in his accounts of curbing prison sentences and the precautionary measures to be taken when punishing inmates. Tasan makes a bold demand when he calls for prisoners to be released, not confined for long periods, and their debts forgiven. Excessive punishment was to be a last resort and displayed the failure of government. In particular, Tasan criticised the use of punishments on the old and the very young, obviously something he had witnessed while he himself was in prison. He writes quite lucidly that prison was like a living hell, where one could not even begin to imagine the torture one had to endure. Tasan exposes the legal system from the inside out: he was someone who wrote books on the law that exposed its injustices, and calls people to lead with humaneness, not merely to blindly follow laws which persecuted the weak. He also draws attention to the plight of those in exile, and considers the shepherd as responsible for their well-being, though they have broken the law, they are still entitled to be treated as dignified human beings. In fact, Tasan (Book Nine, Section Five) proposes the "Prohibition of Tyrannical Abuses", insisting it would lead to peace among the people and suggests that the people who need to be supervised and controlled are the rich and wealthy families. He also compares the abuses of the rich and powerful against the poor and weak like wolves and tigers against sheep, and recommends their removal. In the midst of these proclamations against the wealthy, Tasan comments on the sexual immorality of the people and urges men to stop frequenting female entertainers called *kisaeng* and prostitutes – also prominent Catholic teachings from this period. Of course, he carefully never references Catholic teachings, but he also never criticises Catholicism, despite the fact that he openly criticises the false and 'treacherous' teachings of Shamanism and Buddhism. Tasan is particularly harsh in relation to Shamans, suggesting they be "killed and their shrines destroyed" (818–821). If Tasan had truly abandoned his belief in the outlawed Catholicism as he had recounted in an earlier letter to the king (where he suggested he had mistakenly 'misunderstood' it as another form of Confucianism) which saved his life, would he not have seized the opportunity to criticise it here and to discredit it along with these other 'treacherous' traditions that contradicted Neo-Confucian orthodoxy? If Tasan had rejected Catholicism, then why is it not mentioned here when he specifically criticises "people with wicked words, practicing fetichism", as this was how the Confucians had described Catholics, and why they (and Tasan) were exiled or executed.

What is revolutionary are Tasan's teachings about compassion and charity as the mark of a humane person who empathises with those undergoing hardships, who does not distinguish between people from 'this' village and 'that' village, as "there should be no distinction between inside and outside" (906–907). He is truly a visionary, effectively calling for practical pastoral care, even for those we do not know, even destitute beggars, who can never repay us: valuable lessons for us in the world today, especially when we consider the current global refugee crisis (affecting Korea itself). Tasan harshly criticises the practice of magistrates who coercively solicit contributions of rice even during period of famine, describing this as "cruel and atrocious" (915), while drawing our attention to wealthy Buddhist monks who needed to be persuaded to donate grain to the poor and "to carry out charity for the general populace" (927). These ideas denote what is practical in Tasan's philosophy of the *heart*: changing people's hearts changes lives for the better. This new fellowship depends on those who lead, where leading signifies serving. This ground-breaking text hopes for change and hopes to transform the stoicism of the Confucian officials with some Christian *caritas*.

Conclusion

This chapter has examined the development of Neo-Confucian thought during the early Chosŏn dynasty. T'oegye's *Ten Diagrams on Sage Learning* became an integral text during the entire Chosŏn period, synthesising Zhu's teachings, advocating the importance of education and the need for private academies far away from the capital. Additionally, T'oegye re-oriented his moral views around the idea of mindfulness, *kyŏng*, which now became a serious ongoing practice, to control one's thoughts by curtailing negative feelings, while to reveal one's innate good nature, reflecting the idealistic interpretation of *Principle*. His answer to the Four-Seven metaphysical debate is dealt with in a coherent and straight-forward manner in the text, and is neither a main focus of the diagrams, nor his overall writings, despite the fascination that continues on this subject even today. Yulgok's real-life context as a minister for defence (among other government posts) made him aware of the realities of the state that T'oegye managed to eschew to some degree by withdrawing to the countryside where he focused on teaching. Yulgok's community compacts are an attempt to redress some of the social ills of the time, and recognised the hardship of those in the more rural areas.

Western Learning would also make its way to Korea, and Matteo Ricci's *Catechism*, while initially rejected, was a subject of discussion within Korea from the early seventeenth century, especially after scholars later named as participants of the '*Sirhak* Wave' began to critique them. Scholars such as Yi Sugwang and Yi Ik demonstrated their knowledge of Western ideas, while continuing to write commentaries on Confucianism and remaining faithful to its main tenets. The later attacks against Ricci's text by Sin Hudam and An Chŏngbok highlight that Catholicism had expanded and was being practiced – by elite Confucian men. The early Confucian scholars who became inclined to Ricci's ideas tried to hide it from the king, as well as from rival factions. Yi Pyŏk and Yi Sŭnghun led this early group, shaping their faith in a dangerous doctrine. The Chŏng brothers, including the famous Tasan, were some of the main proponents in spreading the ideas of this heterodox religion and members of its initial pseudo-ecclesiastical order. Soon, realising the burgeoning interest that had spread among women, Chŏng Yagchong wrote the *Han'gŭl Catechism* in a clear cogent style that was accessible to the members of the early Catholic Church, which by 1801 consisted mainly of women and people from the lower classes. Attracting the ire of the Confucian government, the 'Catholics' were rounded up, tortured and executed, as outlined in the *Silk Letter*. Many Yangban Confucians recanted, such as Tasan, with no choice but to do this or die. Many did choose to die, and persecutions would ultimately not stop until the 1870s, giving the church numerous martyrs, among them a considerable number of women, some of whom would be canonised by Pope Francis I in 2014.

Tasan's writings reflect a Christo-Confucian transcultural transformation, whereby Neo-Confucian metaphysics are rejected, while embracing *Sangje* as a monotheistic deity. His vast textual legacy, only compiled during the later colonial period, deals mainly with Confucian themes that have been recalibrated with post-Confucian ideas. As Choi ((trans.) 2010: xxiv) points out in the introduction to his translation discussed above, "The circulation of Tasan's manuscripts was limited to his close family and friends" in particular his older brother Yakchŏn who died in exile. Tasan's ideas were not written as part of some *Sirhak* movement, and he himself correctly suggested that his ideas would not be heeded (xxvii). The *Sirhak* label overshadows his compassionate attempts to redress the Confucian hierarchy's mistreatment of men, women and children, highlighted in the *Heart Book*. Such ideas are at the "heart" of Tasan's call to redress the inequalities of those undervalued and ignored, while elite men in long robes lived in luxury. This text constitutes the foundation of a politics of 'humane rights' and 'humane laws', and reflects ideas that were found in Tasan's own brother's *Han'gŭl Catechism*, and ideas that attracted women and the poor to its teachings, where the actual law had failed them. Soon Koreans would develop new religious path*ways* reacting to socio-political circumstances that were going from bad to worse, and not improved by the so-called '*Sirhak*' ideas. Soon, a period of isolation would be followed by darker times, when the entire country was colonised by its neighbours to the East.

References and further reading

Baek, Min Jeong. 2016. "Moral Success and Failure in the Ethical Theory of Tasan Chŏng Yagyong". *Acta Koreana*, 19(1): 241–266.
Baker, Donald. 1999. "A Different Thread: Heterodoxy, and Catholicism in a Confucian World". *Culture and the State in Late Chosŏn Korea*, eds. Jahyun Kim Habousch and Martina Deuchler. Harvard University Press: Cambridge, MA. 199–230.
———. 2004. "Tasan Between Catholicism and Confucianism: A Decade Under Suspicion, 1791–1801". *Tasanhak*, 5: 55–96.
Cawley, Kevin N. 2012. "Deconstructing Hegemony: Catholic Texts in Chosŏn's Neo-Confucian Context". *Acta Koreana*, 15(1): 15–42.
———. 2013. "In the Name(s) of God: Matteo Ricci's Translational Apostolate". *Translation Studies*, 6(3): 293–308.
———. 2014. "Dis-Assembling Traditions: Deconstructing Tasan via Matteo Ricci". *Journal of The Royal Asiatic Society*, 24(2): 297–313.
———. 2015. "Dangerous Women in the Early Catholic Church in Korea". *Religious Transformation in Modern Asia*, ed. David W. Kim. Brill: Leiden. 76–97.
———. 2017. "The Silk Letter: A Case of Transcultural Religious Conversion and Conflict". *Religious Encounter in a Transcultural Society*, ed. David W. Kim. Lexington Books: Lanham. 139–158.
Cho, Kwang. 1996. "The Meaning of Catholicism in History". *The Founding of the Catholic Tradition in Korea*, ed. Yu Chai-shin. Korean and related Studies Press: Mississuaga. 115–140.
Ch'oe, Yŏngho, Peter H. Lee and Wm Theodore De Bary. (eds.). 2001. *Sources of Korean Tradition*, vol. ii. Columbia University Press: New York.

Choi, Byonghyon (trans.). 2010. *Admonitions on Governing the People – Chŏng Yagyong*. University of California Press: Berkeley.

Choi, Jai-keun. 2006. *The Origin of the Roman Catholic Church in Korea*. The Hermit Kingdom Press: Seoul. Chapters 1–2.

Chon Syngboc. 1984, *Korean Thinkers: Pioneers of Silhak (Practical Learning)*, Si-sa-yong-o-sa, Inc: Seoul.

Chung, Chai-sik. 1985. "Chŏng Tojŏn: Architect of Yi Dynasty Government and Ideology". *The Rise of Neo-Confucianism in Korea*, eds. Wm Theodore De Bary and JaHyun Kim Haboush. Columbia University Press: New York. 59–88.

Chung, Edward Y.J. 1995. *The Korean Neo-Confucianism of Yi T'oegye and Yi Yulgok: A Reappraisal of the 'Four-Seven Thesis' and Its Practical Implications for Self-Cultivation*. University of New York Press: Albany.

De Bary, Theodore Wm. (ed). 1985. *The Rise of Neo-Confucianism in Korea*. Columbia University Press: New York.

De Mendina, Juan G. Ruiz. 1994. *The Catholic Church in Korea: Its Origins, 1566–1784*. Translated by John Bridge. S.J. Royal Asiatic Society – Korea Branch: Seoul.

Deuchler, Martina. 1985. "Attitudes Towards Heterodoxy". *The Rise of neo-Confucianism in Korea*, eds. Wm. Theodore de Bary and JaHyun Kim Haboush. Columbia University Press: New York. 375–410.

———. 1992. *The Confucian Transformation of Korea*. Harvard University Press: Cambridge, MA.

———. 2003. "Female Virtues in Chosŏn Korea". *Women and Confucian Cultures in Premodern China, Korea and Japan*, eds. Dorothy Ko, Jahyun Kim Habousch and Joan R. Piggott. University of California Press: Berkeley. 142–169.

———. 2004. "Neo-Confucianism in the Early Joseon Dynasty: Some Reflections on the Role of Ye". *Korean Philosophy: Its Tradition and Modern Transformation*, ed. Korean National Commission for UNESCO. Hollym: Seoul. 43–54.

Diaz, Hector. 1986. *A Korean Theology – Chugyo Yoji: Essentials of the Lord's Teachings by Chŏng Yak-jong Augustine (1760–1801)*. Neue Zeitschrift für Missions- wissenschaft: Immensee.

Eckert, Carter J. *et al*. 1990. *Korea Old and New: A History*. Ilchokak Publishers: Seoul. Chapter 10.

Grayson, H. James. 2002. *Korea: A Religious History*, revised edition. Routledge Curzon: London.

Han, Hee-sook. 2004. "Women's Life During the Chosŏn Dynasty". *International Journal of Korean History*, 6: 113–162.

Han, Yŏng-u. 2004. "Jeong Yak-yong: The Man and His Thought". *Korean Philosophy: Its Tradition and Modern Transformation*, ed. Korean National Commission for UNESCO. Hollym: Seoul. 357–371.

Hwang, Alexander Y. and Kim, Lidia T. 2009. "The Silk Letter of Alexander Sayông Hwang: Introduction and Abridged Translation". *Missiology: An International Review*, 37(2): 167–179.

Ivanhoe, Phillip J. 2016. *Three Streams: Confucian Reflections on Learning and the Moral Heart-Mind in China, Korea and Japan*. Oxford University Press: Oxford. Chapter 5.

Jorgensen, John. (trans.). 2015. *A Handbook of Korean Practice: A Mirror of the Sŏn School of Buddhism (Sŏn'ga kwigam)*. University of Hawaii Press: Honolulu.

Jung, Ok-ja. 1992. "New Approaches to the History of Ideas in the Late Chosŏn Period". *Seoul Journal of Korean Studies*, 5: 155–176.

Kalton, Michael C. 1985. "The Writings of Kwŏn Kŭn: The Context and Shape of Early Yi Dynasty Neo-Confucianism". *The Rise of Neo-Confucianism in Korea*, eds. Wm. Theodore De Bary and JaHyun Kim Haboush. Columbia University Press: New York. 89–124.

———. (trans.). 1988. *To Become a Sage*. Columbia University Press: New York. Available at: https://faculty.washington.edu/mkalton/10dia%20contents%20web. htm [accessed on 13 June 2018].

———. 2004. "An Introduction to Silhak". *Korean Philosophy: Its Tradition and Modern Transformation*, ed. Korean National Commission for UNESCO. Hollym: Seoul. 293–322.

Keum, Jang-tae. 2000. *Confucianism and Korean Thoughts*. Jimoondang Publishing Company: Seoul.

Kim Habousch, JaHyun. 1985. "The Education of a Crown Prince: A Study in Confucian Pedogagy". *The Rise of Neo-Confucianism in Korea*, eds. Wm Theodore De Bary and JaHyun Kim Haboush. Columbia University Press: New York. 161–222.

Kim, Sunghae. 1996. "Chŏng Yagyong (Tasan): Creative Bridge Between the East and the West". *Confucian Philosophy in Korea*, eds. Haechang Choung and Han Hyong-jo. The Academy of Korean Studies: Pundang. 213–291.

Kim, Sungmoon. 2017. "The Way to Become a Female Sage: Im Yunjidang's Confucian Feminism". *Traditional Korean Philosophy: Problems and Debates*, eds. Youngsun Back and Philip J. Ivanhoe. Rowman and Littlefield Publishers: London and New York. 177–196.

Kwon, Ki-jŏng. 1995. "Buddhism in the Chosŏn Dynasty". *The History and Culture of Buddhism in Korea*, ed. The Korean Buddhist Research Institute. Dongguk University Press: Seoul. 171–218.

Latourette, Kenneth Scott. 1966. *A History of Christian Missions in China*. Ch'eng-Wen Publishing Company: Taipei.

Ledyard, Gari. 2006. "Kollumba Kang Wansuk". *Christianity in Korea*, eds. Robert E. Buswell Jr. and Timothy S. Lee. University of Hawaii Press: Honolulu. 38–71.

Lee Eul-ho. 2004. "Dasan's View of Man". *Korean Philosophy: Its Tradition and Modern Transformation*, ed. Korean National Commission for UNESCO. Hollym: Seoul. 337–356.

Lewis, James. (ed.). 2017. *The East Asian War, 1592–1598: International Relations, Violence and Memory*. Routledge: London.

Mullins, Mark R. (ed.). 2003. *Handbook of Christianity in Japan*. Brill: Leiden.

Mungello, David E. 1982. "The Seventeenth-Century Jesuit Translation Project of the Confucian Four Books". *East Meets West: The Jesuits in China, 1582–1773*, eds. Charles E. Ronan and Bonnie B. Oh. Loyola University Press: Chicago. 252–283.

Nahm, Andrew. 1996. *Korea: Tradition and Transformation*. Hollym: Seoul. Chapter 4.

Oh, Kangnam. 1993. "Sagehood and Metanoia: The Confucian-Christian Encounter in Korea". *The Journal of American Academy of Religion*, 61(2): 303–320.

Pak, Chŏng-hong. 1983. "Historical Review of Korean Confucianism". *Main Currents of Korean Thought*, ed. Korean National Commission for UNESCO. Si-sa-o-yong-sa Publishers: Seoul. 60–81.

Park, Byung-Soo. 1992. "The Deconstruction of Speech Levels". *Korea Journal*, 32(3): 23–30.

Park, Seong-rae. 2004. "Western Science and Silhak Scholars". *Korean History: Discovery of Its Characteristics and Developments*, ed. Korean National Commission for UNESCO. Hollym: Seoul. 327–361.

Ricci, Matteo S.J. 1985. *The True Meaning of the Lord of Heaven (T'ien-chu Shi-i)*, ed. Edward J. Malatesa. Chinese-English Edition. The Institute of Jesuit Resources: St. Louis.

Ro, Young-Chan. 1989. *The Korean Neo-Confucianism of Yi Yulkok*. State University of New York: Albany.

Ross, Andrew C. 1994. *A Vision Betrayed: The Jesuits in Japan and China 1542–1742*. Orbis Books: New York.

Setton, Mark. 1997. *Chŏng Yagyong: Korea's Challenge to Orthodox Neo-Confucianism*. State University of New York Press: Albany.

Shin, Yong-ha. 2000. *Modern Korean History and Nationalism*. Jimoondang Publishing Company: Seoul.

Song, Chu-yong. 1972. "Practical learning of Yi Ik". *Korea Journal*, 12(8): 38–45.

Song, Suk-ku. 1984. "Yulgok's Social Reform Thought". *Korea Journal*, 24(7): 41–50.

Song, Young-bae. 2001. "A Comparative Study of the Paradigms between Tasan's Philosophy and Matteo Ricci's Tianzhu Shiyi". *Korea Journal*, 41(3): 57–99.

Thiébault, Philippe (trans.). 2009. *Anthologie de la Sagesse Extreme-Orientale: Yi Yulgok*. Autres Temps Éditions: Gémenos.

Tu, Weiming. 2004. "T'oegye's Creative Interpretation of Zhu Xi's Philosophy of Principle". *Korean Philosophy: Its Tradition and Modern Transformation*, ed. Korean National Commission for UNESCO. Hollym: Seoul. 75–94.

U, Chŏng-sang. 1983. "Highpriest Hyujŏng". *Main Currents of Korean Thought*, ed. Korean National Commission for UNESCO. Si-sa-o-yong-sa Publishers: Seoul. 39–51.

Wŏn, Yu-han. 1976, "The Monetary Thought of Tasan". *Korea Journal*, 16(10): 41–48.

Yi, Hidok. 1962. "Tasan's Momumental Work". *Korea Journal*, 12(10): 34–35.

5 'Eastern' learning and Protestant Christianity

New religions and a 'Korean' god

Introduction

Though King Chŏngjo had been lenient when dealing with Catholics in the beginning, he was finally forced to take definitive action, especially when Yun Chich'ung and his cousin had replaced Confucian rituals with Catholic ones. When King Chŏngjo died, he was succeeded by Sunjo (1790–1834), who was only 11 years old at that time. The regent appointed for him was the second wife of Yŏngjo, Queen Dowager Kim, known as Queen Chŏngsun (1745–1805). The old 'Noron' faction seized the opportunity opened up by King Chŏngjo's death to expel the Namin and all other challenges to their authority, supported by the Queen Dowager; Catholicism was prohibited almost immediately (Choi 2006: 118–119). The number of Catholics in Korea had risen from 4,000 in 1795 when Zhou Wenmo arrived in Korea, to over 10,000 in 1800, the year King Chŏngjo died. The *Silk Letter* recounted the brutality that was unleashed against Catholics: those who were arrested were initially given a chance to renounce the religion, but if this failed, they were imprisoned, tortured and eventually, if they had not already died of their wounds, executed. Such apostasies cannot be said to reflect the inner beliefs of those who made them: the only alternative was imminent death (Choi 2006: 121; Finch 2009). In Spring of 1801, the Chinese priest, Father Zhou, who had voluntarily surrendered, was then imprisoned and soon executed, as well as Kang Wansuk, the leader of the female Catholics (Choi 2006: 128–132). Upon the execution of Father Zhou, Korea was without a priest again until 1834, and the Koreans themselves continued to propagate the religion. The persecutions of 1801 were followed by further persecutions which lasted for several decades, showing that, though they had gone into hiding, Catholics still practiced in secret, some from influential families. Tasan's nephew, Chŏng Hasang (1795–1839), son of the author of the *Han'gŭl Catechism*, Chŏng Yakchong, was also executed, having written a defence of Catholicism, criticising Confucians for their misunderstanding and ignorance of its doctrines. He and 102 other Catholics were canonised by Pope John Paul II in Seoul in 1984 (Ch'oe *et al.* 2000: 138–140).

'The Great Persecution' between 1866 and 1871, saw up to 8,000 Catholics tortured and executed, including entire families. Among the multitudes that were executed were six French missionaries which initiated a series of 'foreign interferences' as they became known, attempts by the French and the Americans in 1866 to have Korea open itself to the outside world. The Korean government had become quite paranoid, thinking they would be invaded by Westerners, reinforced by the Opium Wars in China during 1839–1842 and 1856–1858. Additionally, the Treaty of Tientsin in 1856 signed with Great Britain, the United States, France and Russia, permitted Christian missionary activities in China, something the Koreans hoped to avoid, especially under the stewardship of the notorious Taewŏn'gun, the title of Yi Ha-ŭng (1820–1898), the regent of Korea, due to the minority of King Kojong (r.1863–1897), who ascended the throne in 1863. The Taewon'gun, as he is usually referred to, was completely xenophobic, of

Figure 5.1 One of the Taewon'gun's 'Anti-Westerner' stone markers

course not without due cause. He had stone markers erected all over the country which read, "Western Barbarians invade our land. If we do not fight them, we must appease them. To urge appeasement is to betray the nation".

Ironically, Korea would soon be forced to sign its first unfair international treaty with Japan in 1876, and from this point it was only a matter of time before Korea became a colony of Japan. Western powers soon followed suit: Great Britain, the United States, France and so on, all signed treaties and soon Protestant Christian missionaries were free to preach in Korea. Soon the chaos of peasant revolts and war between Japan and China brought chaos to Korea, and Koreans sought new ways to protect their own traditions and culture, afraid their identity would be usurped by Western Learning and European aggression. This led to a new movement known as *Tonghak* (東學), meaning 'Eastern Learning', which attempted to help the hopeless poor peasants whose lives were getting progressively worse, especially in the southern regions far from the capital. This new path*way* is examined in this chapter, as well the other new religions which emerged ready to reinvigorate Korea's religious landscape, with visions and messages from a god, that seemed to favour Korea, even descending himself to inaugurate a new era, according to *Chŭngsangyo*. The colonial period imbued these new religions with quite nationalistic overtones, with some Koreans turning towards the Tan'gun myth, redirecting it along a very different 'religious' trajectory. Finally, the early Protestant missionaries and their socio-religious impact on Korean society will be examined, which came after they had decided on their own term for God – in *Han'gŭl*.

Tonghak – 'Eastern' learning

The nineteenth century saw various 'new' religions emerge in China (The Taiping Heavenly Kingdom and Spirit Boxers) and Japan (Kurozumikyō and Tenrikyō), with charismatic leaders who sometimes claimed to receive instruction directly from God. In Korea, the socio-political context inspired a reactionary movement, which placed itself in direct opposition to Western Learning (Sŏhak), and so *Tonghak* was founded by Ch'oe Che-u (1824–1864), known by his followers as Su-un. Choi Dong-bi (1966: 16) states that Ch'oe, like many people at that time had "a sense of hostility towards Western Learning", adding that, quite simply, "He hated Catholicism, which was identified with European aggression in the East". In the Korean context, this link between Catholicism and a European military threat had been implied by Hwang Sayŏng in the *Silk Letter* – he had actually courted European military aid, something the Europeans had no intention of giving. Ch'oe grew up when Catholicism was being spread throughout the peninsula, and its adherents often arrested, tortured and executed. In the countryside where he grew up, Buddhism still had a strong presence, mountains and rivers assured that folk traditions thrived there too, and a belief in the spirits associated with such natural entities, transmitted from Korea's past, enshrined in its myths and folktales. Shamanism, too, was prevalent, and in times of widespread illnesses, *mudangs* would have been consulted for their healing rituals. All these ideas would be reflected in Ch'oe's later teachings. It was a time when the Confucians were gradually losing control of the state and the respect they had been used to. As the *yangban* increased, commoners were decreasing: *chungin* could buy government positions, merchants bought *yangban* status, and slaves could buy their freedom, or at least escape to some new town or city where they could assume a new identity. Genealogical records were creatively crafted and falsified. The citizens of Chosŏn were gradually becoming exasperated by the hierarchical disparities that worked against them. Tasan had already highlighted these inequalities, as had the Catholics who had even dared to free their slaves. As is generally the case, the decline of a culture and the weakening of its state ideology and religious apparatus opens doors for new ideas to emerge to meet the new demands of society.

Ch'oe Che-u suffered first hand as a result of this broken system. Though able to boast of a genealogy which dated back to the famous Silla intellectual Ch'oe Chiwŏn, who himself engaged with several religious and philosophical traditions, Ch'oe Che-u's father, Ch'oe Ok, held no official rank. Ch'oe Ok was aligned with the teachings of T'oegye, which he taught in a local school while living near Kyŏngju, the ancient capital of Silla. Furthermore, as Ch'oe Ok's first wife had no son he adopted a nephew to continue his genealogy: hence, Che-u, who was the son of a third wife who had been a widow (rendering him utterly disadvantaged in Chosŏn), was subject to a meagre inheritance and unable to perform the ancestral rites that his adopted cousin could perform. It is important to point out that men, too, suffered from the Confucian patriarchy that fought so hard to maintain its clearly defined grasp on social order. Though Ch'oe Che-u received a Neo-Confucian education, he was entirely unable to climb the social ladder and so he and his wife fell onto hard times. He spent time moving from place to place, sometimes sojourning at Buddhist temples, engaging in meditation, where he had various spiritual experiences and visions. But, ultimately, he was forced to return to Kyŏngju, to the pavilion he had inherited from his father at Yongdam (which means 'Dragon Pool'), on Mt. Kumi. At this point he changed his name from his birth-name Che-sŏn to Che-u (which translates literally as 'to save the ignorant') while also expounding his spiritual ideas, attracting some followers, foreshadowing his development of a new religion, *Tonghak*, later to be renamed *Ch'ŏndogyo*, the 'Religion of the Heavenly Way' (Kallander 2013: 32–42).

This religion has been described as "the oldest of Korea's 'new' religions" (Weems 1967: 92), and Su-un as "the founder of Korea's first indigenous religion" (Beirne 2009). Baker (2007a: 449) writes that, although Korea had its own indigenous beliefs before *Tonghak/Ch'ŏndogyo*, this was the "oldest indigenous organised religion", with canonical texts and its own rituals. These religious texts were only compiled and printed later by Che-u's successor Ch'oe Sihyŏng (1827–1898), known by the penname Haewŏl, who had apparently memorised his master's teachings by heart, finally writing them down in two collections: *Eastern Scripture* (東經大全, K. *Tonggyŏng Taejŏn*), written in literary Chinese; and *Songs of the Dragon Pool* (영담유사, K. *Yongdam Yusa*), written in *Han'gŭl*. These texts reflect Su-un's own context, having received a Confucian training, hence, writing in the language of the elite, while also writing in the language of the masses he understood and had empathy for, also using the traditional Korean *Kasa* metre in his hymns, something the Catholics had done very early on in theirs. However, Haewŏl would emphasise the Chinese writings, placing them first in the canon, followed by the hymns in *Han'gŭl* (Kallander 2013: 43–44). These texts, along with other writings by Haewŏl himself, and the third leader, Son Pyŏng-hŭi (1861–1922), known as Ŭiam, would be collected and make up the *Ch'ŏndogyo Scriptures* (천도교경전, K. *Ch'ŏnjugyo Kyŏngjŏn*). Haewŏl would even have his own 'Ten Commandments' of things 'not to do to Heaven' (十毋天, K. *Simmuch'ŏn*) (Hong 2015: 120; Kim 1978: 72).

Beirne (2009: 2) highlights Su-un's role as a "religious innovator", who "became the prototype for the founders of Korea's many new religions and religious movement". This new religion was formulated after Ch'oe had a series of revelations from heaven's monotheistic deity, who used different names: (1) *Sangje*, clearly the Confucian 'Lord on High', but more commonly in Ch'oe's central classical Chinese text, (2) *Ch'ŏnju*, the Lord of Heaven, the name used by Catholics for God, and (3) Hanŭllim (한늘님), an honorific Korean term for the ruler of Heaven, and the latter is the most used today by members of this religion (Baker 2007a: 450). Of course, *Ch'ŏnju* was the term Korean Catholics associated with Matteo Ricci's *Catechism*, used by Su-un some 14 times in *Eastern Scripture* (Beirne 2009: 128). Indeed, it was Ricci who had initially suggested that various appellations simply reflected the different traditions' name for God. The Catholic influence on Tonghak has generally been downplayed, and of course Ch'oe criticised Catholicism, despite using its designated name for God, prevalent at the time, which led to the execution of some of his followers, mistaken for being Catholics. This may well be why he wrote a major part of his writings in classical Chinese and incorporated Confucian themes, to appeal to Confucian leaders, and to distance himself from links with Western Learning, which was also distained by the state.

Su-un's encounter with God

Paul Beirne's study (2009: 37–42) points out that Su-un wrote three accounts of his 'encounters' with God, one appearing in the *Songs of the Dragon Pool* and two in the *Eastern Scripture*. Beirne has translated the sections relating to the encounters, meanwhile, the *Eastern Scripture* can be found translated in full in George L. Kallander's text, *Salvation through Dissent: Tonghak Heterodoxy and Early Modern Korea* (2013). The first account in the *Eastern Scripture* appears in the section titled "Spreading Virtue", and the second account is in the following section on "Discussion on Learning" (2013: 157–176). In "Spreading Virtue", Su-un describes men of true virtue, the *kunja*, the Confucian 'gentleman' or distinguished man who became a sage, suggesting it reflected the "principle of heaven", and therefore the "Heavenly Way" (157). He then suggests that recently there has been disorder as people have disobeyed this principle leading to great anxiety. From this point, Su-un then broaches the subject of Catholicism, which he suggests rejected having "wealth and glory" (at least in theory), but which focused on building churches to "promote their Way" (158). This sets up Catholicism as a point of conflict, and then the encounter with God ensues – to clarify that Su-un was not to follow the 'Western Way'. This encounter happened in the fourth [lunar] month of 1860, when Su-un describes how he was beset by an inexplicable illness, where he became cold and his body trembled, when suddenly he heard a voice: "Do not be frightened or afraid. The people in the world call me [*Sangje*]. Do you not recognise [*Sangje*]?". The first point to be made here is that this was the Confucian '*Sangje*', now speaking to Su-un. Why this is curious, is that in the Confucians Classics neither Heaven nor *Sangje* spoke or gave special counsel: Mencius (5A:5) is very clear on that exact point, that heaven does not give detailed and minute instructions, because "Heaven does not speak"! Here Su-un asserts himself as a special chosen intermediary between God, whom he called *Sangje*, and mankind. *Sangje* continues to inform Su-un that he has been "brought into this world to teach the people the correct practices", and when Su-un asks if this is "the Western Way", the reply is a curt "No". From this point on, the *Sangje* of the Confucian tradition, and his adoption by the Catholics who also called him *Ch'ŏnju*, is diverted along an entirely new trajectory, teaching Su-un a new path*way*, to guide, but which must also be practiced. *Sangje* explains to Su-un (158, slightly altered):

> I have a talisman [*yŏngbu/pujŏk*], and it is called the elixir of immortality [*sŏnyak*]. Its shape is that of the Supreme Ultimate [*t'aegŭk*] and the characters *kung*. Receive from me this talisman and save the people from illness. Receive from me this ritual incantation [*chumun*] and instruct the people on my behalf. Then you, too, shall have a long life and shall spread virtue under heaven.

Unfortunately, Su-un did not have a long life and was executed in 1864 for heterodoxy, but before that he had become renowned for his visions and his ability to cure people using the talisman, and for his new ritualistic incantation. The use of a talisman was not something new in East Asia especially among Daoists, nor were incantations, indeed, above what we see are various ideas that blend together Daoist notions of immortality, as well as Shamanistic motifs relating to a spiritual illness that is alleviated when communion with the spirit is made. The use of talismans in Korea can even be traced back to Su-un's ancestor Ch'oe Chiwŏn (Beirne 2009: 70–71). The Supreme Ultimate is from the *Book of Changes*, but its diagram featured as the opening for T'oegye's *Ten Diagrams on Sage Learning*, a text that was prominent during the entire Chosŏn period, and maybe even studied by Su-un. Therefore, this short passage embodies Su-un's very creative adaption of the various religious traditions that he had at his disposal to draw from, to counter the Western Way, which he manages to interlace into a truly original religious brocade. Additionally, as Kallander (80) remarks, Su-un "was careful to secure his preeminent role by claiming to communicate directly with God" and thereby instituting a hierarchy within his new religion from the outset. It should also be noted that in this same section, Su-un writes that it is commanded by the deity "that people be differentiated between the noble and the low", inscribing Confucian hierarchy into his otherwise espousal of equality (161). This also meant that women were supposed to maintain 'proper social relations' and follow Confucian norms by becoming devoted wives (who practiced this new *way*), also producing children and educating them in the home (108–109). These Confucian norms for females were also encouraged by Su-un's eventual successor, Haewŏl, who had specific guidelines for women in his own writings, also advocating "Rules for the Inner Quarters" (Kallander 2013: 195–197).

The talisman and the special incantation were initially two very specific features of this new religion. Su-un further explains that the talisman was supposed to be written out on paper, burned and the ashes then ingested, and that he having done this felt that "it refreshed [his] body and dispelled [his] illness" and that then he realised this could grant immortality. This could be used on other people, but would only alleviate the illness of those who were faithful to *Ch'ŏnju* – though practice has disappeared from the religion (Beirne 2009: 39). This introduces the concept of 'belief' in God as one of the tenets of the religion, an idea that is not generally found in East Asian traditions, unimportant for Buddhists, Daoists and Confucians, but which is of course central to Catholicism. Here, too, it is important to note the use of the Catholic term for God, which Su-un had assumed into his religion, now supplementing it with particular Korean ideas that had currency in his socio-religious landscape, where he attempted to provide security to the masses. In his "Discussion on Learning" (Kallander 2013: 159) Su-un mentions the nine states of ancient China, which is mentioned in the *Classic of History*, as well as yin and yang, and the eight trigrams, again channelling his knowledge of East Asia's religious and philosophical traditions. He is also, once again, critical of Westerners and their technology, which he suggests they only use for destructive purposes, such as war. He does not mention any '*Sirhak*' trends or scholars belonging to a '*Sirhak'pa*' or faction, as a way of counterbalancing the claims of Western technological superiority. As mentioned before, that simply was not even a subject of discussion until later, when Korea had fallen under brutal Japanese control.

In Su-un's second classical Chinese account (159–162) of his encounter with God, this time referred to as the Spiritual Being (or *Kwisin*) in the "Discussion on Learning" section in the *Eastern Scripture*, he again recalls his strange feeling just as the Divine Spirit descended into him, again reminiscent of Shaman spirit possession. This is also similar to the *Han'gŭl* account of Su-un's encounter with "*Sangje*" in the "Song of Reassurance" from the *Songs of the Dragon Pool*, which depicts his wife and children present as witnesses to his Shamanesque 'ecstasy', followed by details of how he then received instructions for the talisman: writing that he consumed thousands of them over several months, regaining his strength and vigour, suggesting that he had become an immortal. However, the second account in the *Eastern Scripture* has some very significant details, as Su-un hears a voice tell him that "my heart is your heart". This is a potent statement and distinguishes this God from the Catholic God, *Ch'ŏnju*, and the distant *Sangje* of the Confucian tradition – now God is an all penetrating spiritual entity, or 'Ultimate Energy' (至氣, K. *Chiki*) as it is described in the incantations (discussed below), that is attuned to (wo)mankind's heart, and so the place to seek this deity is inside oneself. This is definitely a transformation from the previous encounter, and is described by Beirne (2009: 59) as reflective of the "egalitarian nature of the Tonghak religion", where treating each other as God was a way to serve God, suggesting that humans and their deity share the same heart, or emotional psycho-spiritual connection at the deepest level. The idea of serving heaven and serving (or bearing) each other as Heaven was taken up by the next two leaders of the religion after Su-un had been executed.

Firstly, Haewŏl, in his *Discussions on the Teachings* [of Su-un] (with selections translated in Kallander 2013: 189–197), wrote that "People are Heaven, so to serve people is to serve Heaven", developing Su-un's idea that humans should "serve *Ch'ŏnju*". Beirne (2009: 159) goes so far as to add that "Haewol's entire theological/philosophical/ethical theory is outlined" in this single sentence. Secondly, this idea by Haewŏl is taken yet another step in the writings of the third patriarch of Tonghak, Ŭiam, who eventually changed the name of the religion to *Ch'ŏndogyo* (the Religion of the Way of Heaven). Ŭiam's teaching was that "Man is Heaven" (人乃天, K. *in-nae ch'ŏn*), though I prefer to use the gender neutral term, a person is Heaven, as the character '人' is unbiased and does not refer simply to men. This expression is also often written as "[Wo]Man is God", discussed, for example, by Kim (1978) and Beirne (2009) (as well as numerous others scholars), but the term used is Heaven, '天' (K. *Ch'ŏn*), and if Ŭiam had wanted to choose a term for an actual anthropomorphic deity he had many to choose from (in *Han'gŭl* and *Hanmun*) – he did not – instead choosing a more pantheistic and fluid term, Heaven, after which he renamed the religion. Kim (1978: 31) describes this as "the heart of Ch'ondogyo belief [which] expresses the fundamental monism of Ch'ŏndogyo in regard to man and his relation to God [Heaven]".

Also important to note at this point is the preparation required for rev-elations, as Su-un announced that he "cultivated [his] heart and corrected [his] life force" (守心正氣, K. *susim chŏnggi*) (Kallander 2013: 160). The phrase is described in more detail in the section on "Cultivating Virtue" and linked with the Confucian virtues of Humaneness, righteousness, propriety and wisdom (163–166). This critical phrase, which represents an avenue for sagehood in what Su-un refers to as "My Way", distinguishing it from other path*ways*, has been translated by Kim (1978: 98) as "keeping mind and having right energy", linking the bifocal feature of 'self-cultivation' highlighted throughout this book: thought and action. *Susim* literally means "guarding the mind", and so preserving its inherent goodness, or enlighten-ment from a Buddhist point of view, or its good nature for the Confucians, but here linking the mind with the mind of God, whose ultimate energy per-vades it, from Su-un's point of view. *Chŏnggi*, the second part of the phrase, emphasises correcting one's '*ki*', an idea that reflects T'oegye's view on the Four-Seven debate, as *ki*, the material force, can be either good or bad, and shape our external interactions with each other, though here it could be translated as 'spiritual energy'. Su-un also describes his new path*way* in quite Daoist language, noting that it "arises spontaneously, without any action" echoing Laozi's famous image of "*wu-wei*" (non-action) in the Dao De Ching, discussed in Chapter 1. This is a new guide for a 'new' form of sagehood provided by Su-un, who has brought together a new understand-ing of several Korean and East Asian metaphysical interpretations, emblem-atic of his eclectic metaphysical ingenuity, which adds philosophical depth to his religious ideas.

Nevertheless, it was Haewŏl and Ŭiam who drew together Su-un's teach-ings, organising them into a specific religious canon and emphasising the main doctrines for adherents who would also celebrate on a Sunday, like Christians. Charles Allen Clark (1961: 156) also noted how "the interior of their churches resembles very much the Christian churches with a ros-trum and pulpit", a feature that would be adopted by other new religions, including Wŏn Buddhism, discussed in the next chapter. Clark (159–160) also outlines the "Five Things Required of All Believers", described by Kim (1978: 100–102) as the "Five Rules of Practice", (五款, K, *Ogwan*).

The Five Rules of Practice of Ch'ŏndogyo

1 Incantation (呪文, K. *Chumun*): Repetition of the incantation that Su-un received from God serves to open the mind of the believer to the 'Ultimate Energy' (*Chigi*) and their union with the 'Lord of Heaven', using the term used by Catholics in Korea at the time. The incantation is in two parts:

   i   Ultimate Energy here and now, I pray for its great descent.
   ii Serving *Ch'ŏnju*, I am transformed to follow the divine will. Eter-nally not forgetting, I become aware of all.*

2 Sincerity Rice (誠米, K. *Sŏngmi*): This is an offering made to the Church at the end of the month by putting some rice aside at each meal as a sign of one's faith and belief.

3 Clear Water (淸水, K. *Chŏngsu*): An offering of pure water is placed in a bowl at all Ch'ŏndogyo ceremonies and acts as a symbol of the purity one should aspire to achieve for one's heart. Practitioners should observe this every day at 9 pm with their families along with prayer, and at all services.

4 Keeping the Day of Service (侍日, K. *Siil*). This aims at creating a community of followers who meet on Sundays to hear the doctrine and to renew their commitment to their faith. It includes prayers, sermons and hymns, similar to a Christian service.

5 Prayer (祈禱, K. *Kido*): As followers believe that Heaven is in their hearts, prayer is generally silent, known as the *Simgo* (心告) or Heart Address, to focus on the divine presence within themselves.

* there are variations included in the *Eastern Scriptures* (see: Kallander 2013: 168).

Tonghak and the peasant rebellion of 1894

Many adherents of the Tonghak religion became actively involved in peasant uprisings in the rural, underdeveloped areas where the teachings were first spread, hoping to bring about great change in their country, where they felt disenfranchised. Su-un (in the *Song of Reassurance*) had used the term '*Kaebyŏk*' (開闢) to refer to a new time of 'creation' after his encounter with God, which also made him consider his nation, distancing it from China. This term would also be important in other religions that would develop on the Korean peninsula during this time, and this new creation, described by Beirne (2009: 145) as "the beginning of a new era for humankind", would have Korea at the centre, as the leader of a new world order. Interestingly, in this particular '*kasa*', Su-un is greatly critical of the Japanese, recalling the damage they did to Korea during the Hideyoshi invasions during the late sixteenth century. He writes that the current times, too, are "dark and threatening" and how he would be created again by God to destroy the Japanese troops, clearly envisaging them as a viable and serious threat, and ironically, followers drawn to his ideas would come into open conflict with Japanese troops on Korean soil, and as almost prophetic, it would be the Japanese who would colonise Korea, not Western powers as was feared by the xenophobic Taewŏn'gun and other members of the government (Kallander 2013: 182–186). Su-un had already been arrested in 1862, and though he was released, his use of a mysterious talisman, curing illnesses and teachings on serving 'Ch'ŏnju' the Lord of Heaven, had caught the attention of the government already intent upon destroying Catholicism, itself accused of magic and perverse teachings. When Su-un was arrested again in 1863, he portrayed himself as a nationalist trying to protect Korea from the Western-ers through his teachings. Even this could not save him. He was tortured and executed, but his ideas had inspired many in the Southwest, especially the poor, including slaves.

Soon Korea was forced to open up after initial failed attempts by the Americans and French in 1866 had failed had signed international treaties, firstly with Japan (1876), and then with Western countries such as the United States (1882), Russia (1884) and France (1886). Japan's Meiji government had become increasingly aggressive towards Korea, but many Koreans were going to Japan to study its progressive ideas, as Korea developed its own 'enlightenment thought', known as '*Kaehwa sasang*'. During this period, Tonghak ideas had spread and some figures with it were more militant in nature, such as Yi P'ilche (1824–1871), who was eventually captured and beheaded, the same fate as thousands of Catholics. By 1880, Haewŏl had already started compiling Tonghak doctrine, while also petitioning for his master's posthumous pardon by the state, referring to their country as one that had its origins with "Tan'gun and Kija", though Su-un himself referred only to Kija – Korea's identity was clearly under threat and this recourse back to the Tan'gun myth would emerge at a growing pace.

Indeed, due to foreign pressure, religious persecutions had become extremely lax by the 1890s, and the numbers of Tonghak followers appears to have been in the tens of thousands, mainly in the southern provinces from Kyŏngsang in the East to Chŏlla in the West. Peasants were becoming emboldened, tired of local corruption, oppression and mistreatment, even-tually being led by figures such as Chŏn Pongjun (1855–1895), who drew in Tonghak support, instigating several uprisings, taking over major cities such as Chŏnju, while defeating the government's own troops stationed in those areas. When things seemed to get out of control, Chinese and Japa-nese troops were brought in to bring the quell the situation and after the Tonghak Rebellion (as it became known) was over, China and Japan would seek supremacy over Korea leading to the Sino-Japanese War (1894–1895), which Japan won. Haewŏl was initially at odds with Chŏn Pongjun over the use of armed resistance, promoting a more passive approach. Eventually, he hesitantly sent troops to join in the Tonghak uprising, and only when he thought that the religion itself was in danger due to the brutality of Japa-nese troops who suppressed his followers. He ended up being executed as a result of his involvement in the Tonghak rebellion (Beirne 2009: 176–177). With Japan victorious over China, it was only a matter of time before they started to make plans to take total control of Korea. With 'Tonghak' linked to rebellion, it was clearly a motivating factor behind Ŭiam's decision to change the name of the religion to Ch'ŏndogyo in 1905, mentioned previ-ously. Ch'ŏndogyo's membership would grow, as would its influence, espe-cially for Korea's independence movement. (For further historical details on this period see Kallander 2013: ch. 4; Beirne 2009: ch. 9; Shin 1978–1979; Ch'oe 1973).

Figure 5.2 Ch'ŏndogyo main temple in Seoul

One of the political effects of the Tonghak rebellion was the implementation of the Kabo reforms in 1894, which were considered an attempt at modern reforms, and which led to the "dismantling of the Confucian order", and eventually Korea's historically close, but subservient relationship with China (Park 2015: 42). This also opened up a space for new modes of spirituality, including the further development of Ch'ŏndogyo itself, as well as the other religions discussed in the rest of this chapter. The threat to Korean identity was taken very seriously, especially with the Sino-Japanese War bringing disaster to the Korean peninsula, as well as a deepening sense of doom, menacing Korean sovereignty. New religions emerging in this context of antagonism and antipathy would draw upon the nationalistic currents of the time, that sought to continue the work of overturning feudal Korea and its corrupt government, prompting many millenarian aspects, hoping to usher in a new world order. Some would draw on Tonghak ideas, such as Chǔngsando, while others again would create very different path*ways*, like Taejonggyo. But, at the same time, Catholic and, more so, Protestant missionaries, started to arrive in great numbers into Korea, also hoping to take advantage of the changed socio-political situation to spread their own ideas, which many were willing to listen to at a time when chaos surrounded them.

Chǔngsando (Jeungsando): a Korean *Sangje*-incarnate

The founder of the Chǔngsan tradition (which now has different branches) was someone who witnessed the Tonghak rebellion, as well as the failed predictions of Su-un to revitalise Korea as it entered into a new period of creation, or *kaebyŏk*, discussed previously; hence, this is another millenarian religion in essence. Kang Ilsun (1871–1909), known as Chǔngsan (also written Jeungsan), as well as Chǔngsan Sangje, who had been acquainted with Confucian, Buddhist, Daoist and Shamanic ideas, had an avid interest in occult works. After a stay in a Buddhist temple he had an awakening, which meant that he could predict the future, cure illness, soon declaring himself as the Honoured Lord on High – *Sangje-nim* – where 'nim' is simply a Korean honorific form added to the end of *Sangje*. Of course, *Sangje* had been used by the Catholics, but also by the Protestants in Korea at that time as one of the names for their creator God. It was also used along with *Ch'ŏnju* and *Hanŭllim* in the writings of Su-un to refer to God. Kang took the name in a different direction by stating that he himself was *Sangjenim*, Lord of the Nine Heavens who had descended "to teach human beings how to prepare for the Great Transformation" (Baker 2007b: 488). This refers to the *kaebyŏk* that Su-un had failed to usher in. It should be remembered that Matteo Ricci had described *Sangje* as becoming incarnate as a human being to spread his teachings on earth before he returned to heaven – similar to the story Kang's followers believed. But, here, the Creator God of the Universe, as Kang was also referred to in the first scriptures of the religion dating from 1926, was a Korean (Grayson 2002: 206). Hence, this Great Transformation was going to place Korea at the centre of the new era he was going to usher in, a paradise on earth. It also places God as the creator of the universe, diverging from the East Asian metaphysical traditions, such as Principle, the Supreme Ultimate, 'spontaneous arising', and so on.

As James Grayson (2002) points out, this religion was not particularly influential until the 1990s when there was a revival of interest in it, and it now has an important web presence, with its entire sacred texts called the *Dojeon* (or *Tojŏn*) '도전' (meaning 'Transmitting the Dao') translated into English, as well as a substantial amount of information about the religions, its masters and teachings (jeungsando.org). On its homepage it describes itself as "the traditional culture of Eastern Meditation [. . .] the true Eastern Learning", adding that it "is promoting the cultural movement to recover the lost history and culture of Korea" (2002). The use of the term Eastern Learning is interesting, at it is the meaning of 'Tonghak', and its nationalistic goals are quite obvious. The wife of the founder, Ko Pallye, is recognised as its second leader, and was known as '*Taemonim*', or Great Mother, after whom the leadership then passed down to An Unsan who founded a movement to spread the teachings of *Sangjenim* and *Taemonim* called 'Jeung San Do' (which is how they spell the name of their religion in English), and who was then assisted by An Kyŏngjŏn since 1974.

The *Dojeon* was first published in 1992 as the official scriptures of the religion founded by Chŭngsan, and it contains 11 chapters. The first chapter discusses the advent of *Sangjenim*'s descent [into Chŭngsan], and it is linked in with various accounts from various traditions: Christianity, Buddhism, Daoism, even Ch'ŏndogyo, suggesting that all these traditions foretold the coming of *Sangjenim*. It also opens using the term "*Samsin*" or Three Gods, but emphasising it is the one creative God of the universe – a unified Trinitarian God, in the Christian sense. In Chapter 2, verse 20, which discusses the *kaebyŏk* and the Way of the Spirits, Chŭngsan writes that he first descended in the West and then travelled the world before arriving in the East at the Maitreya statue at Kŭm-sa temple, before being born into the Kang family. Here, we see that the founder of the religion gained an overview of the world before being born in Korea to initiate the Great Transformation, hoping to bring together East and West. There is an important section in the same chapter dedicated to none other than – Matteo Ricci (*Dojeon*, ch. 2: 26):

1   Matteo Ricci contributed much to the world. In this age of the resolution of bitterness and grief, he is the head spirit in the spirit world. Those who know this should speak of him with reverence.
2   Yet, people are unaware because he benefited the world inconspicuously.
3   Matteo Ricci, a Westerner, came to the East and offered many ideas for building heaven on earth. His ideals were not actualised because he was unable to correct all the corrupt practices entrenched over the ages;
4   but he did succeed in bridging the boundaries between the East and West, which enabled the spirits of different regions to cross borders unhindered.

This shows the knowledge that the leader had of Ricci's ideas and that he saw him as a cultural pioneer, holding him in great esteem, unlike scholars such as Yi Sugwang, Sin Hudam or An Chŏngbok. It also shows the enduring legacy of Ricci's ideas in this later context, something that has been underplayed and blatantly ignored at times. The other chapters outline details of the history of the religion and its development, but also its main theological and moral values, along with random details, such as when *Sangjenim* quit smoking! (ch. 5, verse 31). Certain parts also provide practical advice, such as ch. 9 on "Blessings, Wealth and Longevity", which has sections on: how to earn your own meal, and how to be clear in financial dealings. Ch. 9 (verse 23) also contains accounts of *Sangjenim*'s healing miracles, which are shamanistic in one sense, but also similar to the miracles of Jesus in the bible, where he could heal with his words, or by laying hands on people, noting that *Sangjenim* "also eliminated evil and cast out demons according to the situation, thereby curing the sick and even bringing the dead back to life". Ch. 10 (verse 1) predicts *Sangjenim*'s ascent to heaven: "I will ascend to heaven to unfold the work of renewal and quicken it. Do not wait for Me. I will return when the work of renewal is complete there". The final chapter is entirely dedicated to *Taemonim*, the 'Mother of All', who "conducted the work of renewing heaven and earth [. . .] thus atoning for humanity's transgression and all bitterness and grief, guiding the world's people to the path of a new life", again not dissimilar to the role of Jesus and the atonement of sin. This important role of *Taemonim*, a woman atoning for humanity's sins is ground breaking, but more so, a woman creating a new guiding moralistic path*way*, rejects the misogynistic bigotry of the Confucian men who only revered male sages, sequestering women to the female quarters, also advised later by Haewŏl in his sermons on Ch'ŏndogyo. This was a radical break in Korea's feudal system and really reflected the times that were calling for women to be liberated from the yoke of subservience that had been placed on them.

Along with the Dojeon, there are several other ideas highlighted on the 'Jeungsando' website under 'teachings' as integral to the religion (jeungsando.org):

1 The Cosmic Year: This recognises time as cyclical, and each cosmic year is made up of 129,600 calendar years. It describes Early Heaven as the cosmic spring and summer, while the Later Heaven is made up of the cosmic autumn and winter. It highlights that *Sangjenim*'s descent coincides with the transition between the time of the Summer-Autumn transition to the period of the Latter Heaven

2 The Autumn *Kaebyŏk*: This is described as the cosmic time's harvest period, the most important time of the cosmic year and this *kaebyŏk* is central to the teaching of the religion – a time of "Glorious Renewal", but when "cataclysmic change will sweep across the world: natural disasters will strike the world, and the lethal qi [ki] of all the unresolved

bitterness and grief in the human and spirit worlds will cause a great war and a mysterious disease that will nearly completely obliterate humanity". This is reminiscent of images from the 'Book of Revelation' in the *Bible*. *Sangjenim* has descended as he was petitioned by the spirits of sages and spiritual beings, Buddhas and so on.

3   *Ch'ŏnji kongsa* (also *Cheongjigongsa*, 天地公事): Meaning the Work of Renewing Heaven and Earth, this is described as the mission of *Sangjenim*, and to usher in a new time on earth free from disease and tribulations, a union of humans and spirits, when the Paradise of Immortality would be realised in the Later Heaven.

4   The Three Tribulations: The Autumn *kaebyŏk* will be accompanied by three 'tribulations: (1) global war; (2) global disease; (3) a pole shift leading "spawning massive upheavals on land and sea".

5   Salvation at the time of *Kaebyŏk*: Practitioners of the religion will help those afflicted during the period of tribulations using "*Ŭitong*", a combination of *ŭi* (醫), meaning medicine, and *tong* (統), meaning unification, hence humanity will be saved and united when the mysterious disease appears during the Autumn *Kaebyŏk*.

6   The Medicine of Life: This is based on the '*Taeŭlju* mantra', a prayer to heaven and earth given by *Sangjenim* to humanity, used in conjunction with *Ŭitong*, it will be able to "heal mind, body and spirit".

7   The Paradise of Immortality: Those who survive the *kaebyŏk* will be a part of the construction of this earthly paradise of "harmony, enlightenment, and ageless longevity", when all people shall live in "mutual life-bettering" relationships, known as "*sangsaeng*", from *sang* (相) meaning mutual and *saeng* (生) which means life.

The overall picture is a holistic one, bringing together the spiritual and human realms, but ultimately recognising the special place of humans in the universe, and the religion suggests that "humans will, in truth, become the most majestic beings in the universe, and thus this epoch will be known as the era of Humanity's Nobility". This is a very anthropocentric religion, where the ultimate end is not God, but humanity, and whereby humanity can realise a heaven on earth, ultimately by unifying – poignant ideas on a now divided Korean peninsula, and in a world where war and suffering is widespread. These ideas would be adapted by another branch based on the teachings of Kang Chŭngsan, known as Daesoon Jinrihoe (with written variations of Daesun Jinrihoe and Taesŏn Chillihoe).

Daesoon Jinrihoe

This branch of Chŭngsangyo, as Baker (2007b: 488) points out, developed from the teachings of Cho Ch'ŏlche (1895–1958), also known as Jo Jeongsan, someone who had never actually met Kang Chŭngsan, but had a vision of him in 1917, leading him to found a religious branch of his teachings known as T'aegŭkto, or The Way of the Supreme Ultimate. Leadership eventually passed to Pak Hangyŏng (1917–1979), also referred to as Park Wudang within the religion. It also has a modern and very comprehensive website in English (http://eng.idaesoon.or.kr/), which is dedicated to 'The Supreme God of the Ninth Heaven', '*Kukch'ŏn Sangje*', Kang Chŭngsan, described as an omniscient and omnipotent God, again drawing on the God of the Christian tradition. The Daesoon Jinrihoe is engaged in a comprehensive outreach programme, in the areas of charity aid, social welfare and education, described on the website as "Three Major Societal Works". This was probably motivated by the social projects of the Protestant Churches in Korea during this period, discussed later in this chapter, especially charity, notably missing from the Confucian canon.

The teachings of the Church are comprehensive and well-organised. It has a precise set of Five Precepts that adherents should follow: (1) Do not deceive yourself, (2) Practice virtuous speech, (3) Do not provoke grievances or grudges from others, (4) Do not disregard the beneficence bestowed upon you by others, (5) Promote the benefit of others. These precepts are aligned with the idea of '*sangsaeng*' or mutual life-bettering relationships, mentioned in the previous section, with the hope of creating a paradise on earth, blending ideas from different religious traditions. Its 'Ethical Rules' bring together the Confucian Relationships linked to the laws of the nation, requiring members to be active moral citizens: (1) You should obey national laws and observe the moral standards for the benefit of your country, (2) Practice The Three Bonds and Five Relationships, where devotion to the king has been replaced with devotion to the nation. The main book of scripture is called the *Chŏn'gyŏng* (典經), or Canonical Scriptures, and it also has several books and magazines available in English on its website. Its temples are more traditional and resemble Buddhist temples rather than the 'churches' of Ch'ŏndogyo, and communal rituals are performed in the temple sanctuary every Wednesday and Sunday, while individuals can perform rituals at their own home altar.

The main doctrines of the religion can be summarised as follows:

The doctrines of Daesoon Jinrihoe

The Four Articles of Faith

Virtuous Concordance of Yin and Yang to resolve conflicts,
Harmonious Union between Divine Beings and Human Beings,
Resolution of Grievances for Mutual Beneficence,
Enlightenment and Perfected Unification with the Dao

The Four Cardinal Mottos

Quieting the mind, Quieting the body, Reverence for Heaven and Spiritual Cultivation.

The Three Cardinal Virtues

Sincerity, Respectfulness and Faithfulness.

See: http://eng.idaesoon.or.kr/app/en/teachings/doctrines

While Chŭngsangyo and Daesoon Jinrihoe drew on terms for God from the Chinese and Western traditions, a much more nationalistic new religion would emerge in 1909, just before the colonisation of Korea by Japan in 1910, that would be based on the Myth of Tan'gun, discussed in Chapter 1 of this book. This new religion, Taejonggyo, the 'Religion of the Great Ancestor', would catapult Tan'gun into the forefront of the Korean psyche, a move which also constituted a challenge to religions and ideas that did not originate in Korea.

Taejonggyo (Daejongism): the return of Tan'gun

From the late 1800s, especially after the Sino-Japanese War, it was clear that Japan sought complete domination over the Korean peninsula and its people. Before the official date of annexation, the Korean people were seeking strategies to maintain their independence. Destroying the Yŏngŭn-mun, or Yŏngŭn Gate, where for centuries they had paid tribute to China, was a deeply symbolic move, noting the end of the unequal relationship that Korea had with China. Protestant missionaries were spreading their faith all over the peninsula, eventually pleading to their own countries to help Korea avoid complete absorption by the Japanese, which seemed only a matter of time as the Russo-Japanese war in 1904–1905 saw Japan as victorious once again. In fact, Frederick Arthur McKenzie already published *The Tragedy of Korea* in 1908, pointing out that the Japanese sought to destroy "every trace of Korean nationality" (McKenzie 1908: 145). The Japanese had been drawing on their own myth of their Sun Goddess, Amaterasu, to consolidate their re-visioning of Shintō, which highlighted the divinity of their emperor, who was cast as a direct descendent of the Sun Goddess. In this context, Na Chŏl (1863–1916), an anti-Japanese activist and low ranked scholar-official, who had spent time in Japan, founded Tan'gun'gyo (the Religion of Tan'gun), soon renamed as Taejonggyo, the religion of the great ancestor, in 1909, a year before Korea's official annexation. Na boasted that "all Koreans were descendants of Tan'gun, the 'imperial ancestor' (*taehwangjo*대황조/大皇祖) and 'heavenly ancestor' (*ch'ŏnjo*천조/天祖)" (Jorgensen 2018: 283). In more recent times this idea has been bolstered in the peninsular collective consciousness as the National Foundation Day (celebrated on October 3), a major holiday shared by both North and South Korea, is designated as the day when Tan'gun founded the ancient state of Kojosŏn in 2333 BCE. South Korea even used that date to create its own alternative calendar system, known as Tan'gi (the Tan'gun era), used from the 1940s to the 1960s (286).

Na Chŏl mainly based his ideas on a text known as the *Pronouncements of the Triune God* (삼일신고/三一神誥, K. *Sam'il sin'go*), regarded as the Taejonggyo Bible, according to the religion's website. Na had received these teachings from an earlier worshipper of the 'Korean' trinity, Paek Pong (d.u.), to whom they were 'revealed' after praying to heaven – in a cave on Mount Paektu, today in North Korea (Jorgensen 2018: 289). The religion also draws on other texts, such as *The Record of Divine Events* (神事記, K. *Sinsagi*) among others, which have been collected and published together as the *Taejonggyo Scriptures* (대종교경전, K. *Taejonggyo kyŏngjŏn*). The religion centred on the Tan'gun Myth and through a creative elaboration attempted to counter the 'Trinity' of Christianity (which was rapidly gaining growing numbers of adherents), with what the early followers of this religion asserted to be Korea's 'original' deity, which they suggested was also triune by nature: Hwanin, the Lord of Heaven, his (secondary) son Hwanung and Tan'gun himself. In fact, An Ho-sang (1963: 9), a subsequent leader of the religion, even argued that this is the religion that Tan'gun himself actually founded, describing him as "the Father, Teacher and King of the Korean people". This highlights the grand nationalistic narrative that has been constructed in Korea in modern times in regards to Tan'gun. The myth had never been used in the way Na proposed, and indeed had not been used in the other new religions which emerged during this period, discussed in this chapter. Na recast the main dramatis personae of the myth as Hwanin, God the Creator/Father; Hwanung, God the Educator; and Tan'gun as God the Ruler, later reinforced by An Ho-sang (1963: 12–13), who discusses the "Trinity of Han-eul", or Heaven, even relating it to Korean history and Korean life. Readers should note that this reinterpretation, whilst triune, is not Trinitarian in the Christian sense, where the three persons in God were consubstantial with each other, an idea elaborated in the *Han'gŭl Catechism* of Chŏng Yakchong, Tasan's elder brother. The earliest extant recounting of the myth in Iryŏn's *Legends and History of the Three Kingdoms*, does not indicate that the three figures in the tale were worshipped – remember Tan'gun finally became a Mountain God – not 'God the Ruler', though he did rule his kingdom until he was forced out and replaced by Kija (who was Chinese!). The Confucians who had rejected Catholicism (for several centuries) never made any link between its God and some 'indigenous' Korean triune entity, or Tan'gun, but they did relate it to *Sangje* of the Confucian Classics. Furthermore, the Korean Catholics who were trying to convert

Koreans, did not make such a tenuous link, nor use any 'indigenous' Korean term for a monotheistic God.

However, this inventive recalibration allowed Na to create a new religion that was deeply nationalistic, and which sought to counter attempts by the Japanese to undermine and destroy Korea's traditional cultural heritage, as well as threats by Christianity to usurp Korea's traditional religious path-*ways*. Taejonggyo attempted to tap into Korea's rich cultural legacy and proposed "Three Rules for *Self-Cultivation*": (1) Control your emotions: listing six emotions as happiness, fear, sadness, greed, anger and hate (recall the Seven Feelings discussed by Neo-Confucian scholars: joy, anger, sadness, fear, love, dislike and liking); (2) Control your breathing: drawing on techniques similar to those of the Buddhists and Daoists (which even led to an offshoot known as Tanhak, with a special focus on breathing exercises related to one's *ki* energy); (3) Control sensory distractions: this requires adherents to bow to Tan'gun and recite a mantra/prayer to their triune God, but also encourages members from indulging in sex and alcohol, and to remove negative thoughts from their mind (embroidering together ideas from Christianity, Confucianism and Buddhism) (see: Baker 2007c; Jorgensen 2018: 286–287). Additionally, the main day of worship or reverence is Sunday, when members of the religion attend their closest '*Ch'ŏn'gung*' ('Heavenly' Temple), where they pray and sing hymns to God.

In 1994, An Ch'angbŏm (in Baker 2007c: 470–475) wrote a critical essay called "Christians have no right to call their God 'Hananim'", which presents the Taejonggyo case against Christians for having misappropriated, what he posits as, the original Korean term for God – though their scriptures generally refers to God as *Hanŏllim* (한얼님). The article describes the God of the Jewish people as jealous and violent, adding that he is therefore immoral, also adding that Christians deny "the unique Korean characteristics of Hananim", hereby drawing Hananim into a nationalistic diatribe against foreign religious practices. The article also notes that Hananim was a Korean term reserved for the three figures from the Myth of Tan'gun, described as "the same God" – this term was not used in the myth. Additionally, only Tan'gun was considered the 'progenitor' of the Korean people, not Hwanin or Hwanung. Indeed, Koreans, for hundreds of years, especially elite Confucians (including Tasan), mentioned Kija as the founder of the ancient Korean state Koguryŏ, and as the figure who brought culture to its people, and while some writers did mention Tan'gun, they did not discuss him as a triune God linked with Hwanin and Hwanung (Cawley 2016). Even the writings of Su-un, referred back to the time of Kija – not Tan'gun – as Kija was considered a real person, unlike Tan'gun, a character in a 'myth'. Haewŏl, though, did mention Tan'gun, as by that time the myth was clearly making a comeback on the back of a new national discourse, perpetuated by nationalistic historians.

This deeply nationalistic article states that the Christians in Korea ignored Korean history and traditions, instead, suggesting they only "teach the history, philosophy, and religion of another race, the people of Judea", which is very inaccurate, as the next part of this chapter clarifies. It links this xenophobic religious attack to the Japanese, suggesting they did the same as the Christians, "by teaching Japanese history, philosophy and religion" (Baker 2007c: 471). There is also mention of the "distinctive racial identity" of Koreans, which has been weakened because the Christians use the Korean term for God, which "threaten[s] the very existence of Koreans as a separate people". The article continues to critique Christians, accusing them of being collaborators with the Japanese, adding that there were never as many Christian Independence fighters as there were "followers of Korea's indigenous religions", suggesting that there were "quite a few Christians" who were pro-Japanese. The facts are scarce, the hatred of Christians palpable. Then there is mention of filial piety, remarking that Christians deny it, seemingly oblivious to the fact that the first Christian commandment after those relating to God, is to honour one's parents. Historically Koreans did not 'worship' the Tan'gun myth trio as one God, or as their original ancestor. Ironically, the Christians in Korea, dating back to the Catholics who first wrote texts to explain Christian God in *Han'gŭl*, described God as their "original ancestor", suggesting this was the God (and Father) of *all* people – not just Koreans, but Na was interested in creating a narrative about a unique and homogenous 'Korean' race with its own specific trinity that was not a salient feature of any of the traditions outlined in this book. In 'The Archaeology of the Ethnically Homogenous Nation-State and Multiculturalism in Korea', Han Kyung-Koo (2007) is wary about descriptions of Korea "as a racially homogenous state with a uniquely homogenous culture and population [. . .] but also that they [Koreans] are descendants of a common ancestor – Tan'gun". This idea gained currency in early modern Korea and was sometimes used to counter the growing influence of Christians, religiously, but also socially and politically. But, what was the role of the Christian missionaries who arrived at the end of the nineteenth century and how did they interact with the Korean people at that time?

Early Protestantism and the name(s) for God

As the end of the Chosŏn dynasty drew near, Protestant missionaries would enter Korea, and make their mark on its modern development. While the Jesuits had appealed to the Confucian elite through their impressive knowledge of the sciences and cartography, the Protestants would engage with the poorer people by focusing on 'modern' education for men and women, and encouraging the use the modern medicine and technology. During the late nineteenth century and early twentieth century, Koreans, looking for a way to deal with the national trauma of pending colonisation, were attracted to this 'different' form of Christianity, which seemed to relate more to the poorer people and appeared more socially oriented. By this stage the Catholics had mass in Latin, and with the predominantly 'foreign' male clergy in control of the affairs of the Church, and the role of women had greatly diminished. As Park (2015: 38) points out, soon after their arrival, the Protestant churches had "built and infrastructure of churches and economic, social and cultural institutions [. . .] at a time when people sought meanings for changes produced by Japanese colonialism".

Protestant missionaries had made a few attempts to enter Korea before the 1880s, but they may well have heard about the fate of the thousands of Catholics who perished, and bided their time, waiting for signs of change. There were a few notable prior interactions. Firstly, Karl A.F. Gützlaff (1803–1851), who was a German Lutheran, travelled as an interpreter for the East India Company along the western coast of Korea, where he encountered some Koreans to whom he gave Christian literature. But, at a time when Catholics were swiftly beheaded, the Koreans were weary of his Christian literature in Chinese. Secondly, a young Welshman by the name of Robert Jermain Thomas (1839–1866) had the misfortune to be aboard the US merchant ship, the 'General Sherman', during what became known as the American disturbance of 1866, as the ship made its way to P'yŏngyang – before it was attacked and burned – having knowingly, illegally trespassed into Korean waters. It appears that the young member of the London Missionary Society had attempted to distribute some copies of the New Testament in Chinese, when he jumped overboard and made it to shore, before his death (Kim & Kim 2015: 55).

However, one figure stands out during this initial preparatory Protestant phase: a Scottish man, Rev. Dr John Ross (1842–1915), a bilingual English/Scots Gaelic speaker, who became a missionary of the United Presbyterian Church. Ross was eventually based in Manchuria, under the supervision of another Scot, Alexander Williamson, an influential figure from the National Bible Society of Scotland, and its first official representative in China. David Kim (2015: 53–54) draws attention to the unique role of the Scottish mission, highlighting that its "influence on the Christianisation of the Korean peninsula (Hanbando) was more exceptional as it offered the foundational literary sources to the post-1885s Christian workers", and in particular, John Ross. The interest in translating the Christian message into Korean, and of having Koreans involved in the leadership of the Church from an early stage, which Ross initiated, was influenced by the Nevius Plan, based on the ideas of the American Presbyterian missionary, Dr John L. Nevius (1829–1893), who was also based in China. Nevius sought to create churches which were run by the native people in order to assure the spread of the religion by locals, rather than 'Westerners', as this would assure a more rapid spread of ideas in the people's own language and would avoid any missionary 'linguistic' mishaps (think back to Francis Xavier in Japan who unwittingly used a Buddhist term for God!). This method advocated churches that were "self-propagating, self-supporting and self-governing" (Kim & Kim 2015: 56). Ross, hoping to convert Koreans in Manchuria whom he met at the 'Corean Gate', started to learn Korean from a merchant named Lee Ŭng-chan and then compiled the first Korean grammar in English in 1877, known as the *Corean Primer*, followed by a history of Korea in English in 1879. This was followed by *Korean Speech, with Grammar and Vocabulary* in 1882. In 1880, Ross (quoted in Kim 2015: 55; emphasis added) described 'Corean' in a letter:

> The Corean alphabet is phonetic, and so beautifully simple that all men, women, and children of years of understanding can read it; for being phonetic it is necessary only to learn the alphabet to be able to read any book printed in that alphabet. *The importance of the Bible translation into such a language of from 12 to 15 million people cannot be over-estimated.*

While the first part of this quote may be read as a eulogy for the scholars who created the alphabet under the guidance of King Sejong the Great, the second part reflected the main goal of Ross, and his ultimate mission: to translate the Bible into Korean, in order to convert the people of the peninsula.

Ross worked tirelessly on the translation of the bible along with Koreans who helped him, shaping its language and use of religious terminology. The Gospels of John and Luke were translated in 1882, with the entire *New Testament* translated by 1887. The most important word that appeared in these editions was the word Ross chose for God – suggested to him by his Korean friends and translators. Initially, in the 1882 text, Ross used the *Han' gŭl* term *Hanŭllim* for God (also one of the terms used by Tonghak/Ch'ŏndogyo). Writing in 1880, Ross (in Kim 2015: 60) suggested that there were two names for use for God in Korea: one of Chinese origin, *Shangdi*, and another one which was 'Corean', *Hanŭllim*, the term he chose, adding that the term "is so distinctive and so universally used, there will be no fear, in future translations and preachings [. . .] even though the Romanists have introduced the name which they employ in China [*Tianzhu/Ch'ŏnju*]". Interestingly, by 1883 when the Gospels of Luke and John were reprinted, Ross chose the term *Hananim* (하나님) – joining '*Hana*', meaning 'one', with the honorific marker '*nim*', hence, 'The Great One'. Had Ross finally heard from his Korean friends that *Hannullim* was in current usage among a growing rival religion, Tonghak? Or had they explained that there were, in fact, more than just two names for God in the Korean tradition, another one which was *Hananim*? Or, were these dialectical variations? Whatever his reason, this latter term, *Hananim*, was generally accepted by the missionaries who arrived in Korea just after this time (also see: Baker 2002). Hong Sung-wook (2008) investigates this process of choosing the term for God in detail in *Naming God in Korea: The Case of Protestant Christianity*. In particular, he (99) notes the importance of Ross's designated term that other missionaries adopted, adding that:

> This decision was very significant for the history of the Korean Protestantism [. . .]. Firstly, it was a valuable and meaningful decision to choose

the Korean indigenous term formed in folk beliefs for 'God' because they recognised that there was continuity between indigenous religions and Christianity, at least so far as the concept of God is concerned. Furthermore, it provided a valuable lesson in theological contextualisation.

Oak Sung-deuk (2013: 49–74) also discusses translations of some of the books from the New Testament made by in Japan by a Korean, Lee Sujǒng, who had been baptised there. He used a transliteration of one of the Chinese terms for a god or spirit '神' (C. *shen*, K. *sin*, J. *kami*), which was not generally used by later Korean Protestants. Ross's Bible was smuggled across the border and distributed in Korea by Koreans who eventually drew others to the religion and who eventually sought baptism from Ross himself. Some of the early Korean converts founded one of the earliest Protestant communities at the village of Sorae in Hwanghae Province, founded by two brothers. It appears that Korean Protestants would spread the faith before missionaries had the chance to do so (Kim & Kim 2015: 59).

Protestant missions to Korea: education and *Bible Women*

Before long Protestant missionaries would arrive in Korea to convert the Koreans, emboldened by the backing and protection of their governments, which had signed treaties with Korea. Dr Horace Allen (1858–1932) arrived in Seoul in 1884, dispatched by the Presbyterian Church in the United States, acting as a physician to foreign residents there, and introducing Western medical techniques. After a few months of Allen's arrival, members of Korea's reform-minded 'Enlightenment' party, the *Kaehwa-dang*, which was led to believe it had the support of the Japanese, led a failed coup d'état, known as the Kapsin coup. Allen tended to Empress Min's nephew, Min Yǒng-ik, who had been injured on the night of the coup, and by the following year, permission had been granted by King Kojong to build the first modern hospital in Korea, eventually training doctors, it became the Severance Hospital Medical School, opened in 1904 (Kim & Kim 2015: 62; Kim 1999: 209). In this atmosphere, Confucianism was also under attack. Reform-minded thinkers such as Kim Okkyun (1851–1894), pushed for the reform of Chosǒn's "political, economic and social institutions", as did others such as Yu Kiljun (1856–1914), who "emphasised the need for national sovereignty [. . .] rights to self-protection, independence, property protection, creating one's own laws" (Keum 2004: 406–407). At the same time many of these scholars were critical of Confucianism, describing it as "hypocritical", with Shin Ch'aeho (1880–1936), an important nationalist historian and independence activist, criticising the Neo-Confucian elite who sought wealth and power, merely 'imitating' sages, while scholars got caught up in trivial matters (such as metaphysics), but not dealing with social issues (407). Park Ǔnsik (1859–1925), also a historian and deeply involved in the independence movement, criticised "the depravities of Confucian literati [who] neglected their social responsibility", which had been a major Confucian critique of the Buddhists (408). However, some reform-minded Confucians did emerge during the latter Chosŏn period, such as Ch'oe Han'gi (1803–1879), who did not fear the adoption of Western sciences, and who was willing to reframe traditional Confucianism to some degree, while focusing on the 'philosophy of experience', sometimes compared to British Empiricism (Chang 2012). However, as Kallander (2013: 30) points out, Ch'oe suggested that both Catholicism and Islam were derived from Buddhism, and that Islam was a 'European' religion, showing the "gaps in Korean awareness of foreign religions", with Ch'oe further writing that "the things outside [the three bonds and five relations] are all cults . . . the West spreads their religion throughout the world, but do not worry. It is not practical to use". In the end his ideas were not enough to cater for the epistemic transformation of Korea that arrived soon after this death, and his ideas did not provide a meaningful way to improve the social conditions of the poor. Social issues were something the Presbyterians and Methodists sought to redress – and they were, contrary to Ch'oe's assumptions, very practical.

In 1885, the head of the Presbyterian mission, Horace Grant Underwood (1859–1916), arrived in Korea, with the head of the Methodist mission, Henry Gerhard Appenzeller (1858–1902), having travelled together from Japan. With many Koreans already looking for ways to ameliorate their lives, and with indigenous religious embracing a millenarian attitude, membership grew at a rapid pace, but the access to education provided in the new emerging school system organised by the missionaries surely had a great appeal, especially to poorer families whose children had very different futures opened to them. Appenzeller and the Methodists, who had opened a woman's hospital, soon opened the first Christian school in Korea between 1886 and 1887, called the Paejae Boys' High School, soon followed by Ewha Girls' High School (now a leading women's university), both in Seoul. Underwood, who married Dr Lilias Horton (1851–1921), also a missionary, would also set up the Chosun Christian College, today known as Yonsei University, one of the top universities in the Republic of Korea. Another Presbyterian missionary, James S. Gale (1863–1937), this time from Canada, also set up schools in Korea, and established the YMCA with Underwood in 1900. In 1890, the first mission of the Anglican Church arrived in Korea under the leadership of its Bishop, Charles John Corfe (1843–1921), and soon set up hospitals and schools, like the other Christian missions, though not growing with as much success in term of numbers of converts (Kim 2013). By this time the Orthodox Church had established a mission in Seoul, which would soon grow, and produce their own Korean deacons and priests (Kim & Kim 2015: 110). Gale and other missionaries formed a board of Bible translators, and he published his own Korean-English dictionary in 1897. Gale also published the first translation into Korean of a work of Western literature, *Pilgrim's Progress* by John Bunyan in 1895 – also, the first Western text published solely in *Han'gŭl*, without

Chinese characters, the norm in Korea now, but only in recent decades (68–70; Grayson 2002: 157). Gale worked on other translations of Western novels into Korean, influencing the development of modern Korean literature, and writers such as Lee Kwang-su (1892–1950), whose novel *The Heartless* (무정, K. *Mujŏng*) is considered the first modern Korean novel. Many of these missionaries also gathered and published academic essays on various topics related to Korean history, religions, the Korean people and their language, in *The Korean Review* and *The Korean Repository*. Additionally, many of them produced books, which informed Westerners about Korea, such as: *Things Korean,* by Allen, *The Call of Korea,* by Underwood, and *Korean Sketches* and *History of the Korean People,* by Gale. Lillias Horton Underwood (c.1904) also penned *Fifteen Years among the Topknots*, referring to the hairstyle of Korean men at the time, before they were ordered to cut off their top knots by the Japanese. Though, many of the accounts of Korea's religious traditions were overly simplistic, sometimes crude and often demeaning, especially in regards to Shamanism and Buddhism, many of them discussed Tan'gun (as a myth), which had regained its importance for Koreans.

Nevertheless, some of the missionaries had grown particularly fond of Korea and were deeply critical of Japan's Protectorate Treaty of 1905, especially Homer Hulbert (1863–1949), who had been in Korea since 1886, initially an employee at the Korean government school, becoming a Methodist

Figure 5.3 (left) Methodist missionary Rev. Henry Gerhard Appenzeller and (right) Rev. Choi Byŏnghŏn, one of the first Korean Methodist pastors, both at Chungdong First Methodist Church, Seoul

missionary only later. He knew the other missionaries discussed above, and was also involved in editing *The Korean Review* and *The Korean Repository*. He published *The Passing of Korea* in 1906, in an attempt to draw attention to Koreans' plight vis-à-vis the Japanese. He dedicated it to the King and the Korean people. Hulbert, who was close to King Kojong, even went to the peace conference at the Hague in 1907 with some Koreans on a diplomatic mission this time, to plead Korea's case, but was not permitted entry as Japan was participating in the talks, as they were concerned with the Russo-Japanese War (Kim & Kim 2015: 92). In the preface to *The Passing of Korea* (quoted in: Park 2012: 89–90), Hulbert was keen to point out America's role in the tragedy that had befallen the Korean people, through inaction and by effectively siding with the Japanese:

> This book is a labour of love, undertaken in the days of Korea's distress, with the purpose of interesting the reading public in a country and a people that have been frequently maligned and seldom appreciated. The American public has been persistently told that the Korean people are a degenerate and contemptible nation, incapable of better things, intellectually inferior, and better off under Japanese rule than independent. The following pages may answer these charges, which have been put forth for a specific purpose, – a purpose that came to full fruition on the night of November 17, 1905, when at the point of the sword, Korea was forced to acquiesce "voluntarily" in the virtual destruction of her independence once for all. The reader will here find a narrative of the course of events which led up to this crisis, and the part that different powers, including the United States, played in the tragedy.

Hulbert may have been indirectly commenting on the image of Korea relayed by books such as William E. Griffis *Corea: The Hermit Nation* (1882), which was generally criticised "as being inaccurate, negative, one-sided, Western, colonial, and (perhaps worst of all) pro-Japanese", written by a man who had never even been to Korea, and who was a friend of some of Japan's leading figures (88). The irony of some of the negative assertions about Koreans in relation to the Japanese was that, as mentioned earlier in this book, the Koreans had brought Chinese characters, Confucianism, Buddhism and Daoism to the Japanese, who had been considered barbarians by both the Chinese and the Koreans. Zen Buddhism, today associated with Japan, of course originated in China and first passed into Korea; the same for Neo-Confucianism. Soon the missionaries were not seen as part of an elaborate scheme to take control of Korea, many were critical of the Japanese, and in a short period of time managed to draw thousands into the Church, and many of these Koreans would have important roles in the struggle for independence.

Ryu Dae-young (2008: 392) notes that one of the key features of missionary work in Korea at this time was "Bible Training Classes", and furthermore, suggests that "the scriptures were, in fact, the single most important contributor to the birth and growth of the Korean Church", where Korean Christianity was even known as "Bible Christianity". This undoubtedly was, to a large degree, due to the spread of the scriptures in *Han'gŭl*, something emphasised in the schools which were starting to open. Women were an important part of this movement, and an important female missionary, deserving of special recognition, is Mary F. Scranton (1832– 1909), the first missionary of the Women's Foreign Missionary Society of the Methodist Episcopal Church, and the founder of Ewha girls' school (Lee 1993: 185–204). Her son, Dr William B. Scranton, had been the first Methodist physician in Korea, arriving there in 1884.

Mary F. Scranton had initiated the Bible Woman System in 1888, which consisted of Korean women who became known as *chŏndo puin* (傳道夫人), literally meaning, wives who transmitted [and lectured on] the *way*: but this was a new 'Christian' path*way*, with very different teachings. These women often travelled all over Korea, especially to remote villages to spread Christianity at a time when hopelessness must have been pervasive. Ironically, the missionary women would have been considered conservative in their home countries (many of them American), but they were considered 'modern' women by Korean women who were still yoked into a patriarchal Confucian-oriented system, which would soon be overthrown. Most missionaries in Korea between 1884 and 1910 were women who held Victorian ideals that also saw men and women as having different purposes in life, and better suited to different realms, but they did open up their Korean counterparts to new ideas and beliefs, which clearly interested them (Choi 2009). This transcultural encounter must have been as fascinating for the Western missionary women as it was for the Korean women who let them into their homes, and into their inner female quarters, the *anbang*. This also makes the important role of the women of the Catholic Church in the late eighteenth century all the more extraordinary as they worked entirely off their own initiative, with no female missionaries to inspire or guide them.

Lee-Ellen Strawn (2012) describes the "Korean Bible Women's Success" in her article of that title, highlighting the use of the *anbang* network, which also, interestingly, started to occupy a space that had hitherto belonged to the *mudang*, the Korean shaman. Strawn (117) elucidates how the Protestant missionary women inevitably ended up "borrowing the accepted female *mudang*'s religious authority in that sphere [anbang], coherently merging traditional women's practices and perspectives with modern Protestant views regarding women and their roles in society". Whereas the *mudang* had been chosen by the spirits after their 'spiritual illness' in the case of non-hereditary *mudang*, the Bible Women themselves, through their own volition, chose to accept the 'Holy Spirit' and shared it with other women, for free, helping their sisters and their children, providing a network of support, especially for those in difficult circumstances, practicing charity. Strawn (118) notes how faith bound these women together, who were often marginalised as they did not measure up to Confucian norms which rejected their female agency, and could not have envisaged their role as interpreters and translators, educators, or as a powerful evangelising force:

> Initially, these women were middle-aged to older women unencumbered by familial and household responsibilities. This meant that these women were often socially and/or economically marginalized as they might have been widows or previously shamans or kisaeng, female entertainers. Not all Bible Women came to their work from dramatic situations, but most experienced difficult life tribulations that their faith pulled them through, such as severe abuse by husband and mother-in-law, and were now able to share these experiences of overcoming difficulty through faith in order to empower other women in the faith.

Eager to overcome hardship, these women took matters into their own hands, despite being faced with hostility, from the men in their own families, as well as those they encountered on their travels. These women initiated the movement for the modernisation for the women of Korea themselves, as they spread education at the same time as they spread the 'Good News' (Chou 1995). This new path*way* coupled self-cultivation with social transformation, encouraging women, men and children to become involved and "to make progress rather than accept the status in life determined by birth" (Kim & Kim 2015: 82). In this sense, Protestantism was much more radical than Catholicism in the Korean context, which, suffering from the trauma of extensive persecutions was much more willing to accept the status quo and to remain out of trouble.

Progressive and influential men started to convert to Protestantism, who would also be involved in Korea's Independence movement, responsible for the first modern Korean newspaper 'The Independent Newspaper' (K. *Tongnip simmun*), which used only *Han'gŭl* (just like Scarth's translation into Korean). They also founded an important political association the 'Independence Club', in 1896, with key figures such as: Yi Sang-je (1850–1927), Yun Ch'iho (1865–1945), Syngman Rhee (1875–1965), elected first President of the Republic of Korea in 1948, and Sŏ Chaep'il (1866–1951), also known as Philip Jaisohn, the first Korean who actually became an American citizen. Many of these men would be imprisoned, where they were visited by missionaries such as Gale, and some converted to Christianity there. Like many others, some would be forced to leave Korea, and the fortunate ones, like those named above, studied in and worked abroad in the United States and would remain actively engaged in Korean politics until they died. Some of them, like Yun Ch'iho, would also be influenced by Social Darwinism, calling for Koreans to strengthen their own country, also drawing on the Protestant work ethic and the social responsibility in the 'social' gospel, clearly unimpressed with the route Korea had been taken along by the way Confucianism was used in his society (for more on Social Darwinism in

Korea, see: Tikhonov 2010). Churches and ministers encouraged Koreans to develop and improve the Korean economy, and to improve the conditions of all its people, and the Independent Club encouraged "self-reliance" to assure that independence could be preserved, an idea that would feature heavily in the political ideology of North Korea, discussed in the next chapter. Sin Yong-ha (2004: 438) outlines the important changes that the Independence Club proposed, including: "elimination of early marriage [. . .] the eradication of concubines and kisaeng, [. . .] the elimination of superstition and divination, the end of geomancy [. . .], the prohibition of gambling". Many of the goals of the Independence Club, and some of those linked with Social Darwinism, also echoed the ideas of the growing Protestant Church in Korea at that time.

Church growth was rapid, mostly down to the hard work and faith of Koreans themselves, proving the Nevius Method worked well. The Korean ministers were active and brought their own ideas to their churches, such as Kil Sŏnju, an elder of the Presbyterian Church in Pyŏngyang, who organised prayers on the mountains, preaching against smoking and drinking. Kil also introduced 'Dawn Prayer' to his Church in Pyŏngyang, now a common feature of Korean Christian churches. In fact, the growth of Christianity was so impressive in Pyŏngyang, it was referred to as the "Jerusalem of the East' and the centre of the revival movement" (Kim & Kim 2015: 85). Revivalism had been a feature of North American Protestantism during the nineteenth century and clearly influenced the missionary strategy in Korea, holding church meetings while making impressive sermons, calling for people to follow the Church's teachings, to look after each other and to ask for forgiveness. This touched a nerve in Korea at a time when people were living in distress. Timothy Lee (2010: 24–25) writes that "the great revival of 1907 was a paradigmatic event for the Korean Protestant Church, a breakthrough in which the Church became grounded in the worldview and ethos of evangelisation" adding that it gave Koreans "the basis for a new normative order and a fulfilling way to orient themselves towards the sacred". These revival meetings encouraged Koreans to explore and express their religious and emotional awakenings for themselves – they did not need a shaman to help them encounter 'the holy spirit', they could do that for themselves, irrespective of gender and age. During the revival in Pyŏngyang, Hong Sung-wook (2008: 81–82) notes that "audiences were stung in their consciences [. . .] many people were alleged to experience 'manifestations of the Holy Spirit' and to feel God's presence", and that "this movement gave the Korean Church a vivid and vigorous experience of the Christian faith, which became the distinctive feature of the Korean Church". As churches grew in numbers, so did Christian schools, and also by 1907, there were twice as many students in these schools than in those run by the actual government, thereby, educating entirely new generation of Koreans in Christian ethos. In 1900 there were under 40,000 Protestant converts in Korea, but by 1910 there were almost 180,000; outnumbering the Catholics who numbered around 75,000, but that came nowhere near the followers of the then recently renamed *Tonghak* religion, *Ch'ŏndogyo* with around 750,000 followers (Lee 2010: 31).

Conclusion

Tonghak emerged in the late nineteenth century as the population sought new ways to deal with the socio-political situation, seeking counter-measures to the influence of Western ideas and the spread of Catholicism. After the revelations of Su-un from God – a god who could be referred to by different names, *Sangje, Ch'ŏnju* and *Hanŭllim* – he brought together different traditions into a new holistic path*way* that Koreans were keen to follow, especially those in more rural areas where life was more difficult and there they felt abandoned and disenchanted by the government, which was growing weaker. Haewŏl and Ŭiam built upon the foundations laid by Su-un and also transformed the idea of God revealed to their master, by bringing it closer to the individual, where God was no longer some distant deity, but one who resided in their hearts, where the Ultimate Energy was to be found and used to transform themselves and their society, along with the talisman and special incantations.

Other religious figures emerged in this atmosphere, able to find a new place among the many religious and philosophical traditions that had shaped the peninsula for centuries. Chŭngsando, clearly drawing on the Christian tradition, presented *Sangje* as an incarnation of their divine God, this time a Korean, Kang Ilsun, who declared himself the Lord of the Nine Heavens, who was able to cure disease and even raise the dead, just like Jesus in the Bible. His authority was then passed down to his wife, *Taemonim*, the Great Mother, showing the more gender-balanced views espoused by the religion, which overturned Confucian norms. Gaining a following much later, its scriptural texts were collected in the Dojeon, and its followers prepared for a new age, or *kaebyŏk*, where paradise would be a place on earth, realising the union of (wo)man and the spirit world, the fulfilment of the 'Work of Renewing Heaven and Earth'. These teachings would also inspire the Daesoon Jinrihoe, another branch of the religion, which also considered Kang Ilsun as *Sangje* incarnate. Veering away from terms that had origins in Chinese traditions, and definitely eschewing Western influences, Taejonggyo was deeply rooted in Korean nationalistic discourse, triggered by Japan's threat to Korean sovereignty and identity. Taejonggyo re-engaged with the myth of Tan'gun, representing the three male characters in the tale as a uniquely 'Korean' Triune Deity.

The growth of Protestantism reflected the changing times, where Christians had greater freedom to spread their ideas in Korea, drawing huge numbers of new adherents to its more socially engaged teachings, who were also impressed by the schools and medical facilities that they opened up, further eroding Confucian ideas, and quickly overtaking Korea's Catholic

Church in size. Missionaries such as Ross immediately sought to translate the Bible into Korean, and the Bible Women, *chŏndo puin*, helped this evangelising work, as they spread the teachings in their countrywomen's *anbang*, an 'inner space' that they would share and sometimes compete with the *mudang*. The revival movement spread ideas around the country where churches were very quickly governed by Korean ministers, thanks to the Nevius Method embraced by Protestant missionaries. As the annexation treaty was signed in 1910, Koreans felt disheartened, but refused to give up their struggle for independence, which would soon bring Buddhists, Christians and members of Ch'ŏndogyo together to protest the plight of Koreans under Japanese Rule. Soon the Buddhists, whose power had waned for several hundred years, sought to reassert themselves and their religion by reconnecting with the Korean people, and they were willing to draw on lessons for growth provided by the Western missionaries themselves, discussed in the next chapter, along with more modern developments and unforeseen path*ways*, due to a divided peninsula.

References and further reading

An, Ho-sang. 1963. "Dae-Jong-gyo: Religion of God and Human Being". *Korea Journal*, 3(5): 9–13.

Bae, Hang-Seob. 2013. "Foundations for the Legitimation of the Tonghak Peasant Army and Awareness of a New Political Order". *Acta Koreana*, 16(2): 399–430.

Baker, Don. 2002. "Hananim, Hanŭnim, Hannullim, and Hanŏllim: The Construction of Terminology for Korean Monotheism". *The Review of Korean Studies*, 5(1): 105–131.

———. 2007a. "The Great Transformation: Religious Practice in Ch'ŏndogyo". *Religions of Korea in Practice*, ed. Robert E. Buswell Jr. Princeton University Press: Princeton, NJ. 449–463.

———. 2007b. "Renewing Heaven and Earth: Spiritual Discipline in Chŭngsan'gyo". *Religions of Korea in Practice*, ed. Robert E. Buswell Jr. Princeton University Press: Princeton, NJ. 487–496.

———. 2007c. "The Korean God Is Not the Christian God: Taejonggyo's Challenge to Foreign Religions". *Religions of Korea in Practice*, ed. Robert E. Buswell Jr. Princeton University Press: Princeton, NJ. 464–475.

Beirne, Paul. 2009. *Su-un and His Word of Symbols: The Founder of Korea's First Indigenous Religion*. Ashgate: Farnham.

Cawley, Kevin N. 2016. "Back to the Future: Recalibrating the Myth of Korea's Homogenous Ethnicity". *Asian Ethnicity*, 17(1): 150–160.

Chang Wonsuk. 2012. "Ch'oe Han'gi's Confucian Philosophy of Experience: New Names for Old Ways of Thinking". *Philosophy East and West*, 62(2): 186–196.

Ch'oe, Tong-Hŭi.1973. "Tonghak Thought and Modernization (I and II)". *Korea Journal*, 13(10): 4–9 and 13(11): 31–36.

Ch'oe, Yŏngho, Peter H. Lee and Wm Theodore De Bary. 2000. *Sources of the Korean Tradition: From the Sixteenth to the Twentieth Century*. Columbia University Press: Columbia. Chapters 27–31.

Choi, Dong-bi. 1966. "Tonghak Movement and Chundo-gyo". *Korea Journal*, 3(5): 14–19.

Choi, Haewol. 2009. *Gender and Mission Encounters in Korea: New Women, Old Ways*. University of California Press: Berkeley and Los Angeles.

Choi, Jai-keun. 2006. *The Origin of the Roman Catholic Church in Korea*. The Hermit Kingdom Press: Seoul. Chapters 3–5.

Ch'ŏndogyo English Website. Available at: www.chondogyo.or.kr/niabbs4/bbs.php?bbstable=chuneng&categori11=4 [accessed on 13 June 2018].

Chou, Fan-lan. 1995. "Bible Women and the Development of Education in the Korean Church". *Perspectives on Christianity in Korea and Japan*, eds. Mark R. Mullins and Richard Fox Young. Edwin Mellen Press: Lewiston. 29–45.

Clark, Charles A. 1961. *Religions of Old Korea*. The Christian Literature Society of Korea: Seoul.

Daesoon Jinrihoe English Website. Available at: http://eng.idaesoon.or.kr/ [accessed on 13 June 2018].

Finch, Andrew. 2009. "The Pursuit of Martyrdom in the Catholic Church in Korea before 1866". *The Journal of Ecclesiastical History*, 60(1): 95–118.

Grayson, James H. 2002. *Korea: A Religious History*. Revised Edition. Routledge Curzon: New York.

Griffis, William E. 1882. *Corea: The Hermit Nation*. W. H. Allen & Co: London. Available at: https://archive.org/details/coreahermitnati02grifgoog/page/n9 [accessed on 16 Dec. 2018].

Han, Kyung-koo. 2007. "The Archaeology of the Ethnically Homogeneous Nation-State and Multiculturalism in Korea". *Korea Journal*, 47(4): 8–31.

Hong, Sung-wook. 2008. *Naming God in Korea: The Case of Protestant Christianity*. Regnum Books International: Oxford.

Hong, Yong-hee. 2015. "Values in the Global Age and the Life Spiritualism of Donghak". *Korea Journal*, 55(3): 103–134.

Dojeon. English translation available at: www.jsd.or.kr/dojeon/readen.php?c=dojeonen [accessed on 13 June 2018].

Jeungsando English Website. Available at: www.jeungsando.org/ [accessed on 13 June 2018].

Jorgensen, John. 2018. "Taejonggyo". *Handbook of East Asian New Religious Movements*, eds. Lukas Pokorny and Franz Winter. Brill: Leiden. 279–300.

Kallander, George L. 2013. *Salvation Through Dissent: Tonghak Heterodoxy and Early Modern Korea*. University of Hawai'i Press: Honolulu.

Keum, Jang-tae. 2004. "Human Liberation in Early Modern Korean Thought". *Korean Philosophy: Its Tradition and Modern Transformation*, ed. Korean National Commission for UNESCO. Hollym: Seoul. 399–419.

Kim, David W. 2015. "From Manchuria to the Korean Peninsula: The Scottish Impact in Late Nineteenth Century Korea". *Religious Transformation in Modern Asia*, ed. David W. Kim. Brill: Leiden. 50–76.

Kim, Sean C. 2013. "Via Media in the Land of the Morning Calm: The Anglican Church in Korea". *The Journal of Korean Religions*, 4(1): 71–98.

Kim, Sebastian C.H. and Kim Kirsteen. 2015. *A History of Korean Christianity*. Cambridge University Press: Cambridge.

Kim, Yong Choon. 1978. *The Ch'ondogyo Concept of Man: An Essence of Korean Thought*. Pan Korea Book Corporation: Seoul.

Kim, Yunseong. 1999. "Protestant Missions as Cultural Imperialism in Early Modern Korea: Hegemony and Its Discontents". *Korea Journal*, 39(4): 205–234.

Lee, Kwang-rin. 1986. "The Rise of Nationalism in Korea". *Korean Studies*, 10: 1–12.

Lee, Kyung-Lim Shin. 1993. "Sisters in Christ: American Women Missionaries in Ewha Women's University". *Spirituality and Social Responsibility: Vocational Vision of Women in the United Methodist Tradition*, ed. Rosemary Skinner Keller. Abingdon Press: Nashville. 185–204.

Lee, Timothy S. 2010. *Born Again: Evangelism in Korea*. University of Hawai'i Press: Honolulu. Chapter 1.

Mc Kenzie, Frederick A. 1908. *The Tragedy of Korea*. Hodder: London. Available at: https://archive.org/stream/tragedyofkorea00mckeuoft/tragedyofkorea00mckeuoft_djvu.txt [accessed on 13 June 2018].

Oak, Sung-Deuk. 2013. *The Making of Korean Christianity: Protestant Encounters with Korean Religions 1876–1915*. Baylor University Press: Waco.

Park, Albert L. 2015. *Building Heaven on Earth: Religion, Activism, and Protest in Japanese Occupied Korea*. University of Hawai'i Press: Honolulu.

Park, Hwan. 2003. "Na Chŏl and the Characteristics of His National Movement". *International Journal of Korean History*, 3: 225–254.

Park, Hyung Jin. 2012. "Heroes and Villains in the Historiography of Missions: A Korean Sketch". *Torch Trinity Journal*, 15(1): 86–110.

Ryu Dae-young. 2008. "The Origin and Characteristics of Evangelical Protestantism in Korea at the Turn of the Twentieth Century". *Church History*, 77(2): 371–398.

Shin, Susan S. 1978–79. "The Tonghak Movement: From Enlightenment to Revolution". *Korean Studies Forum*, 5: 1–79.

Shin, Yong-ha. 2004. "The Social Thought of the Independence Club". *Korean Philosophy: Its Tradition and Modern Transformation*, ed. Korean National Commission for UNESCO. Hollym: Seoul. 421–439.

Strawn, Lee-Ellen. 2012. "Korean Bible Women's Success: Using the "Anbang" Network and the Religious Authority of the Mudang". *Journal of Korean Religions*, 3(1): 117–149.

Tikhonov, Vladimir. 2010. *Social Darwinism and Nationalism in Korea*. Brill: Leiden

Weems, Benjamin. 1967. "Ch'ŏndo-gyo Enters its Second Century". *Transactions* 43. Royal Asiatic Society (Korea Branch): Seoul. 92–100.

6 Korea's complex modernity

Buddhist renewals, post-Christianities, Juche and Shamanism

Introduction

By the late nineteenth century Korea was in threat of extinction, due to Japan's colonial ambitions, which grew steadily. In 1895, the Japanese orchestrated the murder of Queen Min. The following year, the king fled to the Russian legation in Seoul, and after remaining there until 1897, he returned to his nearby palace (known today as Deoksugung/Tŏksugung, opposite the City Hall in Seoul) announcing that the era of Chosŏn would be replaced by the 'Great Han Empire', putting Korea on an equal standing with Japan, but more symbolically, with China. Things got increasingly worse for Korea after Japan waged successful wars against China and Russia, but especially after the Protectorate Treaty of November 17, 1905, which meant that Korea's international relations were controlled by Japan. The treaty, which was issued through force, though signed by several members of the Korean government, was not signed by the Korean 'Emperor' Kojong, who was soon deposed in 1907, making way for the short-lived reign of his much weaker son, Emperor Sunjong (r.1907–1910). Ito Hirobumi (1841–1909) became the first Resident-General of Korea, the highest level representative of Japan in Korea. He was assassinated in Harbin, China, on October 26, 1909 – by An Chunggŭn (1878–1910) – a Korean Catholic. Different nationalists with different religions (or none) would also be drawn into the bloody side of Japanese aggression in Korea, just as was the case in Ireland under the British at this very time, producing its own patriotic 'Catholic' martyrs. But, Korea's fate seemed sealed when the Korea-Japan Treaty of Annexation was signed on August 22, 1910 by the Korean Prime Minister Yi Wan-yong, and proclaimed to the Korean people on August 29, after Emperor Sunjong abdicated, having refused to sign the coerced treaty. As Andrew Nahm (1996: 223) poignantly stresses, the Korean people "lost not only their national independence, but also their lands, their rights, and every aspect of their lives came under the control of the Japanese rules and regulations".

Religious groups sought to counteract the Japanese influence, leading to the growth of newer religions, as discussed in the previous chapter. Soon the

Buddhists would attempt to reclaim their place, with scholar monks such as Han Yongun (1879–1944), who witnessed the Tonghak rebellion first hand, calling for the reformation and revitalisation of Korean Buddhism, which would soon be under threat by the privileged place of Japanese Buddhism under colonial law, examined in this chapter. This new engagement of the Buddhist community would see the emergence of new forms of Buddhism, particularly successful among these, Wǒn Buddhism, which would be affected (consciously or not) by the social activities of the Christian churches. This chapter also outlines the growth of certain religions Post-Liberation in 1945, and in the aftermath of the horrific Korean War (1950–53) which saw millions lose their lives, and the country's infrastructure almost completely destroyed. In South Korea, Christianity would continue to grow, both Protestant and Catholic churches: though Protestants in South Korea *do not* consider Catholics to be Christians!

There would also emerge some new 'Korean' offshoots to traditional Christianity, such as the Olive Tree Church (*Chŏndogwan*), but most significantly, the Unification Church (*T'ongilgyo*), one of the most successful missionary churches of modern Korea, with a particularly significant presence in Japan and the United States, among other countries. To the North of the peninsula, isolated from the southern part and from the rest of the world, Kim Il-sung would wield together a creative synthesis of Maxism-Leninism, known as Juche (Chuch'e), a philosophy of 'self-reliance', which still holds sway over North Koreans as its state philosophy, that has incorporated the veneration of the cult of personality of its 'Dear Leader'. Meanwhile, down south, in urban and rural areas, Korea's religious and philosophical traditions, new and old continue to meet and interact in a vibrant pastiche, where Shamanism continues to maintain an important place (and space), adapting to the needs of its modern clientele, outlined in the final section of this chapter.

The Buddhist renewal: *from destruction to revitalisation*

With a growing body of research on Korea being undertaken by Westerners in Korea, particularly Christian missionaries, Buddhism was looked on unfavourably by new converts, and often described in outdated and condescending terms in lectures and books catering for foreigners. This is clear in Charles Allen Clark's, *Religions of Old Korea*, published in 1961, but based on lectures dating from the 1920s, which considered Buddhism to be close to extinct:

> Buddha's sun seems to be setting in Korea. Korea owes it a debt of gratitude [. . .] vastly superior to the degraded spirit worship and Shamanism [. . .]. As the sun of Buddhism sets, it should be a joy to all lovers of Korea that a greater Sun of Righteousness has arisen [. . .] a Saviour more real than Amida.
>
> (Clark 1961: 89)

This description, which many missionaries would have agreed with at the time, makes the resurgence of Buddhism in Modern Korea all the more impressive. Ironically, the proscription on the practice of Buddhism was removed in 1895 due to increased pressure from Japanese Buddhist groups who had come to Korea after the 1876 treaty between the two countries, when growing numbers of Japanese began to live in Korea, among them monks from the Higashi Honganji denomination, that preached Pure Land Buddhism, and which itself had been persecuted in Japan during the Meiji Restoration, but also missionaries of the famous Nichiren school, devoted to the Lotus Sutra, like the Tiantai school in China; Ch'ŏntae in Korea (Kim 2014: 149–151). Needless to say, in the context of the time, the peninsular Buddhism of the Koreans themselves was in jeopardy for several reasons: (1) the fact that it had been in decline having been proscribed throughout the Chosŏn dynasty, (2) the growth of new Korean religions, (3) the growth of Christianity, and (4) the infringement of Japanese Buddhism into the Korean religious sphere.

Korean Buddhists had two main issues that needed to be dealt with: on the one hand, they wanted to protect their own distinctive Buddhist legacy, which had assimilated doctrinal schools alongside Sŏn schools, advocating sudden enlightenment and gradual cultivation. On the other hand, they wanted to reengage with the Korean people themselves who were suffering under the brutality of Japanese rule, having already been side-lined by Confucians whose claims to being concerned with 'practical' life in the real world had clearly not produced a social reality to boast about. The first issue would be the goal of Sŏn master Kyŏngho Sŏngu (1857–1912), described by Jin Y. Park (2010: 6) as "a radical practitioner of meditation who could confirm the efficacy and relevance of Sŏn meditation in the path to one's enlightenment", dedicated to the *Hwadu* practice, outlined in Chapter 3, and who was also interested in reviving monastic standards, like Chinul. Also like Chinul, he created his own communities at different temples, such as Haein-sa temple in 1899 and Pŏmŏ-sa temple in 1902. Additionally, he and his disciples, including Suwŏl (1855–1928) and Hyewŏl (1861–1937) assured the survival and success of Korea's Sŏn lineage. Meanwhile, the second issue, and probably the most important one, notably during the colonial period, was taken up by Han Yong-un (1879–1944), one of the most important Korean Buddhists in modern times, known as Manhae, who merits a closer study.

As Yom Moo-ung (1999: 91) notes, "Manhae was born during a turning point in history" which shaped his ideas, due to his life in the context of conflict vis-à-vis Japanese colonisation, especially considering his proactive role in Korea's independence movement, drawing attention to the interconnection between religion and society. His role also overturned the anachronistic image of Buddhists as passive bystanders with no function or role in the real world. As a child Manhae had studied Chinese characters (*Hanmun*), and was married in 1892, but when he was but around the age of eighteen he decided to train to become a monk and entered Ose-am hermitage in Sŏraksan Mountain, where he studied Buddhism and practiced Sŏn for several years – clearly neglecting his Confucian familial obligations. In 1904, he travelled to different places, including Vladivostok and Man-churia, before returning to Korea, and later that year, a son was born, his first child. In 1908, he travelled to Japan and after returning to Korea was motivated to renew Korean Buddhism, as opposed to Japanese Buddhism which was gaining some ground in his country, especially after Korea's annexation, leaving Korean monks in a precarious situation. Unlike Korean monks, Manhae actually petitioned so that monks could get married, as they did in Japan, and indeed, Japanese Buddhists would eventually expect this of Korean monks. However, as a Buddhist-nationalist, he was deeply committed to making Buddhism a religion which could once again help his people. "Rather than focusing on the depths of enlightenment [. . .] he focused on the salvation of sentient beings", obviously moved by the con-ditions Koreans were forced to live in under the Japanese, and so he also emphasised liberty and equality, "criticis[ing] monks who went on retreats that cut themselves off from the world" (Huh 2004: 254).

In his progressive work, *On the Revitalisation of Korean Buddhism* (조선 불교유신론/朝鮮佛教維新論, K. *Chosŏn pulgyo yusillon*), written after his visit to Japan, published in 1913, Manhae, though highlighting the imperfec-tions and weaknesses to be found in Korean Buddhism, sought to address them, and to renew Buddhism for a new age. He was vehemently opposed to other Korean monks who sought to engage with Japanese Buddhists as part of the Korea-Japan Buddhist's League, which effectively subordinated Korean Buddhism. He emphasised that "today's world will continue to progress and it seems this pace will not stop until it arrives at the ideal of true civilisation. If Buddhism is not appropriate for future civilisation, its revitalisation will fail" (Manhae quoted in Huh 2004: 243). Manhae's text (see passages translated in Ch'oe *et al.* (2000: 329–331)) demonstrates the 'de-constructive' gesture advocated by his revitalisation movement, where the 'destruction' he suggests, does not mean to destroy, but to intervene, and to take the tradition along a new, revised trajectory, where *Yusin* (維新) literally means thinking/maintaining *anew*. In other words, making Bud-dhism capable of meeting the demands of a new age, where tradition is to be respected, but outmoded aspects of it, are to be re-energised with new breath:

> Revitalisation of Buddhism must be preceded by destruction. What is revitalisation? It is the child of destruction [. . .] revitalisation cannot take place without destruction [. . .] Destruction does not mean destroy-ing and eliminating everything. Only those aspects of the traditional customs that do not suit contemporary times are to be amended and given a new direction. [. . .] Anyone interested in revitalising Buddhism should worry first about the absence of destruction before worrying about the lack of revitalisation.
>
> (329)

This passage could be a description of Derrida's de-construction, or indeed, the inverse: Derrida's de-construction could be a description of Manhae's 'Re-vitalisation', bringing back a renewed vitality, intervening from the inside out. In fact, Derrida (1981: 93; original emphasis) insists, "Deconstruction [. . .] It *intervenes*", but in a positive way. Additionally, the de-construction of Manhae easily relates to the ideas of Heidegger, who influenced Derrida's deconstruction. Derrida (1985: 1) explains that he "wished to translate and adapt to [his] own ends the Heideggerian word *Destruktion* or *Abbau*". In *Being and Time*, Martin Heidegger (2008: 63) discusses "the task of a de-struction of the history of ontology". The language note in the English text translated by David Farrell Krell in *Martin Heidegger Basic Writings* points out that "*Destruktion* does not mean 'destruction' in the usual sense [. . .] The word *destructuring* should serve to keep the negative connotations at a distance and to bring out the neutral, ultimately constructive, sense of the original" (64; original emphasis). Heidegger warns of tradition's attempt "to fix its *boundaries*" (original emphasis), and calls for "a loosening of the sclerotic tradition and a dissolving of the concealments produced by it" (66). This is in fact Manhae's precise goal for Buddhism, which highlights the deeply deconstructive turn in his ideas, and in Buddhism more generally (see: Jin Y. Park's *Buddhisms and Deconstructions*, 2006).

In the same text, Manhae is critical of monks who do not provide for themselves, who do not produce their own food, instead living off the labour of poor farmers, who at this point in time were often starving them-selves, exploited under Japanese colonial rule and excessively taxed, if they managed not to be thrown off their own land. He showed "an understand-ing of the economic basis of social equality", drawing on the ideas of Liang Qichao (1873–1929), the Chinese reformist who witnessed the decline and fall of the Qing dynasty, also a famous journalist known for journals such as *New Citizen* (Huh 2004: 252). One central issue that Manhae takes aim at is the education of Buddhists, calling for it to be reviewed, revised and updated, suggesting that new textbooks need to be published, and he also provides practical advice for reforming Buddhist pedagogy itself to "help Buddhism shine forth brightly" (Ch'oe *et al.* 2000: 330). Interestingly he asserts that students should go abroad to study, to India and to China, which is what had invigorated Korean Buddhism in the first place. Furthermore, he also recommends that "students should study in the civilised nations of Europe and America to learn the history and current conditions of their religions", to learn how to solve Korea's problems for themselves – and this the main purpose of his revitalisation – to solve Korea's problems and to bring about progress through education and peaceful means, not through violence or military acts, which were, unsurprisingly, growing among Kore-ans, who were treated like second-class citizens in their own country by the Japanese. He was also deeply aware of the 'anti-religious' movements that were gaining momentum globally, and Marxism was already starting to gain proponents in Korea, and so he sought to highlight the important place of religion (now a term in popular usage thanks to the growth of Christianity), writing that "religion appears to transcend man, but in reality, it makes man into an authentic person, leading him to an authentic life", asking in regards to Buddhism specifically, "Did Buddhism, then, explain and teach attainment of enlightenment by breaking national laws, destroying families and transcending daily lives? No. Buddhism only emphasised that life existed beyond those things" (Huh 2004: 239).

Manhae continued to work to spread Buddhist ideas, by making Buddhist works available to a growing literate audience, even publishing a monthly magazine *Yusim* (Mind-Only) in 1918, something the Christians had already been doing to spread their own religion. But in 1919, Koreans staged a public and peaceful demonstration to make their will for independence known to the world, and a central figure in this movement was Manhae. In the aftermath of Emperor Kojong's death on January 21, 1919, tired of the brutality of Japan's military police, the Kempetei, who routinely tortured Koreans, and sick of the suppression of Korean identity by forbidding freedom of press and assembly, banning books on Korean history, and targeting the Korean language in schools, members of the independence movement coalesced, members of various religions (and none), to declare Korea's independence. This culminated on March 1, 1919, when the Declaration of Independence was read out in Seoul, and distributed all over the peninsula, leading to mass rallies of well over a million Koreans. The declaration was composed in mixed script (*Han'gŭl* and Chinese characters) by nationalist Historian, Ch'oe Namsŏn (1890–1957), who saw Korea's history as beginning with Tan'gun, clearly drawing on the nationalism infused by Na Chŏl's new religion, which was used "to give a firm foothold to the national identity of Koreans", but also to compete with the Japanese nationalistic reconfiguring of Amaterasu Omikami, the Sun Goddess, whom the Japanese emperor claimed to be a descendent, hence divine (Shin 2000: 214). Meanwhile it is important to highlight that Manhae added three items of agreement to the end of the declaration (Nahm 1996: 582–583):

1 Ours is an undertaking on behalf of life, humanity, righteousness, dignity and honour at the request of our people. Exhibit our spirit of liberty; let no one follow his instinct to agitate for the rejection of others.
2 Let each and every person demonstrate to the end of our people's rightful wishes and desires.
3 Let all our actions be orderly and solemn so that our demands and attitudes may be honourable and upright.

There were 33 signatories of the declaration: 16 belonged to Protestant Churches (Presbyterian and Methodist), 15 were adherents of Ch'ŏndogyo, while only 2 were Buddhists, Manhae and Paek Yongsŏng (1864–1940). The document referred to the mandate of 'Heaven' – not God – taking a more neutral religious stance, avoiding the polemics that 'naming God' would have incurred.

Soon after the 'March First Movement' as it came to be known, Manhae was arrested, and refused to write a letter of repentance to be released early. While in prison he wrote on Korean Independence, but also of the negative effects of imperialism: "imperialism has raised its head. [. . .] Thus, a day doesn't pass when wars of death and usurpation do not take place among nations and peoples" (Huh 2004: 247). In 1921, he eventually was released and went on to remain involved in the independence movement, founding the *Singanhoe* (New People Society), which was anti-Japanese, as well as founding *Mandang*, a new Buddhist organisation that wanted to separate religion and state, and to implement Buddhist reforms to propagate the religion more successfully. To this end he was also involved in the Korean Young People's League, the Buddhist version of the YMCA which contributed to the growth of young Christians, and he was also appointed as president of *Pulgyo* (Buddhism) magazine. He also remarried and had a daughter, and went on to become an author of poems and novels, while criticising the growing Japanisation of Korea, especially the name-change ordinance, which forced Koreans to take Japanese names (228–229). During this period, another approach was taken to renovate Buddhism by Pak Chungbin (1891–1943), a slightly younger contemporary of Manhae, whose innovative approach led to the founding of Wŏn Buddhism.

Wŏn Buddhism: a 'new' religion or renovated Buddhism

There have been ongoing discussions about Wŏn Buddhism as a 'new' religion or as a 'form' of Buddhism, the subject of an article by Michael Pye (2002), who agrees with the adherents of the religion that it is "at one and the same time a new religion and a form of Buddhism" (Pye 2002: 141). A Daoist might not be too concerned about whether it is described as 'this' or 'that', regarding both as constructions reflecting different points of view emanating from a single reality, but would rather be interested in how it is practiced, and how it benefits human beings – and this was the goal of its founder, Pak Chungbin (1891–1943), known as Sot'aesan. The son of a farmer, Sot'aesan seemed to have been a spiritually curious child, and sought to have an experience with a mountain god at Samnyŏng Mountain where he prayed, reflecting the living folk culture of the area he came from in South Chŏlla Province, where he had also encountered Confucian teachings. His enlightenment appears to have occurred one morning at dawn during April 1916, but not in a Buddhist sense, seemingly a reflection of something more universal, and less exclusivistic, leading him to study

Buddhism, Daoism and Confucianism, drawing them together (as we saw in other religions dating from the late nineteenth century), into a more holistic schema (Chung 1984: 19).

This universal conceptualisation of religious truth, refracting the *ilsim*, or 'One-Mind', emphasised by Wŏnhyo (outlined in Chapter 2), was reframed by Sot'aesan when he wrote (quoted in: Chung 1984: 19):

> All beings in the universe are of one nature, and all things (dharmas-elements) are from one origin, in the midst of neither creation nor annihilation and the causal law of retribution, being mutually based on each other, have formed a clear framework.

Sot'aesan suggested that different sages from different traditions viewed the same 'ultimate reality' differently, developing different path*ways* to explain it, and subsequently, different practices arose, shaped by the context of the 'sage' and his/her followers (Chung 1987: 6). This led him to explain this 'clear framework' in a very clear manner, using the symbolism of a circle, ○, known as *Irwŏnsang* (一圓相): where *ir-wŏn* means 'one-circle', and it this 'wŏn' that was later adopted as name of the religion, Wŏn Buddhism, by its second leader Song Kyu (1900–1962), whose religious name was Chŏngsan. This One-Circle embodies the idea of Buddha Nature, which is everywhere, without beginning or end, hence, without discrimination, and for Sot'aesan a (non-)symbol of the 'ultimate truth', and is hung in all Wŏn Buddhist temples. Jin Y. Park (2007: 477) notes that this is "one of the most visible distinctions between Wŏn Buddhism and traditional Buddhism", and Sot'aesan used the *Irwŏnsang* image to move away from the practice of "venerating the dummy Buddha statue", arguing that people mistake "what is only a means instead to be the ineffectiveness of the Buddha's teachings" (483). Chung (1984: 22) explains that *Irwŏn* symbolises "the essential nature of all Buddhas (Dharmakāya)", and so all things in the universe are deserving of respect and veneration, including the emptiness of non-being, which can turn into being – both ultimately void. So, in Wŏn Buddhist temples/churches there are no images or statues of the Buddha, rather, they look more like Christian churches, with a pulpit – complete with Sunday services, held at similar times to Christian services, leading Grayson (2002: 214), himself a Methodist minister, to describe the practices of Wŏn Buddhism as "strikingly Protestant". This reflects Sot'aesan's strategy to reform Buddhism and to bring it back to the ordinary person who did not have the time to leave their jobs to focus on intensive study of scriptures or the complicated *hwadus* of Sŏn lineages. It was also reflecting the influence of Christianity, which by that point was growing in the countryside, as well as the cities, where Christian missionaries themselves, as mentioned previously, spoke of the end of Buddhism, giving an urgency to Sot'aesan's reform movement.

Clearly influenced by Manhae, Sot'aesan compiled his own ideas on how Buddhism should be reformed, culminating in his "Treatise on the

Renovation of Korean Buddhism" (조선불교혁신론/朝鮮佛教革新論, K. *Chosŏn Pulgyo hyŏksillon*), published in 1935 (and partly translated in Park 2007: 480–484). This treatise highlights the basis of this 'new' religion and recalibration of traditional Buddhism, and as Park (479) points out, it was included in the earliest collection of the religion's scripture, in 1943, called the Principal Book (or *Chŏngjŏn*) and also adapted for the *Taejonggyŏng* – The Scripture of the Founding Master, and together the modern editions of these make up *The Teachings of Wŏn Buddhism*. It aimed to readjust Buddhism for modern times and to tailor its needs for modern men and women. Sot'aesan wrote that: "Sometimes, facets of Buddhism were in direct contradiction to life in the secular world. Lay Buddhists were not able to play a principal role on this system and instead remained in the periphery" (480). Like Manhae, he also criticised the way that monks did not work, relying on alms or money they generated from the 'services' they provided, in addition, he also problematised the celibacy required by all monks, asking "How can we call such teachings universal?", followed by "How, then, do we resolve these problems?", which he attempted to answer (481). One thing that he focused on, again echoing Manhae, was the Buddhism curriculum, which he wanted to be condensed, "to create a curriculum that will be suitable for practice in mundane life" and to teach people how to use their own minds to discover the truth (482). This truth does not reflect a single religious figure or a single set of teachings, but reflects the interpenetrating nature of all things, with the goal of helping individuals in their spiritual life, which is sometimes overtaken by the materiality of the modern world that sometimes isolates us from others. This 'openness' also means that the religion sees itself as one with universal teachings for all people. Its teachings may be broken into three sections: (1) Threefold Practice; (2) Fourfold Grace; (3) Four Great Principles.

The Threefold Practice reflects the moral path*way* of Wŏn Buddhism to help individuals recover their inherent Buddha Nature, and it relates to the Sanskrit terms: samādhi (concentration), prajñā (wisdom) and Śīla (precepts/morality), though these have been reformulated in Wŏn Buddhist practices (Chung 1984: 25). These ideas are then realised in three different ways: (1) Spiritual Cultivation, which focuses on a calm mind, and overcoming attachments and negative impulses, through meditation, chanting and prayer; (2) Dharma Study; and (3) Mindful Choice in Action, or 'choice of conduct', which consists of doing what is correct and rejecting what is not (25–26; wonbuddhism.org/threefold – practice). This method correlates to various practices discussed throughout this book: T'oegye, for example, also highlighted the need to promote what is inherently good, the Four Beginnings, as well as the need to block the negative aspects of the Seven Feelings.

As Chung (23) explains, for Sot'aesan, as all things are interrelated, then human beings should acknowledge their indebtedness to what permits their existence, described by Grayson (2002: 213), as the "four factors that make human life possible", known as the Fourfold Grace: (1) The Grace of Heaven and Earth, (2) The Grace of Parents, (3) The Grace of Fellow Beings (including all creatures), (4) The Grace of Laws (religious, moral and civil). This links all people and calls for them to be compassionate, and to protect those in vulnerable positions (old and young, family and strangers) and to express gratitude on a daily basis (23–24; wonbuddhism.org/Fourfold – grace). This synthesises ideas that are on the one hand, very obviously Buddhist, but also Confucian and Christian, bringing them together in a way that avoids conflict by obliging the individual to be grateful for the world they live in, their family and friends, all of nature and the laws that protect them and moral path*ways* that can guide them to the full realisation of the best version of who they have inherently the potential to become.

However, the most important part of Wŏn Buddhism is reflected in the Four Great Principles, which reflect the scope of the religion and its call for more socially pro-active engagement. These principles provide followers of the religion with clear guidelines for humanistic action, which avoids complex doctrinal issues that could lead to disputes, with teachings that are clear and concise (see: wonbuddhism.org/#/four-great-principles):

The Four Great Principles

1   Right Enlightenment Practice
2   Awareness of Requital of Grace
3   Practical Application of Buddha Dharma
4   Selfless Service to the Public

The opposite of these principles are the cause of suffering from a Wŏn Buddhist point of view, summarised by Grayson (2002: 214) as "lack of self-reliance, lack of good leaders for society, lack of education for all people, and the absence of a sense of public service". Finally, the religion lists 'Eight Articles': Four Articles to Develop – belief, zeal, questioning and dedication; and Four Articles to Forsake – unbelief, greed, laziness and foolishness, reflecting the onus is on the individual to practice and cultivate themselves, without relying on any supernatural or transcendental beings or powers (*Scriptures of Won Buddhism* 2006: 36–37).

Since 1992, Wŏn Buddhism has been accredited as a Religious NGO at the United Nations, "supporting human rights, gender equality, religious freedom, cultural exchange and environmental protection", committed to equality and global peace (wonbuddhist.org/united-nations/). The organisation has temples in Chile, Argentina, Canada, the United States, Australia, Brazil, Japan, France, Germany, South Africa, Cambodia and other countries, truly reflecting a global religion with global outreach programmes.

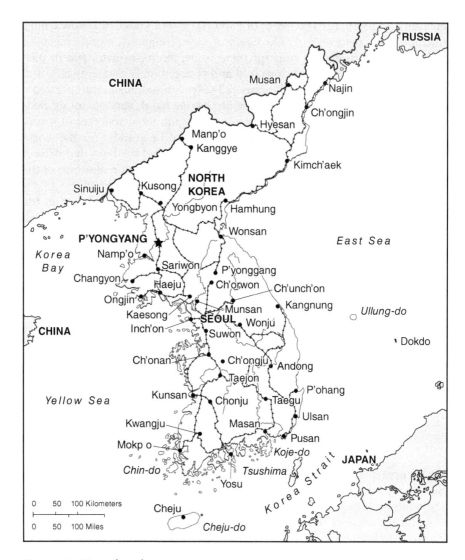

Figure 6.1 Map of modern Korea

In the United States in particular, there is the 'Won Institute of Graduate Studies' (www.woninstitute.edu/), where one can take a Masters in Won Buddhism, as well as other courses, and an impressive retreat centre in New York State, with dharma teachers who are both men and women, Korean and non-Korean (http://wondharmacenter.org/). In Korea, Wŏn Buddhism continues to grow from strength to strength, where it also has its own university and schools. Most importantly, in the age of the internet, it has a very visible web presence, which presents its teachings in an accessible manner, highlighting the effectiveness of Sot'aesan's reformed vision of Buddhism (see: www.wonbuddhism.org).

'New' post-Christian movements

Just as Buddhism had taken some new directions in the aftermath of the Korean War, some individuals were motivated to redirect their Christian churches along quite different trajectories, described by 'orthodox' Christian groups as 'heterodox' organizations and cults. While Grayson (2002) has described these religions as 'syncretic religions', which they are, I have described them as post-Christian as the leaders are the most important figures, seen as either a prophet, or a new incarnation of God, not unlike the leaders of *Chŭngsangyo*, discussed in Chapter 5. Two such groups outlined below are: (1) The Olive Tree Church (*Ch'ŏndogwan*), while the other, (2) The Unification Church (*T'ongilgyo*), has been much more successful in spreading its teachings, amassing huge numbers of adherents internationally.

The Olive Green Church

This Church has been controversial, mainly due to the legal battles and dubious practices of its founder, Pak T'aesŏn (1916–?), after whom it is sometimes called *Park Changnogyo* (Moos 1964). Originally from North Korea, where Presbyterianism was particularly prominent, he had attended church as a youth and after living abroad in Japan, he returned to Korea in 1944, where he once again attended a Presbyterian Church in Seoul, where he became an elder (leader). Grayson (2002: 208–209) describes how Pak had a vision of 'fire and water' descending on him at a rally of the Korean Revival Associations in Seoul, in April 1955, when he then discovered he had great healing powers, leading him to then declare he was the prophet of God from the East foreshadowed in Isaiah 41:2 (*Bible*, NIV):

> Who has stirred up one from the East,
> calling him in righteousness to his service?
> He hands nations over to him
> and subdues kings before him.
> He turns them to dust with his sword,
> to windblown chaff with his bow.

Pak insisted that 'the East' in this prophecy was Korea! Additionally, he asserted himself to be one of two 'witnesses' referred to as "Olive Trees" in the *Book of Revelation* 11:3–5 – hence the title of the religion. Not only was Pak considered to be able to cure through touch, but even drinking the water he had washed his feet with was considered to be able to cure all illnesses, and even grant eternal life (Moos 1964: 116). Members of the Presbyterian

Church soon labelled him a heretic and he was for a brief time imprisoned in 1959 and again in 1960. Nevertheless, in the 1960s, according to Felix Moos (1964: 111), who assessed the Church at that time, suggests that it 'claimed' a membership of over 1,800,000, and was even setting up its own "Christian Towns" to establish a new Zion in Korea, again, fitting in with the new religions that had emerged in the latter part of the nineteenth century, where a new paradise on earth would see Korea as the chosen land, a new heaven on earth. As part of its Zion Educational Foundation, it set up schools ranging from a Zion Kingergarten to the Zion University, and even set up an industrial complex just outside of Seoul, with modern housing. The factories supplied items as diverse as soya sauce and underwear to the Korea Armed Forces (113). Grayson (2002: 208) comments that the white churches belonging to the group were evident throughout the countryside during this period, with church growth so great, at one point it seemed it would "surpass or even supplant orthodox Christianity".

This church, like the Unification Church, as well as some of the Mega-Churches discussed in the Epilogue of this book, would become involved in scandals and a slew of negative press. In this case, the Olive Tree Church could not recover. Pak was accused of evading taxes, excess profit on Zion goods, fraud, bribery, promiscuity with female members of the church, causing death through 'An-Chal' (his curing touch), as well as building churches without building permits (Moos 1964: 118). Moos (119) wrote that "women followers were observed to be especially eager to offer whatever possessions they had – rings, watches, clothing; some ardent believers were even seen shedding their skirts during revival services since they had nothing else to give", clearly highlighting the dubious practices of Pak. Further scandals relating to members of Pak's family led to rapid further decline in the church membership.

A splinter group of this church has emerged since 1984, called 'Shincheonji' (or Sinch'ŏnji, New Heaven and Earth), also called 'Shincheonji Church of Jesus', or 'The Temple of the Tabernacle of the Testimony'. It is sometimes linked with other groups, who initially obfuscate their links with the church, to attract members to 'cultural' events, also targeting foreigners. Founded by Lee Man-hee (1931–), who had at one time been a follower of Pak T'aesŏn, it teaches that Lee had visions of Jesus who revealed he was the "promised pastor", again drawing authority from various passages in the *Bible* (2 Peter 3:13; Matthew 13:31–32; Revelation 14:1–5; Revelation 15:2–5), and preaches that only Lee can discern the true meanings of parables in the Bible (see: http://en.shincheonji.kr/). His book *Creation of Heaven and Earth* (2009) portrays him as this "promised pastor", but one who does not tolerate critics: anyone who disagrees with him is destined for the "fiery lake of burning sulphur", and those who defect will have "seven spirits" descend into them, the latter part clearly drawing on Korea's shamanic tradition, but using it in a negative manner (Lee 2009). The Church is also linked with other organisations as a front to attract unsuspecting followers into its religion, such as Mannam, the International Peace Youth Group (IPYG) and World Peace and Restoration of Light (WPRL) (search these groups online: Yonhap News; Korea Times; Korea Observer). Other Christian denominations have been vociferous in actively denouncing the religion and its followers. This is something the religion has in common with 'The Unification Church'.

The Unification Church

The Unification Church was founded by the infamous Rev. Mun Sŏnmyŏng [Sun Myung Moon] (1920–2012). Once again, it is a religion whose founder was linked with mainstream Christianity before diverging, and declaring himself as a new saviour or messiah, in a way, taking over the role of Jesus in the New Testament, and declaring a new heaven on earth, where Korea would take centre stage. Rev. Mun (often written as Moon, contributing to the negative appellation of the 'Moonies'), like Pak T'aesŏn, was from what today is North Korea, and was also a member of a Presbyterian Church in P'yŏngyang. He, too, studied in Japan and then returned to Korea to lead a reform movement, which he started around the time of Korean liberation from the Japanese (1945) – by then he had married his first wife, Ch'oe Sun'gil, who gave birth to a son the following year. It would later be claimed that Mun had slept with many female members of his early Church, 'to cleanse them', something he always denied. Mun was soon arrested and sentenced to prison in one of the labour camps of the communist authorities of North Korea, who by this stage were persecuting Christians. After his release, an ardent anti-communist, he traversed south of the DMZ (Demili-tarised Zone at the 38th Parallel), which separates the two Koreas, founding his new Church in Seoul in 1954 with the assistance of Yu Hyowŏn (1914–1970), which was called 'The Holy Spirit Association for the Unification of World Christianity'. Despite preaching vehemently on the importance of the family, Mun was divorced from his first wife in 1957. By this time, he and his growing church was already sending missionaries abroad, to the United Kingdom and the United States, but soon this expanded to South America, Japan and other countries, highlighting the global aims of Mun. Having remarried in 1960 to Han Hakcha (also Han Hakja) with whom he had 10 children (who survived), they relocated to Tarrytown New York in the early 1970s, where he set up the world headquarters of his Church and a semi-nary, whose first students graduated in 1977. Again like Pak T'aesŏn, Mun was also involved in business projects to finance his church (and luxurious lifestyle) owning multiple companies (including newspapers in the United States, such as the *Washington Times*), he was investigated for tax evasion, fraud and other charges, but he managed to overcome the negative press which was growing, with further accusations of dubious recruitment drives, brainwashing, breaking up families and so on, making headlines. Neverthe-less, growth of church membership continued, with numbers estimated in the millions (though difficult to verify), and most of that outside of Korea, though membership on the peninsula is estimated to be in the tens of thousands (Grayson 2002: 209–210; The Telegraph 2012).

Grayson (2002: 210) lists four reasons why the 'heterodox' Unification Church is criticised by 'orthodox' Christian Churches: (1) its heretical doctrine; (2) the recruitment methods and education of members, often described as brainwashing; (3) the opulent lifestyle of Mun and his family; (4) the Church's business dealings. But, what exactly does the church teach? Firstly, Mun presented himself as the 'True Father' and his wife as the 'True Mother' (reminding us of the 'Great Mother' *Taemonim* of the *Chŭngsangyo*, discussed in the previous chapter), while both together are considered as the 'True Parents of Humanity'. Mun changed the name of the religion to the 'Family Federation for World Peace and Unification' (FFWPU) in 1994, which, as with the other modern religions in recent times, has an impressive web presence, with its own specific site for the United States (familyfed.org/). Mun, not known for his humility, had himself coronated as 'humanity's saviour, messiah, returning Lord and true parent' at a ceremony on Capitol Hill, in Washington D.C. in 2004, attended by Republicans and Democrats (The Guardian 2004). As he is a self-designated Messiah, he preached that Jesus had failed to accomplish his mission, which was to get married and have children to start the 'True Family', which would usher in a new age for humanity, without sin – which is what Mun and his wife suggest is their goal. A salient feature of the Church is its 'Holy Marriage Blessing Ceremony', which sometimes consists of mass-marriage ceremonies of couples, some who are already legally married, others who have never met before, and in groups numbering up to several thousand couples at a time, with ceremonies taking place in large stadiums. A *New York Times* article from November 30, 1997, describes "an estimated 28,000 couples, most of whom were long married and 2,500 newly matched, gathered today in RFK [Robert F. Kennedy] Stadium here to take part a marriage affirmation ceremony sponsored by the Unification Church". The blessing, Mun taught, would permit 'the family' to enter heaven and assured their children would be free from sin: this is bad news for single people (and single parents!) and non-heterosexual couples (even if married!), as they cannot receive this blessing. An interesting development of this blessing, is the 'Ancestor Liberation Blessing', which might be mistaken for sounding somewhat Confucian – it is not. This blessing is for adherents to have their ancestors blessed and liberated, as Mun taught that they are in hell. In order for this liberation, which then can also cut off any negative connections with the ancestors impacting one's current life, one must apply for blessing and liberation and pay using a Bank Transfer – the amount increasing per generation, on the mother's side and on the father's side, and recommended that one must liberate up to 210 generations! There is also a very disturbing practice of paying to have miscarriages, babies who are still-born, and abortions 'erased' – for a different fee (item 12: en.cptc.kr/subpage.php?p=blessing2). This clearly attempts to generate huge income for the Church and the Mun family, further promoted by a 'USA Ancestor Blessing Tour'. Since Rev. Mun died in 2012, his wife leads the FFWPU, while her son, Mun Hyun-jin (1969–), founded the 'Family Peace Association' (family-peace.org/), which emphasises many of the values of the FFWPU.

Mun's main doctrinal text was first published in Korean in 1966, *The Exposition of the Divine Principle* (원리강론, K. *Wŏlli kangnon*), which had already been translated into English by 1973. The text is divided into five chapters:

1 Principle of Creation
2 The Fall of Man
3 History of Restoration
4 Jesus of Nazareth
5 Christian History

Jon Quinn (2008) has published Mun's ideas in: *Divine Principle in Plain Language: The Basic Theology of Sun Myung Moon* (see: online version). It acknowledges that God created the world, and believes that God is invisible, the "Universal Prime Energy". He suggests that Adam, "the true ancestor of mankind", and Eve were real people, and that Eve's sin was that she had sex with Satan, the serpent, and this 'physical' sin has been transmitted to all subsequent generations. Mun acknowledges that Jesus was the son of God, but not part of a trinity, and not consubstantial with God the Father. The mission of Jesus, according to Mun's teachings, failed because he had not married and produced children, as mentioned previously. Therefore, Mun presents himself as the "Lord of the Second Advent", whose marriage with the perfect woman (his *second* wife), would restore mankind, Mun's main mission, which has produced sinless children. Mun also teaches on patriarchy: that the father is the 'president' of the family, that the family of one small country; that husbands are kings of their families; and that a woman revolves around a man – such ideas clearly stem from *The Great Learning*, and embody Confucian values, which reinforce female submission to males. Through emphasising 'blood' lineage and ancestors, Mun has also tied in other Confucian values, but these values may be viewed as having reached their expiry date, as women strive for equal rights, and where families have taken on new progressive forms, which do not necessarily consist of a married man and woman, and marriage is no longer a prerequisite for having children. Mun emphasises that the primary role of a woman is bearing and rearing children, whereas the primary role for a man is to provide – which sound like ideas that were expected during the Chosŏn dynasty, but not in the twentieth, now twenty-first century. While Buddhism, Christianity and different post-Christian churches developed and grew in South Korea, the Northern part of the peninsula followed a different direction, shaped by the ideas of its 'Dear Leader', Kim Il-sung, who advanced his own path*way*.

Figure 6.2 Modern Christian evangelists' banners displayed in downtown Seoul

Juche and North Korea

North Korea is often portrayed in the West in caricatural terms, but the state ideology is complex and philosophical and, according to some, contains religious elements that move beyond the mere worship of the 'Eternal Leader' Kim Il-sung (also Kim Ilsŏng) (1912–1994). Kim, growing up at a time when Christianity was starting to take root and spread in North Korea, was the son of practising Christians, and his maternal side seems to have been deeply involved in the Presbyterian Church in the 'Jerusalem of the East'. Things would change rapidly after the Japanese colonised Korea, and his family, who had engaged in anti-Japanese activities, fled to Manchuria, as did many Koreans, to escape the discrimination and brutality of the colonisers. By 17 he had already been imprisoned, and had then become involved in Marxist groups, while by 1932 had become a member of a communist group in China, and he soon led guerrilla groups. In 1941, forced to move from Manchuria, he joined the Soviet Red Army training camps, where he met his wife, who had two sons – one of then Kim Jong-il, who would later succeed his father. After the liberation of Korea, it seems that Kim was well-known to the Russians, and selected to lead the northern part of the peninsula, as part of a (much maligned) trusteeship, while the Americans looked after and influenced South Korea, placing Syngman Rhee (the former Independence Club member) in charge, who organised elections in 1948, which the North Koreans boycotted, and this led to Rhee's inauguration on August 15, as the first president of the 'Republic of Korea' (ROK): Kim would lead newly named Democratic People's Republic of Korea (DPRK) until his death in 1994. The DPRK is also referred to inside the country as *Puk-Chosŏn* – 'North Chosŏn', where the Korean language is also called *Chosŏn-mal* (the language of Chosŏn), considering itself as the legitimate heir to Korea's national identity and past. The untenable situation escalated into war, which broke out on June 25, 1950, lasting three years, costing millions of lives, North and South of the border, of more than just Koreans – this was an international war, with soldiers from China backing the North Koreans, while a United Nations' army, including soldiers from 21 countries, was led by the United States. The armistice signed after the war, signed on July 27, 1953, remains in place, as well as the border which divides the North from the South (French 2005: 50–53). To the North, a form of Marxism-Leninism would take a creative turn, shaped by the particularities of the country post-Korean War.

Philosophically and also psychologically, Juche (sometimes written *Chuch'e*), the theory attributed solely to Kim Il-sung, and then developed by his son Kim Jong-il, is what marks a notable departure from the diversity of religions, which can be openly practiced in South Korea, such as Buddhism, Catholicism, Protestantism, Shamanism and so on. Juche, as Eun Hee Shin (2007: 517) explains, comes from Ju (主), meaning 'the main principle' and che (體), meaning, 'body' or 'self', and can be translated as "sovereign autonomy" or "self-determination", though it is often translated as "self-reliance". This "self-reliance" has three aspects, outlined by French (2005: 30–33): (1) *Chaju* (자주), meaning independence; (2) *Charip* (자립), self-sustainability; (3) *Chawi* (자위), self-defence. The latter point was emphasised by Kim Jong-il, especially with the deteriorating economic situation in the 1990s, where it also became known as 'sŏn'gun' (선군) – 'military first' policy, which has been carried forward recently by Kim Jong-un, the third generation 'Kim' leader of the DPRK, a development of 'War Communism'. The first mention of 'Juche' in a documented speech, dating from December 28, 1955, titled, "On Eliminating Dogmatism and Formalism and Establishing *Juche* in Ideological Work", called for Juche to be "firmly established", though it did not clearly explain the term, referring mainly to the "Party's ideological work" (full transcript is available at: marxist.org). Kim Il-sung (quoted in Lee 2003: 105), explained this later as:

> Establishing Juche means, in a nutshell, being the master of revolution and reconstruction in one's own country. This means holding fast to an independent position, rejecting dependence on others, using one's own brains, believing in one's own strength, displaying the revolutionary

spirit of self-reliance, and thus solving one's own problems for oneself on one's own responsibility under all circumstances.

This reflects what French (2005: 32) has described as the "creative application of Marxism-Leninism" for North Korea, which had not been capitalist, but which had been ravaged because of the destruction of the Korean War, making the 'reconstruction' of North Korea the major goal of Kim's state directives.

But, added to this, there were ideas borrowed from Maoism, such as "formal political study, criticism and self-criticism, as well as the role of public campaigns in mobilising the population for specific goals", as well as the cult of personality surrounding the Great Leader, Kim (35). The latter idea would also be bolstered by Confucian thought, which, though not referred to in speeches, had penetrated Korean psyche (and heart-and-mind) for hundreds of years, and this was still North 'Chosŏn' after all. Confucianism was constructed around loyalty (*ch'ung*) towards the king, and filial piety towards parents (*hyo*), and as highlighted before, of tantamount importance in the Korean context. Kim Il-sung appeared in images all over the country as an affable 'father-figure', who was at the same time the 'Great Leader', a veritable sage ruler. Shin (2007: 517) writes that North Koreans view the Great Leader "as 'Father', in the sense of being the national provider, healer and even saviour". French (2005: 40) also emphasises a final element of Juche, which he describes as "a hyper-traditionalist reading of traditional Korean culture [and] much of this is also derived from the general Confucian ethic". Just like the other religious developments examined, both in this chapter and the previous one, Juche also reinforces the idea that Korea is some sort of chosen land (41), reflected in Kim's speech, mentioned above. Kim (1955) stated that "to make revolution in Korea we must know Korean history and geography as well as the customs of the Korean people. Only then is it possible to educate *our* people in a way that suits them and to inspire in them an ardent love for their native place and their motherland". This reflects the ethos of the time, rampant in South Korea as well, which also refers to a collective 'our' (우리, K. *uri*): our country, our people, our language, clearly shaped by its recent history: colonisation, war and a divided country, and where a nationalistic '*uri*' contrasts with the threatening 'other' (see: *Nationalism and the Construction of Korean Identity* (1998), by Hyung Il Pai and Timothy R. Tangherlini).

This idea would be highlighted and expanded upon in Kim's 1965 speech, "On Socialist Construction and the South Korean Revolution in the Democratic People's Republic of Korea". In part four of the speech, Kim (1968: 36–51) focused on "The Question of firmly establishing Juche and thoroughly implementing the mass line", which links together the three aspects of 'independence' relating to Juche, outlined by Paul French previously in this section: *Chaju*, *Charip* and *Chawi*. These also link together the '*uri*-ness', where collectiveness took on a whole new meaning in North Korea as part of its mass-mobilisation project, launched in the late 1950s, known as *Chollima* (named after a mythical horse with wings). Kim (51) describes, "The all-people *Chollima* movement which has been unfolded with untiring vigour in our country is the most brilliant embodiment of the mass line of our Party". If religion is something which links and binds people together, as discussed in Chapter 1, then this is a 'new' religion, which:

> links collective innovation in economic and cultural construction with the work of educating and remoulding the working people [. . .] all the wisdom, enthusiasm and creative energy of our people is brought into full play [. . .] and the building of socialism in our country is greatly accelerated.
>
> (51)

This is a nationalistic ideology without transcendence or God, which unifies the people through collective-cultivation, where the 'self' is overlooked for the greater good of '*uri*', 'our' country and 'our' people. It avoids any eschatology, as what happens here and now is what matters, particularly if it contributes to making North Korea a socialist paradise.

Unfortunately, this is not the case, and North Korea has become synonymous with famine, human rights abuses, nuclear tests and growing numbers of defections by people willing to risk their lives. Hwang Changyŏp (also Hwang Jang-yeop) (1923–2010), who had influenced Kim Ilsung's ideas on Juche, defected to South Korea in 1997, clearly disenchanted by North Korea under Kim Jong-il, as well as the possibilities for Juche's future (French 2005: 44–45). Nevertheless, Kim Jong-il himself has written on and commented about Juche, while always recognising it as his father's unique philosophical thought. In *On the Juche Idea*, published in 1982 to commemorate the birthday of his father, Kim Jongil (1982: 4) wrote, "Our leader created the great Juche idea after acquiring a deep insight into the requirements of a new era when the oppressed and humiliated masses of the people became masters of their own destiny". This places (wo)mankind as central to this ideology, clarified by Kim (60) who emphasised:

> The idea that man is the master of everything and decides everything, in other words, the idea that man is the master of the world and his own destiny and is the transformer of the world and the shaper of his destiny, is fundamentally opposed to idealism and metaphysics.

The Confucians would not be happy with this last statement, which opposes one of their favourite subjects, metaphysics. Kim (59) exaggerates the importance and significance of Juche, suggesting it is "exerting a great influence on the ideological life of humanity", and "gaining strong sympathy from people all over the world". It is also from Kim Jong-il that the *sŏngun* 'military first' policy arose, now being used by Kim Jong-un to negotiate with the current president of the United States, Donald Trump: two anachronistic leaders who have in a short space of time, gone from maligning each other publicly, to holding a 'peace' summit in Singapore on June 12, 2018. North Korea, it seems, wants a place in the world, exasperated by trying to create its own paradise, which has failed, crippling its economy and the lives of many who live there, controlling their religious lives.

But, there are other aspects to North Korea's religiosity than Juche, though these other elements have been controlled, sometimes persecuted, sometimes manipulated and used to 'show' that North Korea permits religious plurality and freedom. These different phases are discussed in a special edition of the *Journal of Korean Religions* (Young 2013), called "North Korea and Religion". What is evident is that the different religions, which had a presence there before the division, mainly Buddhism, Christianity and Ch'ŏndogyo, have membership numbers which are insignificant when compared to South Korea. Not only were the religious orders persecuted, with many executed, but religious buildings were closed down, viewed as a threat to Juche and the control it sought to maintain. By attempting much later to engage to some degree with the outside world, some contacts were permitted between religious groups in the North and South, though Young (6) underscores that this only "held important symbolic value for the North in its public relations", which wanted to portray North Korean citizens as having some sense of religious freedom.

Bernard Sénecal (2013: 9–51) outlines how even though there have been some interactions and projects in North Korea by Buddhists from both sides of the peninsula (funded by South Korea's *Jogye* order), in the North, the *Chobulyŏn* (朝佛聯) order is the only Buddhist group, and it is subordinate to Juche. Nevertheless, there are an estimated 10,000 lay members, led by roughly 300 married monks – there are no nuns. Venerable Pŏpta, of the Jogye order, who has done much work with North Korean monks, has himself been jailed and accused of being 'Pro-North Korean', and sympathetic to communism – South Korea is not the paragon of liberty it would like to have itself portrayed as, and South Koreans do not have access to North Korean websites that can be accessed outside the country. Anyone in South Korea who supports North Korean ideas, such as Juche, can be imprisoned as a result of the 1948 National Security Act, which still exists.

Ch'ŏndogyo, which boasted huge membership before the divide, has suffered a similar fate, with many leaders and members persecuted from 1951, while most seemingly fled South – with members of other religions, especially, Christians. Again, things changed for the better in the 1970s when a new Ch'ŏndogyo worship hall was opened in Pyŏngyang, which Young (64) describes as "more for show than an active community". The religion has also been referred to as the national religion, with members in the country's Chondoist Chongu Party, which is tightly controlled, and clearly subordinate to the state. It is mentioned regularly in news articles on the website of the *Korea Central News Agency* (KCNA), which can be accessed online, though usually only to relay the opinions of the state, such as in 2017, when the party denounced US President Donald Trump: "The rabid dotard Trump cannot evade a merciless divine punishment".

There are also Christian churches (Catholic, Orthodox and Protestant) in the capital meant to demonstrate tolerance and religious freedom, though these too are generally considered as showpieces for special visitors who may be allowed inside, although, as with most things relating to North Korea, nothing is certain. What is sure is that many North Koreans flee and many receive the help of Christian missionaries just over the border in China. Having worked with North Korean Refugees in the United Kingdrom, almost all of those I encountered (around 30) were helped by South Korean Christian missionaries. Though, as Jung Jin-Heon (2013) concludes, the politics of evangelical missionaries in China is not straight-forward, with many refugees clearly feeling the need to convert to receive aid, to avoid the alternative. This is especially the case for many young women, who are vulnerable to human-trafficking, often forced to work in the sex trade, while others are forced to marry men in rural areas. There have also been reports of crackdowns inside North Korea, with random searches for Bibles and hidden Christian paraphernalia, with those found hiding such items, severely punished. The 'World Watch List' currently (2019) has North Korea listed at number one as the country which has the most severe persecution of Christians, according to 'Open Doors', a Christian missionary organisation for persecuted Christians (see: opendoorusa.org). Curiously, there is no data available from North Korea on Shamans, especially as the '*Kangsin-mu*', mentioned in Chapter 1, were originally from the Northern part of the peninsula. Shamans too, have had their own persecution history, but in South Korea, they have risen like a phoenix to meet the challenges of not only globalisation, but the age of the internet.

The Korean *Mudang*: from the 'innerspace' to cyberspace

The history of Shamanism predates the other textual religious and philosophical traditions on the Korean peninsula. During the Three Kingdoms and the early Koryŏ periods, before the rise of the Neo-Confucian elite, Shamanism seems to have coexisted as a prominent traditional path*way*, amenable to both Buddhism and Daoism. It is therefore a 'religion' of tolerance. Indeed, even the celebrated group known as the Hwarang, "reflected a native shamanistic outlook", according to Marshall Pihl (1994: 17), and as seen in Chapter 2, Queen Sondok was described as having Shamanistic powers of prognostication, described by Iryŏn in *Legends and History of Korea* –and, of course, there is the Myth of Tan'gun. Though, during the mid-Koryŏ period, when Yi Kyubo had composed his "Lay of the Old Shaman" (also discussed in Chapter 2), there does seem to have been a growth in animosity towards the *mudang* by Confucians. However, the *mudang* still had a prominent role, even performing rites for the royal family, and the nation, with 'State *Mudang*' (國巫, K. *Kungmu*) resident in the royal palace. As drought was a serious issue, the *mudang* were often summoned to perform *kiuje* (祈雨祭), or rites praying for rain. During the reign of King Injong (1122–1146), this type of rite was performed 16 times (Cho 1992: 4). Cho (5) notes that there was also a national '*kut*' (굿) performed for the wealth and success of the country by the State *Mudang*, something that would have been disdained by the Confucians. It appears that during this same period, the tradition of singing and dancing during the shaman's *kut* became a highly regarded art form, and also at this point, transvestism began with a group known as *Namjang* (남장/男裝), literally 'men's clothes', or 'dressed as men', or in modern parlance – cross-dressers – allowing them to assume the same power and superior position as men. However, towards the end of the Koryo period a change was noted in regards to *mudang*: her '*kut*' was described as '*ŭmsa*' (淫祀), indecent, even promiscuous. The justification was that it encouraged the gathering of men and women in one place, indicating that a new Confucianised Korea was very close at hand.

With the implementation of Confucianism during the Chosŏn dynasty, Buddhist monks and Shamans were reduced to the lowest level in society, and their oppression was particularly harsh during the reign of King Taejong (1400–1418), mentioned in Chapter 3. But also, during the reigns of Sejong (1419–1450) and Songjong (1470–1494) various *mudang* were imprisoned and the '*kut*' was forbidden. There does also seems to have been periods when the oppression was not so harsh, and when some *mudang* were called upon by female members of the royal family: after the death of King Hyojong (r.1649–1659) a shaman ritual was requested by the queen dowager and again Queen Min (1851–1895) was also linked with *mudang* and their rituals (Cho 1992). Despite this downturn and varying degrees of oppression, which never rivalled the persecution of the Catholics during the later Chosŏn period, Shamanism survived. One reason may be that most people (both men and women) could not read the Confucian Classics, and so may have felt that Shamanism was more accessible as it reflected Korea's oral folk tradition, with songs and dances they could appreciate, understand and relate to. Confucian ideals were for an elite few in positions of authority, and even they formed factions and had rivals persecuted, sometimes exiled, even executed – not exactly practicing what they preached. Also, the harsh social reality of women, yoked in by the 'Three Bonds', would have made Shamanism and the *mudang* seem like an escape from suppression, which took place even in their own homes. Women were supposed to remain inside the private sphere, while the man's place was outside, the public sphere. Women were controlled even by a patriarchal interpretation of the metaphysics of yin and yang, manipulated to mean: man-active-high, women-passive-low (see Lee 2005). In such a suffocating context, the *mudang* managed to live beyond the social boundaries, and defied all gender and socio-familial constructs of a patriarchal heterodoxy that codified the inferiority of women and even inscribed it into Confucian laws. They existed beyond the limits of

Confucianised femininity, and indeed their system of 'spiritual' shamanistic inheritance is matrilineal.

Shamans continued to be repressed after the colonisation of Korea by the Japanese. Interestingly, the Japanese saw the influence of Shamanism as a reflection of the ethos of the Korean people and saw its suppression as mandatory. It was through depicting Shamanism as a primitive, unsophisticated series of superstitions that the Governor General sought to destroy the credibility and adherence to Shamanism, accusing it of "having negative effects on the development of the self-help spirit and scientific attitude", while also acknowledging that Shamanistic ideology had "been cherished in Koreans' minds for thousands of years" (Han 2000: 42–43). Shintoism, which was used as a praxis by the Japanese to develop patriotism and loyalty to the Emperor within Japan itself, was partly used in Korea in an attempt to dispossess the Korean 'mind' of Shamanistic influences. Enforced worship at Shinto shrines, especially after 1932, also led to conflict among the Christian churches, with many coerced by the Governor General to attend the rituals. This lead some to take a firm stance against attending rites or bowing at Shinto shrines, considering this worship, hence, idolatrous, especially due to the polytheistic belief associated with Shinto. Some Christians, mainly Presbyterian, but also some Methodists and Catholics were incarcerated, tortured and, in some cases, died for refusal to accept the rites (see Kim 1997). Many of the Christian missionaries also viewed Shamanism as something superstitious and contentious. Clark (1961: 175, 178), quotes several missionaries from the early twentieth century, such as Homer Hulbert, who noted in 1906 that "the native demonology of Korea united with Buddhism and formed a composite religion", meanwhile W.M. Clark highlights that "today [in 1925] it may be safely said that this Shamanism is the strongest power, from a religious point of view in Korea".

Shamanism has great cultural value as an intermixture of all aspects of traditional Korean culture. Kendall (1985: 35) notes that folklorists consider Shamanism "a living repository of indigenous religions and literature". Rye (1984: 8) emphasises that Shamanism "has produced an intricate network of connections relating [to] both the major established religions and to the new religions of today as well". The various '*kut*' ceremonies draw on the richness of pure Korean culture, in addition to imported Daoism from China, or Buddhism from India through China. In particular, it reflects 'women's culture', true 'Girl Power', so to speak. The very place where women lived was inextricably linked to Shamanism, the traditional Korean home, especially the *anbang* 'inner quarters', discussed before in relation to the Bible Women, who endeavoured to share the innerspace that had been shaped by the *mudang*. This 'innerspace' was a female realm, but also an *axis mundi* for *mudang* spirituality. As Yi Chŏng-yŏng (1983b: 195) illustrates, "Besides the festivals and seasonal rituals, most shamanistic affairs are primarily for women [. . .]. Especially the rituals for childbearing and childbirth". Obviously such occasions are beyond masculine apperception and are exclusively comprehensible to women. The most important gods of the home are also deities of shamanistic purport, and "bring home and Shamanism together" (197), for example, *Taegam*, the God of wealth, while the *Sambul Chesŏk* (three Buddhist Chesŏk gods often appearing in *mudang* paintings and on their fans) take care of child-bearing, longevity and happiness: the latter also reflects the way the *mudang* creatively embroidered Buddhist beliefs into their own spiritual culture. On the other hand, Iryŏn also referred to Hwanin as Chesŏk in the Myth of Tan'gun, blending Buddhist ideas with earlier myths – though Chesŏk, noted as a Buddhist guardian – was originally a deity in the Hindu pantheon, demonstrating the religious bricolage that clearly affects all traditions. This is also reflected in Shaman paintings, which are usually hung in the *sindang* (spirit shrine) of the *mudang* in her home, where there is an altar where the *mudang* offers food and drink to her gods. Many shaman paintings have been burned, even buried by the shamans, and so 'antique' shaman paintings are not common. Today, those paintings are collected and on view in museums, representing material *mudang* culture, where the Shaman gods are on full view to the public (see Kendall *et al.* 2015).

Many of these gods also have their own origin myths or folktales related to them, which are recited or sung during the *kut*, for example "The Origin Myth of the Three Buddhist Chesŏk Gods" (see Lee 2000: 70–115). *Myths of Korea* (Lee 2000) presents many of these "Shamanist myths" from the peninsula as well as some from Cheju (Jeju) island, off the Southern coast, which are quite different. Some of these tales present iconoclastic images of women, like *The Story of Princess Pari*, which portrays the protagonist rejecting traditional female roles. The king sought to have a son and in despair after having seven daughters he orders the last child's infanticide. She survives and is brought up by poor people who were Buddhists, displaying the Buddhist incorporation into Shamanism. The Mountain God informs her that the king and queen have an illness and only the young princess can find the medicinal water that can cure them: she must "go to place that even a man cannot go" (Chun 1982: 100). Here the male role of protector is given to a young woman. She is masculinised and the men are feminised–as is the *mudang* during the *kut* when she wears male attire and draws into her male spirits. The princess has to marry a god in order to get the magic potion and hence becomes a Shaman deity. She in turn has seven children, all boys. She finally returns and brings her parents back from the dead. The interesting factor here is the role of Confucianism, which seems to be rejected in one regard, yet is upheld by the princess as a filial daughter, who, loyal to her father, is therefore also loyal to her king.

Some of these tales are incorporated into the ritual chants (or songs) of the Korean shaman, known as *muga* (무가). This has been extensively researched by Boudewijn Walraven in *Songs of the Shaman: The Ritual Chants of the Korean Mudang* (1994). It appears that and there is no way to know if the folktales have influenced the songs of the *mudang*, or if the *muga* have shaped the folktales. These songs "include all utterances of the *mudang*, whether sung, chanted, or spoken, as long as they are part of the *kut*" (Walraven 1994: 16). However, as Walreaven notes, "some songs are nothing more than simple prayers, not exceeding a few lines, while the narrative songs may take three, four, or five hours to sing in their entirety" – something to remember for those who may have the possibility of attending one of these rituals. The other thing to note is that these are entertaining affairs, filled with music, song, dance, food and alcohol. These are, one must remember, spiritual encounters, and should be shown the same respect one would have at a church or a temple, or any other 'religious' space.

The *kut* is where the traditional arts intersect the living culture, and they are known for their traditional improvised music, known as *sinawi* (시나위). In fact, Keith Howard (1989: 174) argues that "court music may have roots in Shaman music such as *kagok*, the classical lyric song repertory". Also noticeable are the similarities between the '*muga*', and *P'ansori* (traditional storytelling where the singer is accompanied by a drum). A closer examination illustrates that "they are based on the same typical Cholla-region rhythmic structures and also employ alternating spoken and song delivery" (Pihl 1994: 61). There is some evidence that the P'ansori has derived from Shaman narratives but they refer to the living world, whereas Shaman narratives and songs are spiritual in content (62). Additionally, Shaman dances have influenced modern traditional dances and the clothes used are traditional Korean clothes. The instruments used are pure traditional Korean instruments complementing the overall "Koreaness" of the *kut* which displays iconoclastic images of women and ambiguous and fluctuating notions of 'sexualities'. The *Mugam*, or dance during a *kut,* is a time of confused identity. During this episode, a bisexual *mentalité* manifests itself: the female becomes male, the woman becomes man, the repressed becomes liberated, and the 'inner' emotions are 'outwardly' expressed. As Kendall (1983: 225) points out, it "affords women one abundantly exploited opportunity to drink, dance, and play among themselves". This is diametrically opposed to 'male' rituals, which were dominated by a contrastingly cautious and composed Confucian control.

In *Maxims and Proverbs of Old Korea*, there is a section dedicated to the 'Sorceress' or *mudang*. They refer to the general amusement value of the *kut* and speak of gatherings of women eating rice cakes to the beating drum whilst dancing and driving out devils (Ha 1964: 134–138). The *mudang* has even permeated the colloquial language and creates a curious female dominated vocabulary of feminine entertainment. Divination is an art form practiced by *mudang*, and sometimes by others who are not *mudang*. Yi Chŏng-yŏng (1983a: 181) underscores that "divination and Shamanism are so intimately related that it is not possible to separate one from the other". One such figure is the *Posal*, "a religious officiant sharing her name with Buddhist officiants", but who occupies a somewhat complicated and sometimes contentious space between the *mudang* and the Buddhist, especially on the internet where some serious debates arise (Bruno 2013: 175). She is someone who can engage in divination, but who cannot perform important *kut*, hence the *mudang*, in this sense has more 'spiritual power' (Bruno 2013). The *mudang* also has more spiritual power than the numerous fortune-tellers, such as *chŏmjaengi* (점쟁이), similar to mediums, and *sajujaengi* (사주쟁이) who predict by analysing 'The Four Pillars' (*Saju*) of destiny: year, month, day and hour. Both groups are a common fixture of modern Korea, from rural villages – to downtown Seoul (even Koreatown LA) – often frequented by young couples who want to find out how their relationships will turn out.

Rather than disappearing, shamanism has evolved and *mudang* have been early-adapters to modern technology (like most Koreans for that matter). While an ensemble of traditional Korean culture, it also fits into the present, making use of the internet and cyberspace, where a growing number of 'cybershamans' wield their power online since 1996 (Kim 2005). In 1998, there was even an attempt made by the Korean company LG to launch a cyborg *mudang* named 'Cysha' – a combination of Cy (from cyber) and sha (from Shaman), outlined by Kim Seongnae in "Korean Shamanic Practice in Cyber Culture" (3). This was eventually pulled as netizens complained, many outraged: some thought it was not fitting for such a famous Korean 'modern' technology company to promote something that seemed anachronistic, while some feared its "cyber-mysticism". Meanwhile, others were happy to have access to electronic talisman (*pujŏk*), which could be downloaded – even used as screensavers – a far cry from the talisman of Ch'ŏndogyo (4). Kim shows how other online shamans, though often criticised, have grown online *mudang* services, where they charge for counselling and talisman. Clearly cyber-shamanic counselling has a valid place in South Korea, which has currently one of the highest suicide rates in the world, though the idea of the *mudang* as a counsellor is not something new. Youngsuk Kim Harvey (1976) discussed the Korean *mudang* as an 'ethnopsyhiatrist', who was a "household therapist", while Kim Kwang Iel (1972) considered Shamanism from a psychoanalytical point of view.

Korean Shamanism has also attracted headlines internationally: "Modern Shamans all the rage in S Korea" (Global Post 2010), or "Shamanism enjoys Revival in Techno-Savy South Korea", which suggests there are over 300,000 shamans in Korea (New York Times 2007), and the TED Blog, "In twenty-first century Korea, Shamanism is not only thriving – but evolving" (TEDfellow 2017). Kim Seong-nae, quoted in the Global Post (2010), underscores that "most contemporary Koreans do not fear shamans or *mudangs*, but instead rely heavily on their counselling for significant life decisions such as birth, marriage, house moving, success, business and politics". Clearly some conservative Christians would criticise these practices, but Protestant theologian, David Kwang-sun Seo (Global Post 2010) highlights how Korean Protestantism has drawn on Korea's pre-existing religious and spiritual practices, adding that "Koreans often interpret 'receiving' the

Holy Spirit as being literally possessed by it – a striking resemblance to *mudang*s, who also claim to be possessed by spirits". Shamanic elements have also been assimilated into the new religions, discussed in Chapter 5. Shamanism, the great assimilator throughout Korean history, has itself been greatly assimilated and continues to hover between and within many of the religious traditions in Korea, cross-fertilising ideas and, most importantly, practices which transforms the lives of those who embrace them.

Conclusion

Buddhism, which had been suppressed during the Chosŏn dynasty, saw its identity undermined by Japanese Buddhist infiltration into the Korea religious landscape. Patriotic Buddhists like Manhae saw an opportunity in recalibrating Buddhism, re-vamping it from the inside out, through a deconstructive intervention. His progressive work *On the Revitalisation of Korean Buddhism* sought to bring Buddhism back to the people, and back from rural retreat centres, while others re-engaged with Sŏn practices. Sot'aesan decided to take Buddhism along a new trajectory, creating a new, modern Korean Buddhist path*way* that eschewed formalism, emulating to some degree Christian churches and their services, opening their temple to laypeople from all backgrounds. Just as Buddhism had renewed itself, different Presbyterian leaders, many of whom originally came from the northern part of the peninsula where Christianity spread like wildfire before the division of the peninsula, before communism, would take their teachings and practices down a new avenue. The Olive Green Church placed its leader at the centre of his new religious configuration, seeking to establish a new Zion in Korea, before his downfall after a series of scandals, some sexual, some financial. This church would inspire several splinter movements, such as the Shincheonji Church, founded by Lee Man-hee, who fronts the religion. Taking this one step further, and gaining a huge international following is The Unification Church (renamed as the Family Federation for World Peace and Unification) of Rev. Mun Sŏnmyŏng, who, along with his wife, are believed by their followers to be the True Father and True Mother of humanity, suggesting that Jesus had failed his mission. Mun, too, though in trouble with the law on many occasions, created the most globalised new religion from Korea.

To the North of the peninsula, Juche has ruled supreme. This state ideology, growing out of Kim Il-sung's interest in Marxism and Leninism, influenced by his time living in China and experiencing its communism first hand, is also combined with overt nationalism, which also draws on Confucian teachings, such as filial piety and loyalty to the king (or Dear Leader). It was developed over time and is studied in schools every day in North Korea, where criticism is met with punishment. Various reports indicate that there are still some forms of Buddhist, Christian and Ch'ŏndogyo churches remaining, though they have suffered greatly from persecution and oppression.

To the South, Shamanism has enjoyed a comeback, having endured centuries of oppression, like Buddhism. The Korean *mudangs*, much maligned in the past, by Confucians, then Christians and later progressives, wield spiritual power in the twenty-first century, and are appreciated, and now protected by the state to some degree, emblematic as living 'Korean' culture. Their ritual *kut* is an engaging, music-filled, singing, and dancing spiritual celebration – represented at the opening ceremony of the 1988 Seoul Olympics. The *kut* draws together indigenous Korean folk culture, bridging the past and the present, the living and the departed, as well as offering psychological relief for those involved. These ritual specialists continue to increase their clientele online, and guide and counsel new generations of Koreans who have new modern complaints and stresses, no longer restricted to the innerspace of the 'anbang'. They share the cyberspace with Buddhists, Christians and all of the old and new path*ways* which continue to make the future of Korea's religious and philosophical traditions an interesting one. But, they are still vulnerable to attacks and criticisms, especially by more conservative Christian groups, who still consider them as sorceresses and heretics, doomed to hell (in the company of all other non-Christians!).

References and further reading

Bernard, Senécal. 2013. "Buddhists in the Two Koreas: North-South Interactions". *Journal of Korean Religions*, 4(2): 9–50.

Bible: New International Version. Available at: www.biblegateway.com [accessed on 25 June 2018].

Bruno, Antonetta L. 2013. "The Posal Between the Mudang and the Buddhist: In-Between and ByPassing". *Journal of Korean Religions*, 4(2): 175–196.

Ch'oe, Yŏngho, Peter H. Lee and Wm Theodore De Bary. 2000. *Sources of the Korean Tradition: From the Sixteenth to the Twentieth Century*. Columbia University Press: Columbia. Chapter 33.

Cho, Hŭng-yun. 1992. "Le Chamanisme au début de la dynastie Chosŏn". Translated by Christian Deschamps, *Cahiers d'Extrême-Asie*, 6: 1–20.

Chun, Shin-yong. (ed.). 1982. *Korean Folk Tales*. Si-sa-yong-o-sa Publishers: Seoul.

Chung, Bong-kil. 1984. "What Is Won Buddhism". *Korea Journal*, 24(5): 18–31.

———. 1987. "The Concept of Dharmakāya in Won Buddhism: Metaphysical and Philosophical Dimensions". *Korea Journal*, 27(1): 4–15.

Clark, Charles A. 1961. *Religions of Old Korea*. The Christian Literature Society of Korea: Seoul.

Derrida, Jacques. 1981. *Positions*. Translated by Alan Bass. The Athlone Press: London.

———. 1985. *Derrida and Différance*. Parousia Press: Warwick.

Family Federation for World Peace and Unification. Available at: http://familyfed.org/ [accessed on 24 June 2018].

Family Peace Association. Available at: http://family-peace.org/ [accessed on 24 June 2018].

French, Paul. 2005. North Korea: *The Paranoid Peninsula – A Modern History*. Zed Books: London.

Global Post. 2010. Modern Shamans All the Rage in S Korea. Available at: www.
globalpost.com/dispatch/south-korea/100125/shamanism-mudangs [accessed on
24 June 2018].

Grayson, James H. 2002. *Korea: A Religious History*. Revised Edition. Routledge
Curzon: New York. Chapter 16.

The Guardian. 2004. Moonie Leader Crowned in Senate. Available at: www.the
guardian.com/world/2004/jun/24/usa.religion [accessed on 23 June 2018].

Ha, Tae-hŭng. 1964. *Maxims and Proverbs of Old Korea, Korean Cultural Series*.
vol VII. Yonsei University Press: Seoul.

Han, Do-Hyun. 2000. "Shamanism, Superstition, and the Colonial Government".
The Review of Korean Studies, 3(1): 34–54.

Harvey, Youngsook Kim. 1976. "The Korean *Mudang* as a Household Therapist".
Culture-Bound Syndromes, Ethnopsyhiatry, and Alternative Therapies, ed. W.P.
Lepra. University of Hawai'i Press: Honolulu.

Heidegger, Martin. 2008. *Basic Writings*. Translated by David Farrell Krell. Routledge and Kegan Paul: London.

Howard, Keith. 1989. *Bands, Songs and Shamanistic Rituals: Folk Music in Korean
Society*. Royal Asiatic Society, Korea Branch: Seoul.

Huh, Woosung. 2004. "Manhae's Understanding of Buddhism". *Korean Philosophy: Its Tradition and Modern Transformation*, ed. Korean National Commission
for UNESCO. Hollym: Seoul. 225–256.

Jung, Jin-Heon. 2013. "North Korean Refugees and the Politics of Evangelical Mission in the Sino-Korean Border Area". *Journal of Korean Religions*, 4(2): 147–176.

Kendall, Laurel. 1983. "Mugam: The Dance in Shaman's Clothing". *Korean Folklore*, ed. Korean National Commission for UNESCO. Si-sa-yong-o-sa Publishers:
Seoul. 224–237.

———. 1985. *Shamans, Housewives and Other Restless Spirits*. University of Hawai'i
Press: Honolulu.

Kendall, Laurel, Jongsung Yang and Yul Soo Yoon. 2015. *God Pictures in Korean
Contexts: The Ownership and Meaning of Shaman Paintings*. University of
Hawai'i Press: Honolulu.

Kim, Ilsung. 1955. "On Eliminating Dogmatism and Formalism and Establishing
Juche in Ideological Work". *Marxists Internet Archive*. Available at: www.marx
ists.org/archive/kim-il-sung/1955/12128.htm [accessed on 23 June 2018].

———. 1968. *On Socialist Construction and the South Korean Revolution in the
Democratic People's Republic of Korea*. Foreign Language Publishing House:
Pyongyang. Available at: https://archive.org/details/Binder1_20170116 [accessed
on 24 June 2018].

Kim, Jongil. 1982. On the Juche Idea. Available at: www.korean-books.com.kp/en/
packages/xnps/download.pg.php?306#.pdf [accessed on 24 June 2018].

Kim, Kwang Iel. 1972. "Psychoanalytic Consideration of Korean Shamanism".
Neuropsychiatry, 11(2): 121–129.

Kim, Seong-nae. 2005. "Korean Shamanic Practice in Cyber Culture". *Inter-Religio*,
46: 8–20.

Kim, Sung-gun. 1997. "The Shinto Shrine Issue in Korean Christianity Under Japanese Colonialism". *Journal of Church and State*, 39(3): 503–520.

Kim, Yong-tae. 2014. *Glocal History of Korean Buddhism*. Dongguk University
Press: Seoul.

Korea Central News Agency. Available at: www.kcna.kp/kcna.user.home.retrieve HomeInfoList.kcmsf?lang=eng [accessed on 24 June 2018].

Lee, Grace. 2003. "The Political Philosophy of Juche". *Stanford Journal of East Asian Affairs*, 3(1): 105–112.

Lee, Man Hee. 2009. *The Creation of Heaven and Earth*. Shinchonji Press: Seoul.

Lee, Peter H. (ed.). 2000. *Myths of Korea: Korean Studies Series No.4*. Jimoondang: Seoul.

Lee, Sangwha. 2005. "Patriarchy and Confucianism". *Women's Experiences and Feminist Practices in South Korea*, eds. Chang Pilwha and Kim Eun-shil. Ehwa Woman's University Press: Seoul. 67–117.

McBride, Richard D. 2010. "Won Buddhism". *Religions of the World: A Comprehensive Encyclopedia of Beliefs and Practices*, eds. J. Gordon Melton and Martin Baumann. Routledge: Santa Barbara. 3121–3122.

Moos, Felix. 1964. "Some Aspects of Park Chang No Kyo – A Korean Revitalisation Movement". *Anthropological Quarterly*, East Asian Series Reprint No 7: 110–120. Also available online.

Nahm, Andrew. 1996. *Korea: Tradition and Transformation*. Hollym: Seoul. Chapter 7, Appendix E.

New York Times. 1997. 28,000 Couples Gather for Rev. Moon Rites. Available at: www.nytimes.com/1997/11/30/us/28000-couples-gather-for-rev-moon-rites.html [accessed on 23 June 2018].

———. 2007. "Shamanism Enjoys Revival in Techno-Savy South Korea".

Open Doors World Watch List. 2018. Available at: www.opendoorsusa.org/christian-persecution/world-watch-list/ [accessed on 23 June 2018].

Pai, Hyung Il and Timothy R. Tangherlini. 1998. *Nationalism and the Construction of Korean Identity*. Institute of East Asian Studies, University of California: Berkeley.

Park Jae-soon. 2004. "Ham Seok-heon's National Spirit and Christian Thought". *Korean Philosophy: Its Tradition and Modern Transformation*, ed. Korean National Commission for UNESCO. Hollym: Seoul. 519–554.

Park, Jin Y. (ed.). 2006. *Buddhisms and Deconstructions*. Rowman and Littlefield Publishers: Lanham.

———. 2007. "The Wŏn Buddhist Practice of the Buddha-Nature". *Religions of Korea in Practice*, ed. Robert E. Buswell Jr. Princeton University Press: Princeton, NJ. 476–486.

———. (ed.). 2010. *Makers of Modern Korean Buddhism*. State University of New York Press: Albany.

Pihl, Marshall R. 1994. *The Korean Singer of Tales*. Council on East Asian Studies, Harvard University: Cambridge, MA.

Publications of the DPRK. Available at: www.korean0020books.com.kp/en/search/?page=work-leader1 [accessed on 23 June 2018].

Pye, Michael. 2002. "Won Buddhism as a Korean New Religion". *Numen*, 49(2): 113–141.

Quinn, Jon. 2008. *Divine Principle in Plain Language: The Basic Theology of Sun Myung Moon*. Available at: www.divineprinciple.com/dp_text_all_2.pdf [accessed on 23 June 2018].

Rye, Tongsik. 1984. "Shamanism: The Dominant Folk Religion in Korea". *Inter-Religio*, 5: 8–15.

Scriptures of Won Buddhism. 2006. Available at: www.wonbuddhism.org/docs/1. principal.of.wonbuddhism/The.Principal.Book.of.Won-Buddhism.in.English.3rd. Edition.by.budswell.pdf [accessed on 23 June 2018].

Shin, Eun hee. 2007. "The Sociopolitical Organism: The Religious Dimensions of Juche Philosophy". *Religions of Korea in Practice*, ed. Robert E. Buswell Jr. Princeton University Press: Princeton, NJ. 517–533.

Shin, Yong-Ha. 2000. *Modern Korean History and Nationalism*. Korean studies series No.16. Jimoondang Publishing Company: Seoul.

Shincheonji English Website. Available at: http://en.shincheonji.kr/ [accessed on 23 June 2018].

TEDfellow. 2017. In Twenty-First Century Korea, Shamanism Is Not Only Thriving – But Evolving. Available at: https://fellowsblog.ted.com/in-21st-century-korea-shamanism-is-not-only-thriving-but-evolving-f1a8862a7bc8 [accessed on 23 June 2018].

The Telegraph. 2012. Obituary of Sun Myung Moon. Available at: www.telegraph. co.uk/news/obituaries/9517193/The-Rev-Sun-Myung-Moon.html [accessed on 23 June 2018].

Walraven, Boudewijn. 1994. *Songs of the Shaman: The Ritual Chants of the Korean Mudang*. Kegan Paul International: London.

Won Buddhism– Official English Website. Available at: www.wonbuddhism.org/#/ [accessed on 22 June 2018].

Won Dharma Center. Available at: http://wondharmacenter.org/ [accessed on 22 June 2018].

Won Institute of Graduate Studies. Available at: www.woninstitute.edu/ [accessed on 22 June 2018].

Yi, Chŏng-yŏng. 1983a. "Divination in Korean Shamanistic Thought". *Korean Folklore*, ed. Korean National Commission for UNESCO. Si-sa-yong-o-sa Publishers: Seoul. 181–192.

———. 1983b. "Shamanistic Thought and Traditional Korean homes". *Korean Folklore*, ed. Korean National Commission for UNESCO. Si-sa-yong-o-sa Publishers: Seoul. 193–210.

Yom, Moo-ung. 1999. "A Study of Manhae Han Yong-un". *Korea Journal*, 39(4): 90–117.

Young, Carl. 2013. "Into the Sunset: Ch'ŏndogyo in North Korea". *Journal of Korean Religions*, 4(2): 51–66.

Epilogue

Christianity continued to grow throughout the twentieth century, as Protestant Churches, in particular, gained ground in the aftermath of the Korean War, with social programmes that extended all over the country, helping orphans and widows, providing medical aid and so on. Today, Korean Christian missionaries are among the most numerous in the world. Of course, South Korea, like the North, experienced a series of dictators, until democracy was ushered in during the 1990s, after massive demonstrations during the 1980s, by 'the disenfranchised masses', known as the *Minjung*, influencing Korea's own *Minjung* theology (see Küster 2010). These complicated times influenced scholars such as Ham Sŏkhŏn (also Ham seok-heon) (1901–1989), a Quaker who encouraged non-violence in violent times, like Ghandi, and who developed his own *Ssi-al* (씨알) philosophy, where *ssi-al* (a pure Korean word) means 'seeds'. It was "a symbol of life and nature", but also "linked to the democratic, grassroots-centred thought", and used by Ham to refer to "unprivileged ordinary people" (Park 2004: 534, 535). Under such dysfunctional socio-political conditions, it is hardly surprising that the main tenets of Korea's evangelical churches has been wealth and health, very this-worldly, a common trope in the religious and philosophical path*ways* outlined in this book, with the added bonus of salvation. Catholics, too, became involved with the *Minjung* movement, as priests became more actively engaged with the people, and during the Park Chung-hee (1917–1979) dictatorship of the 1960s and 1970s, Cardinal Kim Suhwan (1922–2009) famously protected demonstrators inside Myeongdong Cathedral – the site where Kim Pŏmu's house used to be, where the earliest Confucians turned Catholics used to gather in secret. In 1984, Pope John Paul II would visit Korea, and, in 2014, Pope Francis I arrived to huge fanfare: both recognised the suffering and hardship of the earliest martyrs of the early church, men and women, discussed earlier in this book.

The Buddhists, who were subsumed under the control of the Government-General through the 1911 Temple Ordinance of the colonial period, sought reforms, led by monks such as Manhae and Sot'aesan, outlined in Chapter 6. It was not until 1941 that a unified Korean temple system was put in place, with the order called Jogye-jong, mentioned before in relation to the

Koryŏ monks, Ŭich'ŏn and Chinul, though there was no direct descent line from that time. As soon as Korea was liberated in 1945, Korean Buddhists organised a National Convention of Buddhist Clerics to discuss reforms, including the removal of the vestiges from Japanese Buddhism, such as marriage, calling for the 'purification' of Korean Buddhism. In fact, it was a Methodist, President Syngman Rhee, who issued the order to expel married monks in 1954, hoping also to appear patriotic by removing traces of the colonial period, though this led to increased antagonism between married and celibate monks. This continued even after the founding of the 'Jogye Order of Korean Buddhism' (대한불교조계종; 大韓佛敎曹溪宗, K. *Taehanbulgyo Chogyejong*) in 1962, now the largest Buddhist order in Korea, which also lists an impressive 149 temples internationally (see: koreanbuddhism.net/). Eventually, in 1970, the married monks formed their own order, the T'aego-jong (태고종), currently the second largest order in Korea, which also has a growing presence abroad, with its own American-European Parish (see taegoaeparish.org). These different branches of Korean Buddhism introduce foreigners to Korean Sŏn practices, but in some cases they have programmes that lead to ordinations for those who are more serious, outlined on their websites. It should be noted that the Buddhist nuns (or bhikkuni, pronounced *biguni* in Korean) of the Taego Order must remain celibate – maybe reflecting the legacy of Chosŏn morality, and the gender inequality that exists in modern Korea. However, there are two important organisations run by female Buddhist nuns and founded by women: (1) the Pomun-jong (보문종), founded in 1972 by Ŭnyŏng Sŭnim (1910–1981), and (2) the Hanmaŭm Sŏnwŏn (한마음 선원, literally 'One-Mind' Sŏn Centre), also founded in 1972 by the very influential Daehaeng Sŭnim (1927–2012) who has many books published in English (for more on these important women, see Sunim 1986; Yi 2006; Go 2010). Meanwhile, more recently on the peninsula, just before the 2002 World Cup, Buddhist temples launched the 'Temple Stay' Programmes "to provide a space for foreigners as well as Koreans to experience and feel traditional Buddhist culture", usually for two nights, often at temples in the countryside, up in the mountains (Jang 2009: 192).

Religious conflict, something that has arisen throughout history, also manifests itself today in Korea. As some Korean Christian groups emphasise exclusivistic teachings, i.e., that one can only be saved through Jesus, some more radical adherents have decapitated Buddhist statues, even burned down Buddhist temples in recent years, and are often found parading outside Buddhist temples with banners and speakers, threatening hell to all those who do not follow Jesus. If Muslims, who have a growing, yet minor presence in Korea, perpetrated similar acts against a Christian Church, would they not be maligned as acts of terror? (For an overview of Islam and Islamic Studies in Korea, see Chang 2010.) But Christianity holds much political sway in Korea today. Non-mainstream religions, especially offshoots of Christianity, are quickly called 'pseudo-religions' or 'cults', deemed dangerous or unhealthy, and known as '*saibi chonggyo*' (사이비종교/似而非宗敎),

often making the headlines in Korea. These are the 'heterodox' or 'heretical', '*idan*' religions of the modern age, just as different religions were in the past. Shamanism, too, has suffered due to its wrongful association with cultic groups in the past few years, implicated in the biggest political scandal in modern East Asian history.

On October 27, 2016, the *New York Times* ran the story of a scandal about South Korean President Park Geun-hye and "an adviser accused of being a 'Shaman fortune-teller' by opposition politicians" (Choe 2016). This adviser, Choi Soon-sil, was not a Shaman, but her father, Choi Tae-min (1912–1994), who had been a mentor to Park after her mother's assassination in 1974, had led one of Korea's many new religions, called Yŏngse-gyo (Church of the Spirit World), which apparently blended together different aspects of Buddhism, Christianity, Ch'ŏndogyo and Shamanism – though only the 'apparent' Shamanic aspect was picked up by the media, even in South Korea. The next day, a story in *Korea Joonang Daily* ran the headline, "Shamanistic Cult Linked to President" (Ser 2016). The real story was much less spiritual: it was actually about the undue influence Choi had over the president, made privy to private government business, in turn leading to bribery and corruption, which eventually escalated into the 'real' scandal, which was about influence-peddling for millions of dollars, that lead

Figure E1.1 A Presbyterian Church in Busan warns people against the '*idan*' or 'heterodox' Sincheonji Church

all the way to the de facto head of Samsung, Lee Jae-yong, who as head of Korea's most important conglomerate, wielded a different sort of power, in the form of money and wealth. President Park, her confidante and the Samsung boss (and others involved) were all arrested, and Park was disgracefully impeached. Things got much worse for her. On April 6, 2018, almost exactly four years since the events of the Sewol tragedy unfolded, which opened this book, Park was sentenced to 24 years in prison. Choi had already been sentenced to 20 years in February, meanwhile Lee, the businessman, was at first sentenced to five years in prison for having paid millions into Choi's foundations: Choi would then influence the President in his favour – quid pro quo! However, in February 2018, Lee was freed from prison, his jail term suspended. Some might say Park reaped the karma she sowed, never having recovered her legitimacy or moral authority as leader, after her mishandling of the Sewol disaster. Some might say that Park and Choi both got what they deserved. Others might add that their sentences reflect a patriarchal Confucian legacy in modern Korea, which discriminates against women, and is lenient on powerful modern 'yangban' men. People who violate laws should be punished, that is something we might all agree on. Meanwhile, the dictator, former President Chun Doo-hwan (1931–), who orchestrated the Kwangju Massacre in 1980, where thousands were wounded and died, was pardoned, free to live in luxury. Should his pardon be revoked? After all, he was involved in the mass murder of his own citizens, much more serious than Park's own immoral behaviour. What initially made the headline in regards to Park, Korea's first female President, was her misreported religious proclivities, and a slur campaign to undermine her for consulting a shaman, linked to a cult. In twenty-first century Korea, religion matters and can sway public opinion very quickly.

The 2015 South Korean census revealed the percentages of adherents to the main religions as: Protestant Christianity, 19.7 percent; Buddhism, 15.5 percent; Catholicism, 7.9 percent; with other religions all coming in under 1 percent. Since the 2005 census, only Protestant Christianity had grown slightly from 18.3 percent, and Buddhism has declined from 22.8 percent, and Catholicism from 10.9 percent. Another important statistic is that those with no religious affiliation has also increased from 46.5 percent in 2005, to 56.9 percent in 2015. Since the 1990s, there is no doubt that the influence of Christianity in politics has been immense. There have been both Protestant and Catholic Presidents in South Korea – none have been Buddhist. Lee (2010: 143–145) provides statistics for two studies conducted in 2000 in relation to politics and religious affiliation: one study concluded that out of the top 100 governmental positions, 42 were Protestant, 20 were Catholic, 9 were Buddhist – only 3 were linked with 'other' religions, while 26 had no religion. The second study examined the religious affiliation of members of the 273 members of the National Assembly: 39 percent were Protestant; 25 percent were Catholic; while only 11 percent were Buddhist. This shows that Protestants hold more political sway, even more than non-believers who make up the majority of South Koreans. This is all the more staggering if one is reminded that at the beginning to the twentieth century, less than 1 percent of Koreans were Christian. Korea's religious landscape has changed dramatically – it will continue to do so – and its philosophical traditions also hold sway, not articulated in any census.

Confucianism is not considered by most Koreans to be a religion, but more a cultural *modus vivendi*, which shapes their social interactions, reinforces filial piety, puts a strong focus on education and success – where male heirs are still preferred (many of these are the topics of Korean Dramas, now watched internationally). The Korean language itself reverberates with Confucian hierarchical appendages, which still distinguish a superior person (윗사람, K. *wit saram*) from their subordinate (아랫사람, K. *araet saram*), and women have not yet received the equality of their counterparts in many other developed countries. The LGBTQ community in Korea also struggles against Confucian norms which reinforce heterosexuality and procreation, as does Christianity, a forceful critique of homosexuality in Korea. Marriage (between a man and a woman) is still often linked with the union of two families, not love between two individuals, though divorce is now common – no longer based on the 'seven evils', and more often than not initiated by women, who more and more are refusing to be subjected to different standards than men. Confucian deference to authority lacking moral guidance and 'humanity' is also being challenged, as the aftermath of the Sewol tragedy painfully highlighted.

Korea's religious and philosophical teachings, outlined in this book, are still relevant today. The philosophical underpinnings of Buddhism and Confucian sagehood can help us to lead better, more consciously aware lives, if we take the time out for some self-cultivation. These path*ways* can be self-transformative, and to transform ourselves, we inevitably have to change the way we think, and also how we interact with others, shaping how they think about us too. It has been repeatedly shown throughout this book that self-cultivation, making ourselves more compassionate, humane human beings, needs to be practiced every day, so that gradually, our bad habits are transformed into good ones. While Confucian and Buddhist teachings emphasise our innate goodness and innate Buddha Nature, they both teach us that we have unlimited potential to be better human beings, and that actualising that potential should be our daily goal. These different teachings also show us that happiness *is* how we 'think' about things, not the things themselves, and so it is something that comes from the inside out, requiring self-reflection, coming from meditation or mindfulness. We should, on the one hand, guard ourselves against negative thoughts, which could lead to negative actions, while promoting our good characteristics (i.e., watch out for anger and ego) and embrace kindness and humility. The scholars discussed in this book recognised that we have the potential to be perfect, whereby perfection means to be the most morally responsible and socially engaged human beings we can be – which is why it requires a continual

Figure E1.2 Altar for the victims of the Sewol Tragedy in Seoul

and mindful practice. We may falter, but we can learn from our mistakes and then practice some more. These ideas reflect the collective wisdom of Wŏnhyo and Chinul, but also T'oegye and Tasan, and so many others not discussed in this book, awaiting discovery. They all have things to teach us today – whether we are Korean or not. Wisdom does not discriminate, it provides us with a path*way* to help ourselves, and more importantly, each other.

References and further reading

Chang, Byung-Ock. 2010. "Islamic Studies in Korea". *International Area Studies Review*, 13(1): 3–21.

Choe, Sang-hun. 2016. A Presidential Friendship Has Many South Koreans Crying Foul. Available at: www.nytimes.com/2016/10/28/world/asia/south-korea-choi-soon-sil.html?_r=0 [accessed on 25 June 2018].

Go, Chong. 2010. "Sŏn Master Daehaeng's 'Doing Without Doing'". *Makers of Modern Korean Buddhism*, ed. Jin Yi Park. Suny Press: Albany. 227–242.

Jang, Eunhwa. 2009. *Journey to Korean Temples and Temple Stay*. Her One Media: Seoul.

Kŭster, Volker. 2010. *A Protestant Theology of Passion: Korean Minjung Theology Movement*. Brill: Leiden.

Lee, Timothy S. 2010. *Born Again: Evangelism in Korea*. University of Hawai'i Press: Honolulu.

Park, Jae Soon. 2004. "Ham Seok-Heon's National Spirit and Christian Though". *Korean Philosophy: Its Tradition and Modern Transformation*, ed. Korean National Commission for UNESCO. Hollym: Seoul. 519–552.

Ser, Myo-ja. 2016. Shamanistic Cult Linked to President. Available at: http://korea joongangdaily.joins.com/news/article/article.aspx?aid=3025424&cloc=etc%7Cja d%7Cgooglenews [accessed on 25 June 2018].

Sunim, Samu. 1986. "Eunyeong Sunim and the Founding of Pomun-jon, the First Independent Bhikshuni Order". *Spring Wing: Buddhist Cultural Forum*, 6: 129–162.

Yi, Hyangsoon. 2006. "Pomunjong and Hanmaŭm Sŏnwŏn: New Monastic Paths in Contemporary Korea". *Out of the Shadows: Socially Engaged Buddhist Women*, ed. Karma Lekshe Tsomo. Indian Book Centre: Delhi. 228–234.

Index

Page numbers in *italic* indicate a figure and page numbers in **bold** indicate a table on the corresponding page.

For Product Safety Concerns and Information please contact our EU
representative GPSR@taylorandfrancis.com
Taylor & Francis Verlag GmbH, Kaufingerstraße 24, 80331 München, Germany

www.ingramcontent.com/pod-product-compliance
Lightning Source LLC
Chambersburg PA
CBHW071424050326
40689CB00010B/1975

* 9 7 8 1 1 3 8 1 9 3 4 0 6 *